The Multi-Talented Mr. Erskine

THE MULTI-TALENTED MR. ERSKINE
SHAPING MASS CULTURE THROUGH GREAT BOOKS AND FINE MUSIC

Katherine Elise Chaddock

Beto,

With huge thanks for your partnership in research and your friendship in everything,

Katherine

palgrave
macmillan

THE MULTI-TALENTED MR. ERSKINE
Copyright © Katherine Elise Chaddock, 2012.

Portions of chapter 9 were previously published in: Katherine Chaddock, "The Making of a Celebrity President: John Erskine and the Juilliard School," *Perspectives on the History of Higher Education: Iconic Leaders in Higher Education*, 28 (2011), 115–136. Copyright © 2011, Transaction Publishers. Reprinted by permission of the publisher.

First published in 2012 by
PALGRAVE MACMILLAN®
in the United States—a division of St. Martin's Press LLC,
175 Fifth Avenue, New York, NY 10010.

Where this book is distributed in the UK, Europe and the rest of the world, this is by Palgrave Macmillan, a division of Macmillan Publishers Limited, registered in England, company number 785998, of Houndmills, Basingstoke, Hampshire RG21 6XS.

Palgrave Macmillan is the global academic imprint of the above companies and has companies and representatives throughout the world.

Palgrave® and Macmillan® are registered trademarks in the United States, the United Kingdom, Europe and other countries.

ISBN: 978–0–230–11775–4

Library of Congress Cataloging-in-Publication Data

Chaddock, Katherine E.
    The multi-talented Mr. Erskine : shaping mass culture through great books and fine music / Katherine Elise Chaddock.
        pages cm
    Includes bibliographical references.
    ISBN 978–0–230–11775–4 (hardback)
    1. Erskine, John, 1879–1951. 2. Authors, American—20th century—Biography 3. Musicians—United States—Biography. 4. Scholars—United States—Biography. 5. College teachers—United States—Biography. I. Title.

PS3509.R5Z65 2012
813'.52—dc23   2011047540
[B]

A catalogue record of the book is available from the British Library.

Design by Newgen Imaging Systems (P) Ltd., Chennai, India.

First edition: May 2012

10 9 8 7 6 5 4 3 2 1

Printed in the United States of America.

To Robert Wiebe, who turned the sleepy coed in row 29 into an interested student. And to L. Jackson Newell, who turned her into a historian many years later.

Contents

ILLUSTRATIONS

ACKNOWLEDGMENTS

During the research and writing of this book, I was blessed with friends, family, colleagues, students, and others who assisted and encouraged me each step of the way. Additionally, crucial funding aid was provided by a Research Opportunity Grant from the University of South Carolina and by an Everett Helm Fellowship from the Lilly Library, Indiana University. This volume could not have happened without the support of these individuals and institutions.

Two generous friends who contributed exceptional time and assistance were Bob Toy, who spent many days combing through archival files with me at the Butler and Low Libraries, Columbia University, and John McCormack, who read every word of each manuscript chapter to uncover errors and suggest essential improvements and whose expertise continued through proofing and indexing. Additionally, my friend and colleague Iris Saltiel helped me on a final trip to New York to search for photo images and tie up loose ends. My incomparable coauthor on three previous volumes, Carolyn Matalene, offered ideas and advice—especially on curing mixed metaphors. I am amazed and grateful for the time and patience of these smart and gracious individuals.

Other caring academic colleagues and friends who continued to prove that I can always count on their encouragement and advice included: Christian Anderson, Beverly Bower, Vivian DeRienzo, Linda Eisenman, David Fleisher, Roger Geiger, Scott Henderson, Jim Hudgins, Bob Jones, Zach Kelehear, Craig Kridel, Michelle Maher, Jana Nidiffer, William C. Rice, Bob Schwartz, Ken Stevenson, John Thelin, and Wayne Urban. Several professionals who were pursuing graduate degrees at the time shared writing weekends with me as we interacted in cyberspace about goals and progress, including Willette Burnham, Eddie Dille, Stephanie Foote, Mateel King, Amy Scully, and Jenny Williams. Jean Weingarth joined me both online and on campus for mutual support on our historical research projects. Two new friends, musicians Roberta Rust and Philip Evans, advised on musical aspects of the book and suggested just the right concluding chapter title: "Coda."

For nearly five years, a string of University of South Carolina graduate assistants helped with library errands, fact checking, organizing files, finalizing endnotes, and launching the bibliography. The first of these, Courtney Thain Molony, was soon followed by Amber Stegelin Falluca who coined the term "Erskineville" to describe how she spent a healthy portion of her PhD student life. Later, Erskineville benefitted from the expert graduate assistance of Elizabeth White-Hurst, Telesia Davis, and Helen Halacz. Additionally, I thank Kathleen (Kate) Watson of the University of Pennsylvania for taking on archival research at that campus and Brett Reynolds who searched archives at the Newberry Library when he was a student at the University of Chicago.

The research portion of this work depended on the guidance and good graces of librarians and archivists whose work is vitally important to all scholars of history. I owe a special debt of gratitude to several who hosted me on a number of occasions and took my emails and phone calls in between. Jeni Dahmus at the Juilliard School went far above and beyond my expectations by giving expert advice, readying boxes and files for my visits, and suggesting that I review items I would have missed. Tara Craig and Jocelyn Wilk at Columbia University, Butler Library, made their Rare Book and Manuscript collections not only available, but comprehensible—right through my search for photo images and my emails with last-minute questions. The personnel at other institutions who gave crucial assistance are those at the Amherst College Library; the Annenberg Rare Book and Manuscript Library, University of Pennsylvania; the Houghton Library, Harvard University; the Library of Congress; the Lilly Library, Indiana University; the Low Library, Columbia University; the Newberry Library, Chicago; the St. John's (Annapolis) College Library; and the Regenstein Library, University of Chicago. My own home libraries, the Thomas Cooper and South Caroliniana Libraries at the University of South Carolina and the Addlestone Library at the College of Charleston, provided me with books, articles, electronic sources, and exceptional service as I sought ideas, information, and answers throughout this project.

In navigating the publishing world, I was fortunate to have the early help of Adam Chromy of Artists and Artisans, Inc., and the assistance throughout of Chris Chappell and Sarah Whalen of

Palgrave Macmillan. Superb anonymous reviewers offered insightful comments that greatly enhanced the final work. I thank Transaction Publishers for granting permission to use words and several sentences from my work "The Making of a Celebrity President: John Erskine and the Juilliard School" published in 2011 in *Perspectives on the History of Higher Education: Iconic Leaders in Higher Education*.

I dedicate this work to two wise historians and superb teachers, L. Jackson Newell of the University of Utah and Deep Springs College and the late Robert Wiebe of Northwestern University. How fortunate I am to have had their guidance at various stages of learning to love history. Finally, my daughter and son, Adrienne and Brett Reynolds, have continued into adulthood to be my most essential and enthusiastic cheerleaders.

INTRODUCTION:
MERCHANT OF ACADEME

When John Erskine and his former Columbia University student Lloyd Morris selected the Brevoort Café for a long-overdue reunion lunch, the setting could not have been more appropriate for the two practitioners and critics of all things literary. Wedged into the basement of the Brevoort Hotel, a Greenwich Village landmark that opened in 1851 and shared its block with the Fifth Avenue town house once home to Mark Twain, the café had become a busy watering hole for New York's writers, artists, and activists. By 1925, Erskine and Morris could enjoy the French character and fine wines provided by owner Raymond Orteig, who would gain fame two years later as the man whose $25,000 reward inspired Charles Lindbergh's legendary soar across the Atlantic.[1]

Erskine, a dynamic 44-year-old Columbia literature professor and a widely admired poet and essayist, arrived with bulging briefcase in hand and a ready supply of news from campus. As a postwar stewpot of intellectual intensity and internal political turbulence, the college fueled heady exploits by students and faculty alike. Graduate students and new faculty were honing their teaching skills by instructing sections of Erskine's popular course, General Honors, a "great books" course that was the first of its kind in American higher education. Among their undergraduate charges were Leon Keyserling, a 17-year-old history major on his way to an appointment as President Truman's chief economic advisor; Lionel Trilling, a budding literary and cultural critic; Jacques Barzun, preparing for a distinguished career as a historian and eventually provost at Columbia; Clifton Fadiman, a future author and popular radio and television personality; and Whittaker Chambers, already becoming a determined and controversial communist. Lou Gehrig, a Columbia undergraduate for two years, had recently moved on to greener fields. The Columbia faculty, of course, had bragging rights to its own star power. In 1925, John Dewey, although singularly unimpressive in the lecture hall, graced his publisher with *Experience and Nature* to further solidify his already sturdy international reputation in pragmatic thought and progressive education. Columbia's first professor of anthropology, Franz Boas, could count Zora Neale Hurston and Margaret Mead among his current students. Recent faculty addition Mark Van Doren was attracting attention and bright students with a poetry course he described as "a study of long and short poems, with special attention to tragedy and comedy as forms in which the human understanding states itself."[2]

While the Columbia gang provided ample luncheon conversation for Erskine and Morris, it was clear that Erskine had more on his mind. The erudite professor—complete with prominent bow tie, pale blue eyes, and bushy brows that underlined a remarkably high forehead—explained to Morris that he had decided to abandon his most recent academic writing project, a volume about John Milton. However, in consenting to cancel that contract, the editors at Bobbs-Merrill had agreed to consider his idea for a substitute work. He was now putting finishing touches on a book titled *The Argument of Helen*. The manuscript just happened to be in that briefcase sitting by his feet.[3]

Lloyd Morris, 32 years old and already a well-regarded literary critic with two books to his credit, agreed to listen to a chapter over coffee and to contribute his opinion of the style. The writing experiment was so new to Erskine that when a Bobbs-Merrill publicist asked if his submission would be biography or fiction, he had hesitated before admitting, "I guess it's fiction."[4]

Erskine read to Morris in a deep voice with little modulation and a slight patrician inflection, letting each finished page drop onto the table. Neither of the men tasted their coffee. Morris later would recall the portions he heard as "an extended Platonic dialogue." He noted that Erskine brought to the work "all his wit, dialectical skill, and mastery of paradox. It was light and gay in tone, and full of laughter."[5] His immediate response was unbridled praise for the professor who had guided him and many other promising Columbia undergraduates toward love of poetry, disciplined use of criticism, and enthusiastic reflection in interpreting literature and life. To students, this tall, slim teacher was self-assured and imposing in the extreme; so Morris was somewhat startled when Erskine seemed surprised and humbled by his pupil's effusive approval of the new manuscript.[6]

Morris's reaction was destined to seem remarkably understated in light of the nationwide excitement that greeted the November, 1925, publication of Erskine's first novel—with its working title, *The Argument of Helen*, changed to the more commercially viable *The Private Life of Helen of Troy*. Reviewers raved, and the public purchased. To the literary critic at the *New York Times*, the novel was "rather shocking and very amusing...a humorous, wise and beautiful book."[7] Within 6 weeks, nearly 20,000 copies had sold to enthusiastic readers who discovered that a breathtaking and brainy Helen returned from Troy with Menelaus to live a fully domestic married life punctuated with wit and wisdom that could apply to contemporary spouses.[8] A year later, with its titillating suggestiveness for fun seekers and stimulating satire for the literati, the volume remained on the list of the country's 20 best-selling books. Its motion picture rights had sold, and Ethel Barrymore was examining the script.[9] Professor Erskine, much to the stunned amazement of his Columbia colleagues, was at work on two new manuscripts titled *Galahad: Enough of His Life to Explain His Reputation* and *Adam and Eve, Though He Knew Better*.[10] Over the next two decades, Erskine would evolve into a fully formed "celebrity professor"—the first to deserve that title in the age of mass communication and mass culture.[11]

* * *

Although *Helen* and its many successive volumes in the genre of historicized popular myth launched him as an early twentieth-century household name, by 1925 Erskine was already a well-known scholar among intellectuals. He was a respected nonfiction author who regularly contributed to *Harpers*, *North American Review*, and the *New Republic*; a highly acclaimed teacher; and a noteworthy academic thinker. He had garnered further accolades for creating Columbia's General Honors seminars, in which students read and discussed a classic of Western literature each week. According to Lionel Trilling, "It was from this course that the movement of General Education in the humanities took its rise and established itself not only in Columbia College but in numerous colleges throughout the nation."[12] The Great Books course also defined Erskine as a key proponent of sharing widely the emblems once reserved for highbrow culture—especially in literature and the arts—among all classes that could enjoy them.

However, as *Helen* was arriving in book stores, Erskine was forging yet another path toward popular eminence. He determined to revive his earlier promise as a concert pianist—a talent and passion that had occupied much of his youth. Among his teaching and writing, he had begun to practice two to four hours a day in preparation for symphony appearances and live radio performances. Three years later, as a recognized academic innovator and musician, he was named the first president of the Juilliard School of Music. While serving at Juilliard for nearly a decade (1928–1937), he also maintained a busy schedule of public lectures and piano performances throughout the country, continued publishing historical fiction in books and short stories, and appeared frequently as a celebrity guest on radio and in newspaper columns. His name seemed to be everywhere. Yet, the distance from noted academic and accomplished artist to national icon would prove to be a great divide.

*   *   *

Erskine learned from childhood the art of juggling multifaceted talents and interests, and he appeared to smoothly navigate the transition from the age of Victorian stringencies in which he spent his early years to the age of postwar liberties in which he later thrived. Born in New York City of Scottish descent, he also became adept at straddling the boundaries between classes. While he adopted the Victorian proprieties adhered to by the managerial class, which characterized his family situation, he was a fascinated observer of the more freewheeling ways of workers who populated the silk ribbon factory owned and directed by his father. Fine music, literature, art, and items manufactured by Steinway and Tiffany made their way into the Erskine household, which moved to Weehawken, New Jersey, when John was five years old. Early education for John and his sisters was in the hands of a series of governesses. But the aristocratic accessories of that life could not survive the late nineteenth-century downslide of a Victorian culture steeped in romance, sentimentality, and faith in restrictive moralism, and that downslide took the market for fine bows and shimmering ribbons from the Erskine mills with it.

With the family in greatly reduced circumstances, the adolescent Erskine began making a nearly two-hour trip each day into Manhattan. There he confronted the classical curriculum of Columbia Grammar School, complete with Latin and Greek grammar and prose, as well as French, literature, and mathematics.[13] Outside of class and commute, his major focus was on the piano lessons and practice he had begun at five years old. In a study of individuals whose work represented the movement toward mass culture, Joan Shelley Rubin concluded that the fate of his father's business demonstrated to Erskine the triumph of commercial forces over refined artistry and "cemented his allegiance to the genteel stance of alienation from the marketplace."[14] However, his eventual ability to balance both aesthetic and commercial impulses in pursuing literature and music indicates that his father's reversal of fortune also may have provided pragmatic lessons about succeeding in that marketplace.

Columbia College and Columbia University Graduate School followed, and Erskine entered as a freshman in 1896 with the essential support of merit scholarships. Through master teacher and mentor George Woodberry, he developed a taste for poetry and a commitment to Woodberry's endangered humanistic notion that taught "how to live is the main matter, whatever else we may study."[15] From prominent pianist and composer Edward MacDowell, recently hired to chair Columbia's music department, he discovered that music was an art worthy of study "not primarily to make money, but to live out a philosophy."[16] The undergraduate Erskine performed and composed at the piano, wrote poetry for the student literary journal and beyond, and adopted Elizabethan literature as his own specialized area of study and analysis. At a time when the idea of liberal education had begun a long uphill battle for survival among the growing popularity of vocational subjects and degrees, Erskine clearly favored the efficacy of studies in arts and humanities. Again, however, he would prove adroit at juggling genteel cultural interests with working-class professional realities—a balancing act made possible by faculty appointments, first at Amherst (1903) and then at Columbia (1909).

*   *   *

Erskine launched his career in higher education at a time of substantial debate among academics, particularly those in humanities disciplines, about the necessity for relevance, the nature of analysis, and the extent of interpretation. Columbia faculty readily joined the debate, occasioned both by broad cultural changes experienced throughout American higher education and by individual differences of opinion on the campus. The 1910 retirement of longtime dean of Columbia College John Howard Van Amringe, never favored by President Nicholas Murray Butler, ended the influence of "that venerable embodiment of the Columbia of another era."[17] Indicative of how steadily the undergraduate college would then move beyond its classical education emphasis, President Butler quickly began work to align course offerings and admissions practices with market demand and with New York City public high school fare. Latin was removed as a requirement for the bachelor of arts degree in 1916, an event that a later Columbia director of admissions, Frank Bowles, interpreted as "the abandonment of the entire system of education of which the classics were a symbol."[18]

In numerous universities throughout the early years of the twentieth century, factions within humanities disciplines divided and subdivided on approaches to contemporary American preferences. In addition to the usual departmental politics about hiring, curriculum, and decision-making influence, faculties disagreed on how to confront the modern realities that J. David Hoeveler summarized as "the triumph of relativism in philosophy and social thought, of materialism in daily living, and of romanticism and naturalism in literature."[19] In terms of scholarly methods of analysis, Jacques Barzun noted that also at that time: "In the hope of rivaling science, of becoming sciences, the humanities gave up their birthright. By teaching college students the methods of minute scholarship, they denatured the contents and obscured the virtues of liberal studies."[20]

The new humanists of the era worried about growing signs of democratic excess that could mean anything is as good as anything else. Their answer was to attempt to recapture earlier traditions of restraint in order to curb willful pragmatic and naturalistic notions. However, the humanist impulse was rarely consistent among its individual proponents whose "core of belief was in fact capable of immense variety in its application."[21] In departments of language and literature, the most evident ideological split was between what Gerald Graff called " 'generalists,' ...who upheld the old college ideal of liberal or general culture against that of narrowly specialized research" and " 'investigators,' who promoted the idea of scientific research and the philological study of the modern languages."[22] Graff summarized the differences, which began in the late nineteenth century, as "the polarities of hard investigation and soft appreciation, of specialized research and general ideas."[23] At Columbia, for example, English professor Joel Spingarn, an activist for academic freedom and racial equality, supported the call for the scientific treatment of literature—a "new criticism" that would include counting and calculating stylistic devices used in written works. Given his experience with MacDowell and allegiance to

Woodberry, Erskine was firmly rooted in the generalist camp. There he found a platform from which he could let literature speak for itself, encourage his students toward refined understanding through the practice of writing poetry and essays, and "give my boys the spirit of the authors, and let them judge between them for themselves."[24] His own critiques of literature, summarized in his well-received 1915 volume, *The Moral Obligation to Be Intelligent,* visited the climes of ideas and artistry rather than the neighborhoods of metaphors and symbols.[25] In 1916, his proposal for a "great books" course that would entail reading works in their entirety also addressed the humanist fear that "with the development of survey courses and near-encyclopedic syntheses there was every danger that literature and philosophy would be treated merely as literary and philosophical history."[26]

* * *

As it did for many individuals and for many elements of American lifestyles, World War I proved a watershed happening for Erskine. Historian Robert Wiebe, summarizing the effects on Americans in general, aptly depicted Erskine's experience: "The crisis of war, by stripping away a veneer of restraint, allowed Americans to translate assumptions into actions, to express normal feeling with abnormal directness; and the beneficiaries were those few with simple, persuasive answers."[27]

Erskine's immediate personal answer was to temporarily decamp from campus, as had so many wartime faculty, and head for France as part of a loosely formed plan by the US Army and the YMCA to launch traveling educators to the troops. He waved his good-byes to family (by then a wife and two young children) in January, 1918, and, except for one brief return trip, spent the next year and a half in France. Heady times on foreign shores among the recent victors in a great war undoubtedly hastened his plunge from the confines of reflective moralism into the seduction of new experiments. At Beaune, in the Burgundy region of France, he founded and directed a temporary and short-lived American university for soldiers waiting for ships to deliver them home. Faculty members, at one point numbering nearly 800, represented almost every prominent US college. Students, numbering close to 10,000 at the height of registration, were able to use their credits at US institutions when they returned. Program areas ranged from agriculture and engineering to fine arts, education, and law.[28] Erskine quickly came to adore the French culture and language, and before he returned, he had formed a friendship with General John J. Pershing, who decorated him with the Distinguished Service Medal. A very different John Erskine arrived back at Columbia for fall semester, 1919.

Fortunately for Erskine and many others changed by wartime experiences, nearly everyone on the American scene seemed prepared to welcome a new era. "Gaiety was the main item on the agenda, a taking hold of life with both hands, feeling tolerant toward human vagaries (including one's own), and under stress, showing nonchalance," observed Jacques Barzun, who dubbed the tendencies of the time as "the cult of the new."[29] Similarly, a number of analysts have noted that the post–World War I era spawned an outer-directed regard for "personality" that supplanted the more inner-directed focus on "character" of the nineteenth century. From there, the concept of people as "personalities" was a small step, and the notion of "celebrities" would not be far behind.[30]

Postwar patriotism and national enthusiasm for Western civilization enabled Erskine to revive his earlier proposal for a course based on great books; although he found that lingering faculty objections prompted his colleagues to "protect the students—and themselves—from it by decreeing that my course should be open only to the specially qualified, who would take it as an extra, or as they like to say, as 'honors'."[31] But it was postwar social, material, and personal expansiveness that would soon help to propel Erskine beyond the confines of a sparkling academic career that boasted a half-dozen books, successful initiation of a "first" in college curriculum, and a reputation that brought him several queries about college presidencies.[32]

Erskine himself guessed at the possible downside of a commercial venture when he sent the last of his manuscript for *The Private Life of Helen of Troy* to his publisher. Later, he would recall thinking: "I wondered whether I was God's masterpiece in fools. So far my life had been fortunate and happy...I had made friends and a more than respectable name; would this little book spoil it all?"[33]

*   *   *

Erskine's arrival on the American scene as a popular intellectual who achieved academic celebrity status was well timed for the early twentieth-century cultural shift toward ideas, goods, entertainment, and education that recognized the tastes of a bulging middle class. The national move to "mass culture" supported his multimedia reach into the public consciousness—ranging from popular novels to piano concerts, and eventually from radio quiz shows to advice columns.[34] Although not quite a legacy to the highest rungs of aristocracy, Erskine demonstrated how to successfully partake in what Janice Radway termed the "American attempt to come to terms with the process of massification."[35] As an intellectual whose resume included pursuits contrary to the notions of repressive American gentility well established in the nineteenth century, his experiences and ideas reflected the curious national paradox of creating access to elements of culture for the middlebrow many while honoring the preferred exclusivity of the elite. Richard Hofstadter summarized the conundrum by identifying the dual nature of the American intellectual class as elite "in its manner of thinking and functioning," but democratic in intent. "Intellectuals in the twentieth century have thus found themselves engaged in incompatible efforts: they have tried to be good and believing citizens of a democratic society and at the same time to resist the vulgarization of culture which that society constantly produces."[36] While Hofstadter asserted that most could not do both, Erskine demonstrated the outcomes of attempting just that.

John Erskine was destined to be a Renaissance man without a Renaissance. The varied accomplishments and successes that distinguished him as an extraordinary individual were supported by the early twentieth-century spread of cultural trappings beyond the domain of the highbrow few, but without a context of genuine vitality or uplift in the essence of American culture or in the direction of American institutions. David O. Levine pointed to scattered efforts toward such revitalization in higher education, citing the honors movement spearheaded by Swarthmore president Frank Aydelotte, the "great books" plan rooted in Erskine's courses and advanced by University of Chicago president Robert Maynard Hutchins, and the calls for educational humanism over utilitarianism by Harvard philosopher Irving Babbitt. But, while such endeavors succeeded briefly as a "counterattack (that) established the distinctiveness and prestige of the elite liberal arts college," they were not long lived or comprehensive.[37] Helen Lefkowitz Horowitz noted that the general education movement "led by Columbia after World War I" was followed by the efforts of individual educational reformers, including those named by Levine. However, "as vital as these efforts were to students who chose to submit to them, because intellectual integration went against the grain of both the professoriat's academic training and its principal routes of professional advancement, these programs remained the individualized creations of mavericks, admired abstractly but seldom flattered by imitation."[38]

Far more than other academic innovators who assisted the masses to poach on territories once reserved for the socioeconomic elite, Erskine employed the full range of what Joan Shelley Rubin labeled "sources of refinement." In explaining the late nineteenth- and early twentieth-century diffusion of genteel culture into the ranks of the middlebrow many, she noted four key platforms: Theaters and concert halls; the publishing business; higher education; and the public lecture.[39] These arenas prompted popular enthusiasm when theaters and concert halls added moving pictures to their repertoires; publishing included paperbacks, reprint series, and photo-filled periodicals; higher education embraced more students (including women), more courses (including electives), and more degree and certificate programs (including advertising and sales); and public lectures benefited from better transportation for lecturers and opportunities for listening from home on radios. Erskine embraced all these as his own instruments of dissemination, tapping into the mass culture desires of a class of Americans who clamored for the refined trappings that had once been denied to them for lack of money, time, and/or interest. However, while the new paths for spreading those upper-class trappings sometimes announced truly excellent art or thought, Rubin found there was still a tendency "to present refinement in unabashedly commodified form."[40]

* * *

Inevitably, Erskine would struggle to reconcile professional endeavors of intellectual interest with the commercial realities of popular pursuits, and not always successfully. As a regular contributor of racy fiction to *Cosmopolitan* magazine throughout the Depression years, including stories such as "Afterthoughts of Lady Godiva" and "The Candor of Don Juan," he may have earned less respect—but larger recognition—than he deserved when he performed as a solo pianist with the Philadelphia Orchestra and the New York Symphony or served as chairman of the Metropolitan Opera board of directors. Navigating the seeming inconsistencies was a lifelong challenge.[41]

The path that Erskine traveled beyond the intersection of academic achievement and popular acclaim presented enormous struggles in balancing competing values and demands—particularly in the areas of commercial interests, personal desires, professional expertise, and intellectual curiosities. Although his popular fiction earned him the ability to purchase and then renovate a large weekend and summer home in Wilton, Connecticut, that property eventually became a convenient place for his wife and children to live full time, while he remained at his Manhattan apartment and romanced other women. His love for his son and daughter was unconditional, but he had limited time to develop close relationships with them. He was passed over for chair of the Columbia English Department, and his Columbia colleagues expressed little regret when he left them to accept an appointment as the first president of the Juilliard School of Music.[42]

In the dozen years after the success of his first novel, he published more and more fiction to keep pace with his growing financial needs—at least a book each year and many short stories. But he became more and more testy with personnel at Bobbs-Merrill when foreign and film rights did not sell quickly enough or the Book-of-the-Month Club snubbed his latest novel. By the mid-1930s, his writing ability could not keep pace with his own productivity demands, and reviewer comments on book manuscripts stung with examples as: "It reads as if Erskine were purposely juvenilizing it" and "this is so completely unworthy of its distinguished author that it is hard to believe he wrote it." By 1938, after more than 20 books and years of close friendship with his editor, Laurance Chambers, the author, peeved that Bobbs-Merrill hadn't made him more money, turned to new publishers.[43]

Yet, as an educator who would rise to celebrity, Erskine managed to create a personal legacy that did not altogether disappoint himself. His "General Honors" course at Columbia was suspended in 1928, but revived three years later by Jacques Barzun and retitled "Colloquium on Important Books." Columbia teaching assistant Mortimer Adler convinced his friend Scott Buchanan, then working in community education at Cooper Union's "People's Institute," to use Erskine's General Honors course as a model for presenting "great books" seminars in the city's public libraries. Buchanan would later install the idea at St. John's College. Adler would carry it to the University of Chicago. Additionally, through his books, lectures, and appearances as a piano soloist with dozens of symphony orchestras,

Erskine managed to bring to a general citizenry enjoyment in litera-ture and music once reserved for only the highbrow few.[44] From 1928 until his resignation in 1937, he set the Juilliard School on a path to prominence that has continued through successive administrations. In 1945, after at least 15 years of separated living, Erskine and his first wife divorced. He married his longtime companion, Helen Worden, the next day and stayed closely by her side until his death in 1951.

Erskine's own attempt to summarize, but not explain, his life jour-ney found its way into a trilogy of episodic memoirs: *The Memory of Certain Persons* (1947); *My Life as a Teacher* (1948); and *My Life in Music* (1950). These largely unembellished volumes provided both too much information and not enough information about a com-plex and very full life. Sometimes overlapping, but only occasionally conflicting, the memoirs offered much detail about various episodes and people that populated Erskine's academic and artistic worlds, but they shared little about his personal interactions, his writing life, his integration of motivations and actions, and the consequences of his transition from scholarly academic to celebrity professor.

Published descriptions of the Erskine who authored popular fic-tion cast him as a pop icon who had figured out a way to escape the boundaries of boring professorial duties. A 1927 *New Yorker* writer noted: "This benign personage is constantly being asked for his opinion, and giving it, on love, rolled stockings and the younger generation...One of his most conspicuous duties as a professor of English at Columbia is autographing his novels at the request of awe-struck coeds."[45] Several years later, another interviewer was herself so awestruck that she found it necessary to include her reaction in her article, gushing: "His suit was so deep a grey, his shirt so mellow a blue and his tie so neat a red and blue polka-dot that I capitulated just the way any woman worthy of the name capitulates before a man with an enchanting smile and symphonic clothes."[46]

More serious observers, however, noted the conundrum of "a dif-ferent John Erskine" encountered in his fictional works and contrasted to the refined professor and author of serious poetry and essays. The writer in that case asked: "How, then, to explain a confessedly conserva-tive professor of English literature indulging in such 'insinuendoes' (as Humpty Dumpty might say), so frequent in *Helen* and *Galahad*?"[47]

Apparently, however, many of his students considered him a bit of a mystery even before his career move into racy fiction. Lloyd Morris concluded: "The professor would have been surprised, possibly displeased, to learn how thoroughly his students discussed him; how much he puzzled and attracted them; how often he was debated in fraternity houses, at lunch counters, or over nocturnal beers in Morningside saloons. He showed a warm, though detached, interest in whatever was alive and quick...But he was personally reticent, and there was a strain of aloofness." Nevertheless, concluded Morris, his chief attraction was "the lively play of his mind, usually unpredictable, but always exhilarating."[48]

This volume addresses the many facets of John Erskine, with particular focus on his aim in bringing fine taste to the masses and the intersection of "celebrity" with his many other defining roles—professor, administrator, husband, father, community leader, concert pianist, essayist, poet, novelist, friend, and lover. It demonstrates the complex interplay of context and person as an academic reaches outside the campus to accomplish personal objectives while garnering attention from the general public. And it depicts the struggle of an individual divided against himself in seeking personal and intellectual gratification in popular arenas.

CHAPTER 1

GIFTED BOY OF THE GILDED AGE

New York City in the last two decades of the nineteenth century was the place to be. There, the very wealthy quickly became the enormously wealthy. The upper middle class became the somewhat wealthy. The middle class became hopeful. And the working poor worked. Urbanization, immigration, and industrialization spawned unprecedented economic and population growth, mechanization and marketing, factories and mansions, and skyscrapers and inventions. In 1869, Leland Stanford hammered a golden spike into a railroad tie in Utah to connect New York to the West Coast. New York City's Grand Central Depot opened a year later, followed shortly by the opening of the Metropolitan Museum of Art on Fifth Avenue. In Manhattan, Alexander Graham Bell demonstrated his telephone by speaking with his assistant in Brooklyn in 1877. The Metropolitan Opera House was dedicated in 1883. The *Wall Street Journal* arrived at newsstands in 1889.

The Erskine family also grew in size and status during those heady, gilded years. Six years after John Erskine's 1879 birth in Manhattan, his family of five moved across the Hudson River to the tony town of Weehawken, New Jersey, atop the New Jersey Palisades. John and his older sister Anna were by then joined by younger sister Helen. The next seven years produced siblings Lois (who died at age six), Robert, and Rhoda. Two aunts, sisters of Mrs. Erskine, also moved into the large, rambling home adjacent to impressive estates that stretched along the Palisades.

The residence, a new house that the young Erskine later labeled "architecturally atrocious," testified to the success of the John Erskine

Figure 1.1   John Erskine, age six, ca. 1885.

and Company silk ribbon and sash factory, a second-generation family business begun in New York City in 1841 and expanded with a move to Union Hill, New Jersey.[1] The largely German settlement of Union Hill, neighboring elegant Weehawken, was a fast-growing brewery and factory town that proved a steady source of German and Swiss weavers for the silk mill. John Erskine's father, James Morrison Erskine, heir to the management of the silk business, was born and raised in Manhattan and was of Scottish descent. His mother, Eliza Jane Hollingsworth Erskine, had mostly Irish roots and parents who had settled in Lansingburg, New York.[2]

Erskine and his siblings grew up among political and economic opinions that were upper-crust liberal and still somewhat regionally influenced. Boot strapping was possible and even preferred for families that had made their way across the Atlantic within the past generation or two. The working class was not so far chronologically from where the aristocrats had recently been; therefore, polite interaction was not impossible and philanthropy was essential. The South, where Eliza Erskine's favorite brother died during the Civil War, was viewed by the family as a misguided place that might have left things better for everyone if simply allowed to secede. The adjoining communities of dense, busy Union Hill and grassy, tree-lined Weehawken underscored both the distances and dependencies between social classes shaped by rapid social and economic change. That larger context, at times isolating and at times humanitarian, forged the bedrock values of piety, discipline, routine, and etiquette that guided day-to-day life among the Erskine family and their refined neighbors. Weehawken's upper class modeled what George Santayana identified as the dual nature of the American mentality: Half clinging to the "genteel tradition" of old-fashioned morality and culture in "all the higher things of the mind," and half moving forward with "aggressive enterprise" in active and commercial life.[3]

John Erskine would spend a lifetime straddling the incongruities of Santayana's dichotomy, attempting to enjoy both adventurous contemporary experiences and genteel comforts in his professional and his personal lives. However, during his family-centered youth, traditional gentility easily held sway. Music and the Episcopal Church were the key factors in the Erskine family life in Weehawken. Fortunately, the two quickly melded together, first at Trinity Episcopal Church in Hoboken, where James Morrison Erskine dedicated his impressive tenor voice to choir solos, and later at the new Grace Episcopal Church in Union Hill. At Grace Church, its pews full of most of Weehawken's prominent families, James Erskine organized the choir and financed the organist, Frank Fruttchey. After a few years of casual piano lessons from his father and then the family governess, seven-year-old John Erskine began twice-weekly lessons with Fruttchey, a teacher who greatly inspired his love of music, if not of practice. Yet, practice he did on the square grand family piano, until it was replaced by a more elegant Steinway baby grand. He soon also played the violin and the organ, and at age 12, when instructor Fruttchey moved away, John took over as the prodigy organist for the Grace Church choir.

Since musical ability extended to most of the Erskine family members, Sunday evenings were typically spent singing together with piano and violin accompaniment. Clearly, musical interest was the chief pastime for young John, although it was interspersed with schooling by governesses in the mornings, reading from a well-stocked family library, and fairly lengthy family suppers. The children were required to wash and change into dress clothes for dinner each evening, but they might find themselves in a separate room if there were adult guests.

Erskine later recalled a children's version of *Pilgrim's Progress* as his first reading, followed by some British boys' series. However, he insisted: "The authors who seized my imagination first were Scott, Dickens, and Tennyson. The title 'Rob Roy' on the back of a cover haunted me for some years before I had the courage to pull down the book and try it. I think I was twelve years old at the time. It has remained one of my favorite novels in English...The book which puzzled me most in my childhood and early youth is the one I now think the greatest of all novels, 'Don Quixote.'"[4] His early interest in poetry "began with three and a half lines from the *Idylls of the King*... how the old green-bound copy of Tennyson was transfigured as I read:

> 'Long stood Sir Bedivere
> Revolving many memories, till the hull
> Looked one black dot against the verge of dawn,
> And on the mere the wailing died away.'"[5]

Perhaps best demonstrating the embrace of comfort, security, and responsibility that marked his upbringing, an earnest 11-year-old John Erskine requested to Santa Claus in a brief note: "This Christmas I would like a nice [riding] whip with a short lash for Robert, and a little trumpet. And for myself I would like a drawing pen, a few other drawing instruments, and some books. I hope you will send something to the poor children and that you and your wife are well."[6] His childhood interest in carpentry soon translated into a small, shaky wooden table that he pounded together as a Christmas gift for a relative, and eventually into a series of model boats for himself.[7]

Only later would Erskine acknowledge that his fortunate, if sheltered, childhood had "kept me for years from observing real life, from seeing the America of the moment, which foretold the future." Of the most aristocratic Weehawken citizens, he decided: "They were well-to-do and cultured, but they were trying to live in an age which was already passing. I remember them as charming ghosts."[8]

* * *

At the start of his adolescent years, Erskine's musical life took a leap forward, both in performance and enjoyment, when a New York musical friend of his father's took over his piano instruction. Carl Walter, who had played the organ at St. Bartholomew's Church when James Erskine was in the choir, was a German immigrant who had hoped for a concert career in New York City. While noted for his agility—running long trills with both hands—and his expert interpretations of Mozart, Bach, and Beethoven, he somehow never gained a solid foothold in the concert scene. Instead, he became a sought-after teacher whose students were among the best because his limited patience and blunt candor allowed him to quickly weed out those with no real musical promise.

For nearly five years, young Erskine commuted weekly to Carl Walter's Manhattan brownstone, learning from his "superb technique and a repertoire of a virtuoso" and enjoying his humor and his dapper demeanor punctuated by flowered waistcoats.[9] Finally, Walter announced: "You have learned everything I can teach you. Now you must go to Europe and study under the great masters."[10] He was convinced that after piano study abroad, Erskine could have a stellar concert career. However, the youngster was both thrilled and dubious. His adored mother was unenthusiastic. The final decision was to stay home and continue to mix music with academic interests. "Perhaps the decision was wise, perhaps not," Erskine later concluded. "I think I would have been a composer."[11]

While young Erskine had been polishing his piano repertoire, his father had been expanding his business. Good earnings from the Union Hill factory inspired him to open a new mill in Norwich, New York, and to rent a home nearby, which became the family's summer residence. However, as styles began to change and demands for ribbon trim began to slow in the last decade of the nineteenth century, the two operations needed more than their earnings to stay afloat. The Depression of 1893 added to the grim picture, with sinking European investments putting US banking and the stock market into disarray. Depressed prices, falling wages, and high unemployment followed throughout the decade as James Erskine tried valiantly—and ultimately, hopelessly—to keep his business afloat. The family realized that the further education of the three oldest children would not likely be in the hands of governesses and would be close to home. For John, that meant working toward college at Columbia University.

*   *   *

If a nineteenth-century boy were to become a Columbia man, the best place to start was Columbia Grammar School, the beginning of a pipeline of well-bred adolescents who would become well-educated gentlemen of letters and of the world. Aimed at instilling its students with a solid grasp of classical languages and literature and at reinforcing the Victorian manners and morals they should have learned at home, the school also served as an entryway to Columbia College. Its location on East Fifty-First Street, just off Madison Avenue and a block away from Columbia's midtown Manhattan campus, put it squarely in the category of the many American college preparatory schools founded to assure a steady stream of the right kind of college applicants with the appropriate early groundwork for success. With no apparent fear of failure, the boys at Columbia Grammar School walked over to the college during June of their eleventh- and twelfth-grade years to sit for preliminary and then final entrance examinations.

When John Erskine entered Columbia Grammar School at age 14, the institution still reflected the character of its 1830 founding. Its first rector, brilliant classical scholar and Columbia graduate and adjunct professor Charles ("Bull") Anthon, populated the school with rules, penalties, inspirational teaching, and a commitment to training in Greek and Latin languages and philosophies. His students held him in equal amounts of fear and affection—a father figure with real power.[12] Sixty years later the school clung fast to its classical curriculum and Victorian methods, wavering little to prepare for the inevitable changes that would greet graduates confronting the twentieth century.

In 1893, the three oldest Erskine children, John and his older sister Anna and younger sister Helen, began making daily journeys from Weehawken to their schools in Manhattan—the sisters to Comstock School for Girls, about 18 blocks from Columbia Grammar School. John, with two years of weekly trips to study with Carl Walter, was already a seasoned commuter. Attendance at Columbia Grammar School required a combination of ferry, cable car, and two different horse-drawn cabs—a nearly two-hour trip each way. However, Erskine would later recall that the "formidable distance" was well worth the exposure to fine teaching, classmates who would become lifelong friends, and learning in subjects that would undergird much of his academic career.[13] Tall for his age, known for his hearty laugh, and almost immediately popular with his classmates, Erskine was also a very serious student.[14] By the end of his second year, when he sat for the Columbia College preliminary entrance examinations, he had obediently, sometimes even enthusiastically, mastered coursework in Latin and Greek grammar and prose, French, history, literature, composition, arithmetic, geometry, algebra, and declamation.[15]

Erskine found that he had a facility for Greek beyond even his strong natural ability in foreign languages, and he credited the formal and humorless Dr. Richard S. Bacon, who was nevertheless widely admired as a superb teacher, with "planting in me an enduring love of Greek civilization and culture."[16] He would later enjoy four more years of Greek as an undergraduate at Columbia College. Another memorable teacher George C. D. Odell, who would one day become a colleague of Erskine's in the English department at Columbia, sparked Erskine's interest in poetry as well as his confidence, at age 14, in his ability to criticize poetic work. He especially appreciated Italian and English sonnets, but quickly announced that he didn't think much of Henry Wadsworth Longfellow.[17] Eventually, his work in poetry would infuse his PhD dissertation and a number of published works. At Columbia Grammar School, poems constituted his first attempt at formal writing to be read by others, garnering him a reputation as a writer among his student peers. His editorship of the school newspaper followed, as did the junior class prize for composition. He recalled of his fast track to a love of writing, "At the end of my third and last school year another composition prize was offered, and again I came out ahead. After that I was incurable."[18]

Like any good early American prep school, Columbia Grammar School was a place where the notion of developing "old school ties" could be taken seriously. The same youngsters who shot spitballs at their headmaster together would later become the baccalaureate group that marched in tandem at college commencement exercises and the graduate student cohort that met over beer at someone's off-campus apartment to exchange dissertation research horrors. For Erskine, who would matriculate to Columbia College with a substantial number of grammar school buddies, the most notable of these early and long friendships were with Alfred Cohn, who later earned accolades as an early pioneering cardiologist, and Melville Cane, eventually a well-known New York lawyer with a respectable writing career on the side. At Columbia College, Erskine and Cane would join clubs together and collaborate on original campus musicals. Cane later described their 58-year friendship as: "It was close from the start and never suffered the slightest lapse in warmth or depth."[19] Another of his close friends, Harry St. Clair, would eventually join his family by marrying an Erskine cousin. By the time they all received their acceptances to Columbia College, Erskine decided that Columbia Grammar School had favored him with "double good fortune in having extraordinary classmates as well as rare teachers."[20]

CHAPTER 2

THE COLUMBIA STAMP

Students who entered Columbia College at or near the divide of the nineteenth and twentieth centuries would find their environments greatly changed by the time they completed their undergraduate experiences. The manner of arriving to register as freshmen still echoed a Gilded Age of pace and tradition that would soon be forgotten amid the new cultural stratifications and commercial commitments of twentieth-century progress. Erskine, for example, traveled with his father to register at Columbia's Forty-Ninth Street location in 1896, both shouldering into a family buggy drawn to the Forty-Second Street ferry and on to the college by their faithful old horse, Bessie. Many other new students of the era, such as Barnard-bound Virginia Gildersleeve and grammar school buddy Melville Cane, resided with their families in downtown Manhattan and could make the trip to the college by a combination of coal-burning, steam-propelled elevated trains and horse-drawn cabs.[1] Ludwig Lewisohn, arriving from Charleston, South Carolina, landed at night by steamer ship, disembarked at a Lower West Side pier, and observed about the city: "Coming from the bland and familiar South and from a life that touched reality so feebly, it seemed brutal, ferocious, stark."[2] As if to underscore the jolt of change waiting for late nineteenth-century students, by the time they graduated even their campus had relocated—to its current site at Morningside Heights.

In the fall of 1897, Erskine's sophomore year, the move to the six initial buildings of the new Columbia campus (not including two additional buildings vacated by the site's previous occupant, Bloomingdale Asylum for the Insane) on Manhattan's Upper West

Side undoubtedly invigorated a shared sense of community among faculty and students. Together they had come through the collective tedium and worry of pre-move planning to confront what one student recalled as "a sense of grandeur and confusion, of the smell of plaster and muddy footpaths, of magnificent but inconvenient distances between classrooms, and memories of the crowded but convenient and familiar home we had left."[3]

While Frederick Keppel, eventually dean of Columbia College, recalled the campus's physical detail, Erskine's grammar school friend Melville Cane noted that the new and somewhat chaotic environment, with much still under construction, inspired boisterous behavior: "The boys were unruly. [In physics class] they threw chalk around the room. It was a very unpleasant atmosphere, and I didn't understand anything."[4] Virginia Gildersleeve, however, a Barnard College student who later served as dean of that college, took in the larger horizon: "In those early days there was nothing on Morningside Heights except empty fields, a few squatters' cabins, and plenty of goats. No apartment houses cut off our view. We could see far up and down the great stretches of the Hudson…, the sunset flare over the darkened Palisades, and the far lights which sprang up calling us home at day's end. Amid these beautiful surroundings, in gay comradeship, I lived two happy years."[5]

From the pioneering spirit of settling the new campus, as well as from the reality of generous physical space, grew a determination among the settlers to initiate new clubs, teams, courses, and programs. Resident student numbers grew from 1,753 in 1890 to 4,440 in 1901, while faculty increased from 203 to 393 and library holdings climbed from 100,000 to 315,000.[6] For John Erskine and his fellow students, this was a heady time of near-frantic activity, experimentation, and discovery. The undergraduates published three student periodicals and a yearbook: *Spectator*, the daily newspaper; *Literary Monthly*, a source of student stories, essays, and criticism; *Morningside*, dedicated to verse and fiction; and *Columbian*, the annual. Student groups presented plays and musical shows regularly. More than a dozen fraternities were immediately active at the Morningside campus; Erskine eventually joined Delta Upsilon. One sorority, Kappa Kappa Gamma, opened a chapter for women students whose "coordinate" attendance at Barnard College allowed them many of the curricular and extracurricular advantages of the Columbia men while preserving the clubby tradition of an all-male campus.

The largest club, King's Crown, was founded by students and faculty after a year at Morningside "to promote sociability and to foster a love of letters, but above all to afford a common meeting place for the discussion of undergraduate movements and the institution of collegiate reforms."[7] Promoted primarily by literature professor George Edward Woodberry and his students, the somewhat shifting group met twice a month—once with a structured program, usually in the form of an address by one of Woodberry's scholarly friends followed by beer and pretzels at College Tavern, and alternately with informal talk around a keg of beer on the second floor of College Tavern. Woodberry and Professor of Greek A. V. Williams Jackson were regulars among the faculty at these sessions, as was graduate student and tutor Joel Spingarn, who would later become a noted literary figure and civil rights advocate. Erskine rarely missed a meeting. He would later recall the collegial contribution to his undergraduate years: "How much of my education I owe to the Tavern! I grieved when it was torn down to make way for the Union Theological Seminary. Woodberry and Jackson kept the talk on worthwhile topics, and drew us into it. We learned then, if we had not known before, how to be both cultured and comfortable. It would be hard to exaggerate the value of an undergraduate 'bull session' where boys speak their minds and unconsciously help each other in their gropings."[8]

*   *   *

Erskine found outlets in classes and beyond for his growing interests in writing. He joined Frederick Keppel and Virginia Gildersleeve on the board of editors of *Morningside*, which was headquartered on the dusty top floor of one of the two old buildings originally occupied by the Bloomingdale Asylum. Among their editorial colleagues were Will Bradley, one of Erskine's grammar school friends, and Hans Zinsser, whose expertise in the written word eventually would be eclipsed by his prominence in medicine and his breakthrough development of a vaccine against typhus. Other committed writers whom Erskine counted among his friends in the class of 1900 included Henry Sydnor (Syd) Harrison, whose novel *Queed* made a substantial splash only 11 years after graduation, and Henry G. (Hank) Alsberg, a determined political radical who later directed the Federal Writers' Project.[9]

Erskine was thrilled in his sophomore year when several of his verses appeared in *Morningside* and caught the attention of Professor Thomas R. Price, a nationally prominent scholar of literature and languages. A committed Southerner by virtue of birth and upbringing in a wealthy Virginia family, the courtly professor had interrupted his university studies in Germany and France at the outbreak of the Civil War to serve the Confederacy as an aide to his cousin J. E. B. Stuart. He had then determined to help the defeated South through education, first by opening a college preparatory school in Richmond, Virginia, and then through faculty appointments at Randolph-Macon College and the University of Virginia. After compiling a noteworthy college teaching record in English, modern languages, Greek, and Hebrew, he moved North in 1882 to accept an appointment as chair of English at Columbia.[10]

When Price invited Erskine to his office, and later to tea at his home, to praise his poetry, the young sophomore was struck for the first time with the possibility that he might become a writer. The timing was excellent; Erskine had discovered limited enthusiasm for his courses in the sciences and mathematics, and he doubted that even his expertise in music could sustain a career. He later recalled, "Professor Price, before I had accomplished a thing, believed in me and taught me to believe in myself."[11] Writing, especially poetry and essays, and reading great writers quickly became his passions.

Price was less successful in inspiring his pair of English Department colleagues at that time, Professors George Edward Woodberry and Brander Matthews, and he was continually pained by the infighting that swelled between the two. With divergent backgrounds, temperaments, and approaches to English language and literature, the two colleagues shared no common ground beyond the corridor that led to their offices in Fayerweather Hall. Matthews, an urbane sophisticate who enjoyed theater and clubs in New York, Paris, and London, was first brought to Columbia in 1891 to fill in when Professor Price took a year of leave. A brilliant conversationalist whose students enjoyed both his "shrewdness and good-fellowship,"[12] he stayed on when Price returned, and he quickly initiated new courses in drama and modern fiction. Upton Sinclair, who arrived in 1897 with a master of arts degree in mind, labeled Mathews "the beau ideal of the successful college professor, metropolitan style; a club-man, easy-going and cynical, but not too much so for propriety; wealthy enough to be received at the dinners of trustees, and witty enough to be welcome anywhere...a bitter reactionary."[13]

George Edward Woodberry, however, was a dreamy idealist and stubborn traditionalist who struck the normally iconoclastic Sinclair as "a master not merely of criticism but of creation; also a charming spirit and a friend to students."[14] Even his fleshy face, sloped shoulders, and drooping mustache contrasted with his nemesis Matthews's high cheekbones and erect posture. Entrenched in his Beverly, Massachusetts roots, Woodberry had studied at Harvard under Henry Adams, Charles Eliot Norton, and James Russell Lowell. He had attended Ralph Waldo Emerson's last lecture. An accomplished poet, he embraced the genteel literary approach of discovering the intersections of life and art in order to express ideal ways of being. He had no patience for the coming wave of realism in any literary form.[15] Following a faculty stint at the University of Nebraska, he came to Columbia in 1890 after Norton and Lowell recommended him to President Seth Low. In 1891, when the English Language and Literature Department was reorganized into three areas, Woodberry was appointed head of the Department of Literature. Devoted students, such as Hans Zinsser, found him "unquestionably one of the greatest teachers this country has ever seen, inspiring with his own passionate sincerity a large and diverse group of young men, few of whom, whatever their subsequent occupations, ever lost entirely the imprint of his personality."[16] Joel Spingarn noted that "he attracted around him all the most alert elements in undergraduate life, athletes as well as scholars, and not only aroused in them a new interest in literature, but gave them a new point of view with which to interpret it."[17] Summing up Woodberry's effect on student habits, Lionel Trilling added, "He was distinguished by the undergraduates from all their other professors—he alone was waited for if he was late to class."[18]

The differences between Woodberry and Matthews reflected changes rippling through the field of English language and literature on many campuses. The old guard represented by Woodberry kept alive the spirit of liberal learning in foundational areas that called for the study and enjoyment of classic literature for its sound and form, as well as its enduring philosophical meanings. According to Joel Spingarn, Woodberry exhibited a "narrowness of sympathy which brushed aside the racier writers like Walt Whitman, Thoreau, Mark Twain, and Herman Melville."[19] Matthews, on the other hand, represented a growing trend toward curricular specialization, allowing students to delve deeply into smaller slices of subject matter and concluding, "Specialization of function is the mark of advancing civilization."[20] He preferred to expose students to newer literary types, what he called "cosmopolitan classics," that actively represented contemporary culture and innovative forms.[21]

Inevitably, students leaned toward either Matthews or Woodberry, with Erskine firmly in the camp of the latter. His undergraduate sensitivities resonated with Woodberry's welcome assertion that literature was best understood with regard to readers' own emotions, experiences, and instincts. To prime the use of those individual powers, Woodberry recommended early reading of the "greatest books of world literature...Such books are landmarks of the intellectual life and give proportion to all later reading."[22] The 1899 publication of Woodberry's well-received volume of essays, *Heart of Man*—"grave and noble in the extreme,"[23] according to William James—further amplified students' affection for their earnest professor. His classes drew students in ever-larger numbers that, according to a *New York Times* reporter, resulted in "thus exciting, it is said, various jealousies in the faculty."[24]

Erskine was less taken with Brander Matthews, although he was impressed with Matthews's vocal demonstrations of allegiance to Columbia and his presence as "a skilled and graceful man of letters." However, he was uncomfortable with the stylish professor's inclination to poke fun at his old-guard colleagues, recalling Professor Price's frequent embarrassment because "Brander was not above telling jokes at the expense of the old and defeated South."[25]

Students, of course, could not have known the extent of the growing bitterness between Mathews and Woodberry as it spilled over to issues of faculty service, teaching hours, time spent on campus, and administrative influence. The depth of the rift as it slid toward juvenile mudslinging is clear in a memo from Woodberry to President Low at the beginning of Erskine's junior year, stating:

> I must request you to communicate directly with Professor Matthews on all matters concerning him, he having explicitly forbidden me to address him. I shall, with your permission, conduct the department for the present without communication with him.[26]

When Low asked Matthews to resign in 1899, he received a curt refusal that stated: "I cannot consider for a moment your suggestion that I resign. Under no circumstances will I do so."[27] The president then opted for the usual administrative solution, shuffling departmental responsibilities through reorganization. He dealt the chair designation of the new Department of Comparative Literature to Woodberry and the chairmanship of the new Department of English to Matthews. Course overlap and petty jealousies helped assure that the discord would only continue to escalate.

* * *

Erskine, however, was too delighted with his discovery of poetry and classic literature, as well as with his own abilities with the written word, to concern himself with faculty battles. He thrived on Woodberry's long Socratic dialogues in his undergraduate literature course—a semester of study that presaged the concept, if not the formalized content, of a "great books" course. Woodberry's class started with a discussion of Aristotle's *Poetics* covering several weeks. Homer, Lucretius, and Virgil followed. All were the subject of heady discussions prompted by Woodberry's probing questions, which, according to Erskine's fellow student Ferris Greenslet, assured that "understanding and appreciation were drawn out from the inner consciousness of the respondent and so felt to be wholly his own."[28] The following semester, the class moved forward in time to *Song of Roland* and works of epic and romance by Ariosto, Tasso, Cervantes, Spenser, and finally Milton. Most of the very mesmerized young men quickly signed up for Woodberry's undergraduate course on Shelley the following year.

Woodberry also taught some large lecture classes, with as many as 90 boys in attendance, in which he displayed "his unusual gift for speaking of a poet in the very mood of the poet's own work."[29] Erskine and a steady stream of youthful enthusiasts like him were thrilled to find unexpected meaning in literature that had typically been taught in ways far less consequential to their limited experiences. He recalled of Woodberry, "He had a unique gift for making even an unread youth appreciate, at least to a degree, how in some passage of Shakespeare or Keats a very human experience produced in the poet a poetic emotion, and how that emotion dictated the form of the poem."[30]

Equally impressive to young Erskine was the internationally renowned composer and pianist Edward MacDowell, who taught all areas of music appreciation and practice. Hired by President Seth

Low at the occasion of a $150,000 gift to start a music department at Columbia, MacDowell had arrived at Columbia in 1896 after prolonged studies in music that had taken him to New York and Paris, where he counted Debussy among his classmates, and eventually to Frankfort, where he found a mentor in Franz Liszt. By 1890, he had settled with his family in Boston and had kept a regular schedule of teaching, performing, and composing. He was attracted to Columbia by the opportunity to start a music program from scratch and by support from President Low for the notion that the program could eventually become a School of the Arts that included art and architecture, as well as music.[31] Apparently, MacDowell failed to comprehend that in academic terms a "program" might simply mean an instructor with a few related courses and a handful of students. He was determined that Columbia's new music endeavor should teach composition, technique, and theory to serious musicians and should teach music aesthetics to others as well. But, with no other assistance for the first three years, he discovered he needed to do all of this by himself. And he needed to attend to administering the fledgling program, establishing a music library, admitting students, securing space and equipment, and negotiating curricular issues with the Faculty of Philosophy, which housed his program. He dedicated himself to the daunting challenge, no doubt convinced that help was on the way.

Erskine was happily amazed at the fortunate coincidence that had brought him and MacDowell to Columbia in the same year. Still toying with the possibility of pursuing a second career in music that might complement his literary ambitions, he was convinced that at the very least the piano would be an important part of his life. The courses he immediately undertook in composition and in harmony and counterpoint introduced him to "the first topflight genius" he had ever met. Joining Erskine in MacDowell's classes were students who ranged from those with musical careers in mind to those with only vague ideas about the finishing effects of some musical understanding. Fortunately, they found in MacDowell a fine teacher who managed to fascinate students from all areas of the university as he shifted from lectern to piano and back again in demonstrations of music theory, counterpoint, harmony, and orchestration.[32]

When the campus moved to Morningside Heights, MacDowell was rewarded with some relief from his overloaded teaching schedule in the form of two assistants who instructed elementary classes and took the lead with the university orchestra and Barnard chorus. This allowed the great musician to unleash some of his most creative, if not always tightly focused, teaching on advanced students. Erskine later recalled: "I had the impression always that his point of departure was not the precise frontier of his students' knowledge or ignorance, but some musical problem which at the moment engaged his interest...He'd ask one of us to write a theme on a blackboard and to do something or other with it, but it wasn't always clear what the theme and its development would illustrate, and as soon as we began asking for information about it, our questions were likely to suggest new directions of thought, which however brilliant, left us somewhat breathless."[33] Erskine, his love of piano reinvigorated, frequently accompanied Columbia Glee Club rehearsals.

Wondering about his future in music, young Erskine pressed his teacher about whether he had any special talent as a composer or pianist. MacDowell admitted he saw "nothing special, but enough to make a good craftsman if you work hard." He also admonished, "Would a law student ask his teacher the chances of his becoming a member of the Supreme Court? An honest, hard-working lawyer has a creditable place in society...Until we have thousands of well-trained musicians, there will be no adequate foundation for genius to build on when it arrives."[34]

For Erskine, being part of a competent foundation was not enough. Further, MacDowell's candid appraisal came at a time when he was beginning to envision the possibility of a life in literature. After his sophomore year, he took no more music courses and never again considered a career as a musical talent. He did, however, continue to work with the Glee Club as needed, to sing in the all-male campus choir, and to provide organ accompaniment for nearby church services whenever needed. He continued to attend the recital performances that capped MacDowell's composition classes. And in his senior year, he penned and composed the Columbia "Marching Song."[35]

The capstone to the undergraduate experience for the 93 graduates of the Columbia class of 1900 was the traditional "Varsity Show," an original musical production written and performed by the graduating seniors. Erskine composed and scored for the university orchestra a play and libretto by Melville Cane and Syd Harrison titled "The Governor's Vrouw." Among the graduating seniors in the cast was future film director William C. De Mille. The historical spoof concerned an early New York governor, William Kieft, his rotund wife, and his beautiful daughter—all embroiled in a caper of political mishaps that involved Indians and Connecticut Yankees in wars over tobacco taxation and the use of wampum as legal tender. The production played for a week at the Carnegie Lyceum and then at the Brooklyn Academy of Music. Spring commencement followed, with Erskine and Melville Cane again collaborating as composer and librettist on the class song, "To Stand by Thee, Columbia," sung at the close of commencement ceremonies.[36] At commencement, Erskine was awarded the Proudfit Fellowship in Letters, which assured his ability to remain at Columbia for graduate school.[37]

*   *   *

For most Columbia graduate students in the earliest years of the new century, education was a matter of attending advanced classes, determining topics of research interest, sticking close to faculty mentors, and interacting with friends from undergraduate years and those few new faces who were able to quickly fit in with established groups. For the Columbia faculty, those same years were more turbulent. In 1901, Seth Low resigned from his 11-year presidency to run for, and then serve as, mayor of New York City. He left a legacy of accomplishment at Columbia that included exceptional growth in faculty, students, and academic programs; the campus move to Morningside Heights; greatly expanded endowments; initiation of summer sessions and extension courses; the inclusion of Teachers College; incorporation of the College of Physicians and Surgeons as an integral part of the university; and the end of required chapel. Low was typically viewed as a busy progressive spirit who brought money and modernity to Columbia without unsettling the delicate balances of interpersonal relationships on campus. He was succeeded by Columbia alumnus and faculty member Nicholas Murray Butler, whose remarkable energy and decisiveness would ignite both great achievements and great controversy during his more than 40 years in the Columbia presidency.[38] Dubbed "Nicholas the Miraculous" by his friend Theodore Roosevelt, he more than lived up to the title in vision, in university fund-raising, and in personal demeanor.

Then, as now, the graduate students' experiences varied widely, even within a single discipline. In graduate seminars, Erskine enjoyed his acquaintance with students he later recalled as "a number of unusual characters"—future noted writers and academics Ludwig Lewisohn and William Ellery Leonard, future University of North

Carolina president Edward Graham, and social activist and writer Upton Sinclair. In his studies in English and literature, John Erskine was delighted to continue his association with Professors Woodberry, Price, and Matthews and to welcome the new faculty addition William Peterfield Trent, a Virginian who had most recently taught at the University of the South where he founded *The Sewanee Review*. Erskine quickly came to know Trent as "a beloved figure...full of courtesy and humor." Woodberry's lectures were still "extraordinary," and Matthews's classes were always "scintillating."[39] Erskine also admired the brilliant activist Joel Elias Spingarn, who had just completed his PhD at Columbia and was immediately appointed Woodberry's assistant in comparative literature.

Ludwig Lewisohn, working with the same professors at the same time, was far less sanguine. "The lectures of these excellent professors were dull and dispiriting to me" he recalled 20 years later in his autobiography. He maintained that his undergraduate years at the College of Charleston had familiarized him with the literature relevant to his graduate English studies, and he had expected graduate classes to build on that knowledge with more complex meanings and interpretations. Instead, he discovered that professors simply "ladled out information," and he "found no master" among the faculty. "So, I drifted and occasionally 'cut' lectures and wrote my reports and passed creditable examinations without doing a page of the required reading. I had done it all!"[40]

Upton Sinclair, pursuing a master of arts degree with tuition money earned from nearly a dozen dime novels he authored by the time he was 22 years old, found "the same dreary routine"[41] he had endured in his undergraduate years at New York City College. However, instead of cutting classes, he simply registered for courses, went to 1 or 2 classes, and then quickly dropped those he didn't like—by his own count eventually completing only 5 or 6 of the more than 40 courses he started. Clearly, the future political activist, socialist, and Pulitzer Prize winner sought livelier company than he found among the students and faculty who John Erskine so thoroughly appreciated. Sinclair would later recall Erskine as a student "whom I knew as a timid and conventional 'researcher.'"[42]

Erskine easily settled into a graduate student life defined by his continuing set of friends, his poetry writing, his dissertation research, and his piano playing. His doctoral pursuit started just when his father, after overextending his business at the start of a recessionary national economy, sold the Erskine factory and the big house in New Jersey. The family moved to a large apartment on West Eighty-Fifth Street and enjoyed the company of new cosmopolitan neighbors and evenings singing around the piano. They repaired to Norwich, Connecticut, each summer.

Erskine met regularly with a group of literary friends who called themselves the Society of Bards and Prophets and who frequented Upper West Side breweries to chat and peer review each other's work. The contacts were invaluable. Among them was Woodberry's assistant, Joel Spingarn, who served as the founding editor of the *Journal of Comparative Literature*. William Bradley and George Hellman, a year ahead of Erskine at Columbia, also frequently attended the occasions and had recently begun publishing a respectable literary magazine *East and West*. Erskine's first paid writing, $2.50, was for a poem titled "Parting" that appeared in *East and West*.[43] During his first year of graduate school, he won a national competition held by the *Century Magazine* for the best poem written within a year after college graduation. His idyllic poem "Actaeon," a modernized interpretation of the Greek myth, soon paved the way for publication of his work in the *Atlantic Monthly,* where recent Columbia graduate Ferris Greenslet served as associate editor.[44]

Erskine's coursework during graduate school was centered in literature and languages. He studied seventeenth-century literature with Professor Trent, Molière's drama with Professor Matthews, Middle English literature with Professor Price, and literary epics with Professor Woodberry. Already adept at French, Latin, and Greek, he tackled Italian and German (required for the PhD at that time) in his graduate years.

*   *   *

Reflecting the character of American higher education in general, Columbia at the turn of the century experienced accelerated growth and differentiation. New faculty titles—for example, lecturers, instructors, and assistants—cropped up on campuses throughout the country. New curricular specializations divided and subdivided departments into constellations of academic interests. Large areas once under single professorships, such as political economy or natural science, fractured into subspecialties narrowly defined by faculty pursuits and student attention. As Abraham Flexner lamented about the consequences of multiple departments and units in early twentieth-century American colleges: "They no longer revolve around a central sun; they do not even freely intersect."[45]

At Columbia, where the full-time faculty numbers had increased greatly during campus expansion on Morningside Heights, English literature had been split off from its placement under the professorship of moral philosophy. It soon bifurcated into dramatic literature and comparative literature, with a separate rhetoric and composition division for undergraduates. Erskine remained devoted to Woodberry and convinced that "not only in undergraduate teaching but in the promotion of graduate studies, he had no rival in the English department."[46] However, for reasons related to the dividing lines of curricular specialties within the English Department, his dissertation in Elizabethan literary concerns required the guidance of Professors Price and Trent.

Combining his love of music and love of poetry, Erskine set out to analyze the history and form of Elizabethan lyrics in terms of both their literary and musical qualities, including their rhythm, cadence, and metrical forms. In 1903, a slightly amplified version of his dissertation was published as *The Elizabethan Lyric: A Study* by the Columbia University Press. An effusive review in the *New York Times* welcomed Erskine as "one of the very, very few students of literature who have taken the trouble to know anything about music, recognize its significance, and treat it intelligently when the two arts come into contact. This one act alone gives his book an almost unique place in literary research and scholarship."[47]

Erskine earned his PhD at a time of substantial disagreement among academics—especially those in the humanities—attempting to respond to the growing encroachment of research and utilitarianism and to the expanding enthusiasm for democracy and progressivism. The waning prominence of a genteel elite in academic life had opened wide the campus doors to not only new students, but also new aims and new subjects. The twentieth-century enthusiasm for the present, and even the future, bore with it questions about the relevance of the past. What of enduring culture, tradition, and values?

Thus, one group of professors avidly defended liberal culture, and the new humanists among them particularly railed against the increasing eminence of science, materialism, and relativism. In 1908, Alexander Meiklejohn, then a professor at Brown and soon-to-become president of Amherst, summarized the stance of liberal culture advocates when he insisted that the aim of higher education "is not primarily to teach the forms of living, not primarily to give practice to the act of living, but rather to broaden and deepen the insight into life itself, to open up the riches of human experience, of literature, of nature, of art, of religion, of philosophy, of human relations...so that life may be fuller and richer in content."[48] On the other side, of course, were battalions of academics and students concerned with contemporary life, both in and outside campus boundaries, and excited by the possibilities of discovery and the realities of professional practice.

Erskine, upon graduation, was fully schooled in the more traditional camp. Therefore, when he considered his teaching invitations from Amherst College and the University of Kansas, he quickly accepted the offer at Amherst. Yet, his disciplined practice as a budding concert pianist and his experience in writing for publication had drawn him toward an active, rather than contemplative, approach to learning and teaching liberal culture. Laurence Veysey, in his classic account of the rise of the distinctive American brand of higher education, cited Erskine as one of "a younger breed of professors [who] began appearing in American institutions of higher learning around the turn of the century...These represented more fully a new cordiality between culture and intellect."[49]

As Erskine prepared to take his place among that new breed, he was struck by the unsettling realization: "This time I had indeed come to the end of my youth."[50]

CHAPTER 3

THE GOWN IS THE TOWN

That Amherst College and many fellow institutions dedicated to undergraduate liberal learning still thrived in 1903 was somewhat of a puzzle. Amidst an avalanche of late nineteenth-century industrial prominence and material enthusiasm, American higher education had tilted toward the new, the big, the multifaceted, and the mega-endowed. The real excitement was for the ascendancy of notable names, new graduate programs, innovative research, and expansive spending at places like Johns Hopkins, Cornell, University of Chicago, Vanderbilt, Stanford, and Columbia. Richard Hofstadter applauded the large and fortunate campuses founded or remodeled late in the nineteenth century as "a system of genuine universities," made possible when the "intellectual community began to detach itself from the leisured class."[1]

Yet, colleges in the liberal tradition—reluctantly backpedaling from strict classicism and religious dogma of earlier years, but still committed to teaching moral conduct and spiritual cognition—continued to attract students and faculty who collectively harbored a healthy suspicion of materialism and an earnest embrace of education for growth and citizenship. Amherst College was founded in 1821 when the surrounding central Massachusetts community determined that Williams College was too far west to survive and Harvard was far too estranged from its Puritan roots. However, after a half century of proud attachment to piety and intellect, Amherst slowly shed its evangelical leanings and its emphasis on classical mental training. By the turn of the century, it was a well-endowed all-male college with an excellent academic reputation and a distaste for the national academic tendency toward professional preparation and utilitarian knowledge. Laurence Veysey explained: "At Yale and at such smaller colleges as Amherst and Bowdoin, the closing years of the century brought a definite expectation of change. As the notion of mental discipline slipped ever further into the background, these institutions moved into the camp of liberal culture—thus retaining their posture of aloofness from the major trends of educational reform."[2] In full agreement, Amherst aimed, according to its president, "to make broad, cultivated men, physically sound, intellectually awake, socially refined and gentlemanly, with appreciation of art, music, literature, and with sane, simple religion, all in proportion—not athletics simply, not scholars simply, not dilettantes, not society men, not pietists, but all-round men."[3]

Erskine arrived at the tiny college in the quaint New England town of Amherst as both a literary intellectual in the well-worn tradition of appreciation and criticism and a working poet committed to writing and publication. The bifurcation of his commitments reflected an American cultural divide of the early twentieth century that straddled both the world of thought and ideals and the world of action and material gain. Van Wyck Brooks identified the new duality as especially conflicting in "the university man," observing: "The theoretical atmosphere in which he has lived is one that bears no relation to society; the practical atmosphere in which he has lived bears no relation to ideals."[4] Literary practitioners and teachers, in particular, had not yet reconciled what Hofstadter later defined as "the divorce in American writing and thinking between sensibility, refinement, theory, and discipline on one side and spontaneity, energy, sensuous reality, and the seizure of opportunity on the other—in short, a painful separation between the qualities of mind and the materials of experience."[5]

Stubbornly embracing a middle path, new Amherst instructor John Erskine aimed to position himself as a deep thinker who could instill literary passion and knowledge in his students and also as a poetic practitioner who could carve new paths in creative work. In the classroom, where he was to teach composition and English literature, he would fashion himself after the sensitive Woodberry, complete with "stimulating lectures which would create in the hearers a passionate love for the best authors."[6] In his writing, spurred on by glowing reviews of the book version of his doctoral dissertation, *The Elizabethan Lyric: A Study*, he would add to the poems that had so successfully begun with the publication of his award-winning *Actaeon*.

*   *   *

Upon arrival, Erskine quickly realized that Amherst was most promi-nently a country college. Situated on a rise just a few Main Street blocks from the center of town, the small cluster of campus buildings crowned a classic New England village where residences, churches, a hotel, business offices, and retail stores gathered side by side in the harmony of relatively small proportions and consistent red brick and white board architecture. The Reverend Doctor George Harris, Amherst class of 1866 and president of the college from 1899 to 1912, impressed Erskine as "neither a teacher nor a scholar...He was not an educator. He was a very kind gentleman, a retired minister."[7] Harris had bumbled through the recruitment interview with the young Erskine, asking little more than his denominational status, his marital status, and his hometown. He noted that Erskine's instruc-torship offer came with a $1,500 annual salary and responsibility for teaching all sections of freshman English for 120 boys who badly needed more challenging coursework than the limited fare of recent years. They also needed to be inspired to graduate; in the first decade of the twentieth century, Amherst classes generally lost about half their students before graduation.[8]

Although Erskine was not surprised by the size difference that distinguished Amherst from Columbia, he was disappointed at the disparities in spirit that separated a country college from an urban university. He lamented the dearth of cultural entertainment in the town of Amherst, and he felt that the young college boys missed the maturing influence of having graduate professional students on their campus. Most disturbing was the almost complete lack of research or productive scholarship among faculty, resulting in "no great intel-lectual stir on the college campus."[9] Still aglow with memories of fine teachers like Woodberry, MacDowell, Price, and Trent, Erskine was convinced that the teacher, not the curriculum or the pedagogy, was the key to student learning. And he was firm in his assertion that "a first class teacher should begin by being a first class scholar."[10]

Only about a half dozen of approximately 40 faculty members were not Amherst graduates when Erskine arrived, adding to the provin-cialism that the college would work hard to shed in coming years.

A large number of notable veteran faculty members had been graduate students in Germany and gravitated toward scientific study in their approach to their disciplines. But, since most faculty published little or nothing at all, their analyses generally were disseminated only to their students. New faculty were expected to shoulder the burden of large classes in foundational areas, while senior faculty scheduled themselves into more specialized work with upperclassmen.

Erskine's two colleagues in the English Department, Professors John Franklin Genung and George Bosworth Churchill, did not deviate from the typical pattern of hierarchy. The venerable old rhetoric and composition professor Genung ("Nungie"), with his commanding position among the dwindling old guard of noteworthy faculty who put Amherst on the map, had earned the privilege of teaching when and what he wanted. Erskine understood that immediately. However, he entertained thoughts that Churchill, only 13 years his senior, might become an early career mentor. But it soon became apparent that Churchill was not a frequent presence on campus outside his own classes, and he bristled when Erskine tried to urge him into duties with student clubs or advising. Their chilly relationship left Erskine still fuming six years after he left the Massachusetts campus for a post at Columbia. When a new Amherst president Alexander Meiklejohn asked him to consider returning, Erskine retorted: "Why should anyone who went through what I did with him [Churchill], and who has seen other men in the department subject to the same experience, voluntarily expose himself to a repetition of such an ordeal?...Any reform in Professor Churchill's attitude might just as well begin before you get additional instructors. In fact, I think it will have to, for the situation in the department is pretty well known throughout the country, and I believe I am not singular in my reluctance to make part of my life work the rejuvenation of Professor Churchill."[11]

*   *   *

From 1903 to 1909, Erskine did learn to enjoy the small-town environment and the company of many students and colleagues who became lifelong friends. He first gravitated to the local Episcopalians at Grace Church, where he eventually played the organ, served on the vestry, and became the choir master. Other early friendships were among his fellow young bachelor instructors who roomed at the large house of Mrs. Baxter Marsh, where Erskine had a study and a bedroom (although not on the same floor). There, he became friends with Ernest H. Wilkins, an instructor in Latin and romance languages who would later become president of Oberlin College; William J. Newlin, instructor in mathematics; and Curtis H. Walker, instructor in history. His closest friendships, which endured for many years, were with associate professor of romance languages William Nitze, and professor of music William P. ("Biggie") Bigelow. Bigelow, a connoisseur of good literature and music, managed a large chorus of approximately three hundred singers drawn from Amherst students and faculty, the local community, and even nearby high schools. Erskine and Wilkins were among the faculty who sang with the chorus, which rehearsed every Monday night with the college orchestra. For final performances of any given work, guest artists appeared from the Boston Symphony and beyond. These, including international piano virtuosos Josef Hofmann and Olga Samaroff, became the beginning of a network of professional musical talent that Erskine would build upon throughout his life.

Bigelow was a native of Amherst who had studied music in Europe before returning to teach. Like Erskine, he was unmarried during the years they shared at Amherst, and Erskine often walked the few blocks to Bigelow's home for long and stimulating chats late in the evenings. Later, Bigelow claimed Erskine as "a sort of amazing protégé of mine" and recalled their close friendship in "those early days in Amherst of late hours, of mutual bachelordom, mince pies at 2 am, courting letters, Churchill."[12]

Faculty teas, dinner parties at faculty homes, visiting lecturers, and college theatrical and musical performances—along with church and chorus activities—easily occupied the limited spare time Erskine found available when he was not teaching, grading papers, or writing poetry. The tall (approximately 6 feet, 2 inches), gangly bachelor with prominent dark hair and thick eyebrows was a favorite of faculty wives, who undoubtedly enjoyed speculating about his marital prospects.

Of course, as a tiny town still full of original settler families and back-fence communication, Amherst bustled with talk about the activities of its local citizens. Among these, special fascination aimed at the descendants of Emily Dickinson, whose ancestors were at various times key to the founding of the town, the church, and the college that defined Amherst. The square New England brick house, the Homestead, where the reclusive poet had resided, still stood separated from Amherst's Main Street only by a hedge, a slight elevation, and a short walkway to the front door. Emily's brother, Austin Dickinson, had moved next door to a large, multilevel Italianate villa, the Evergreens, built by their father to assure that his son and daughter-in-law would not move away from Amherst. Austin's widow, Susan, and daughter, Martha, still lived there when they weren't traveling in Europe. Erskine eventually got to know the two women and enjoyed their hospitality and conversation on many occasions. He became an especially avid fan of the worldly and quick-witted Susan, who had been a close friend of Emily's during their teen years and later was considered more a sister than sister-in-law. To Erskine, Susan was "cultured, intelligent, and kind." Emily's niece, Martha, he viewed as "unconventional and unforgettable."[13] He recalled the atmosphere in their home as one of "satiric illumination," which sometimes targeted celebrated intellectuals or their own neighbors for barbed comments. But, he maintained that "the targets they selected certainly deserved to be hit."[14]

Generations of Dickinson family members traditionally provided entertaining gossip for their Amherst neighbors. When Emily's father renovated the Homestead and built the Evergreens, speculation about the amount and source of funding became a local pastime. Austin Dickinson's lengthy affair with faculty wife Mabel Loomis Todd proved yet another source of whispered outrage. During Erskine's time, Amherst tongues wagged over Martha Dickinson's brief marriage in 1905 to a Russian military captain, Alexander Bianchi. And they continued to wag about the debate over the right to edit and bring to publication Emily Dickinson's poetry. Volumes of the work were willed to Martha by Emily's sister, Lavinia; but other volumes were possessed by Austin, who willed the editing work to Mabel Todd. When various books of Dickinson poetry appeared in print, arguments raged over who was the better editor, Martha Dickinson or Mrs. Todd.[15]

Erskine was convinced that local gossips had treated Dickinson descendants unfairly, and he remained protective of Martha until her death in 1943. In her frequent letters to him, she referred to him as "my god son," and in 1926, he inscribed one of his novels to her with a reminder of "my devoted friendship."[16] A dozen years later, George Whicher, a student of Erskine's at Amherst and later at Columbia, published a biography of Emily Dickinson, and Erskine fumed about sections he considered an attack on Martha.[17]

*   *   *

Erskine originally had been scheduled to teach two sections of freshman English, composition and literature, to Amherst's 120 first-year students. Predictably, sections of 60 students quickly proved unwieldy. The earnest young instructor then doubled his classroom time to divide the boys into four sections, with each section required to meet twice a week. Each student was required to submit a weekly theme paper and to consult with Erskine about it. Soon, shocked by the mistakes on the themes he read, he also organized a spelling class "for the benefit of the near illiterate" among the Amherst matriculates.[18] He also recorded a zero on any paper with four spelling errors on its six pages. Thankfully, Erskine was a high-energy 24-year-old when he reported for duty at Amherst. Although his youth left him little leverage in the area of classroom discipline, he was able to keep up with a teaching and grading schedule that none of his older colleagues would have managed.

While he spent most of the composition teaching time correcting rudimentary grammatical and spelling errors, Erskine did manage to introduce real development and interest into his English-literature teaching. He attacked that subject as he had learned from Woodberry at Columbia, aiming for lectures that would stimulate interest in all his students and even a lifelong passion for fine literature in some. He stuck to British poetry and prose only, with no introduction of American literature or of authors from elsewhere in Europe. Authors from other continents—Africa, Asia, and Latin America—were almost never mentioned in American classrooms of the early nineteenth century. At Amherst, Erskine started with Chaucer, moved on through Blake and Burns, and eventually guided his classes to Thackeray, Dickens, and Tennyson. He covered a score of authors each semester, stopping short of Thomas Hardy, Rudyard Kipling, and other live British authors because, as he later recalled of his youthful sentiment, "To be great, a writer must be dead."[19]

Erskine considered the books he taught to be among "the great books," and he used that phrase liberally. He firmly believed that through exposure to volumes of fine literature, without sidebar discussions about literary forms or author biographies, students would learn to delight in ideas and in creative expression. In an essay published in the *Nation* during his Amherst years, he summarized his convictions:

A college course in literature should provide for two things—the direct contact of the student's mind with as many books as possible, and the filling in of any gaps in his sympathy with what he reads. Almost all the great books were intended for the average man, and the author contemplated an immediate relation with his audience. There is room for the annotator or teacher only when time has made the subject remote or strange, or when the reader's imagination is unable to grasp the recorded experience.

. . . If the pupil's task is to read great books constantly, the teacher's part, to connect the reading with the pupil's experience, is large and difficult. When we consider the wide knowledge he must have of boys and of books, we need not be surprised if the successful teacher is rare.

. . . Finally, the teacher of literature should if possible be a writer. The creative habit of mind, no matter how modestly exercised, is the surest of all protections against pedantry.[20]

It could not have been an easy sell to inspire in Amherst undergraduates a love of great poetry and prose by tapping into ideas and emotions that might parallel their own experiences. President George Harris, always distrustful of intellectual life, clung fast to the idea that the college aim was to develop each student into the all-around man—a well-networked, well-liked guy who was neither too scholarly nor too backward.[21] Erskine's teaching, however, drew upon individual intellectual habits and emotional identity. Further, Erskine's courses demanded greater time in solitary reading and writing than the freshmen had expected, just when Amherst students had become evermore committed to busy extracurricular lives. Fraternities and athletics were the key features of early twentieth-century college life, and new student clubs popped up like weeds each year. As one analyst noted of that Amherst period: "Life was shallow and diffuse . . . And the college was clearly in the hands of the students."[22]

While adhering to the best of what he had experienced in his Columbia professors, Erskine experimented with pedagogical adjustments geared to large groups of underclassmen. He eventually assigned each student in his English-literature courses an essay on the author to be discussed in class, to be submitted before that class began. In this way, the classes became more concerned with group discussions and arguments, while less concerned with lectures and follow-up questions. "In a sense," Erskine later recalled, "the students gave the course; I criticized their presentations."[23]

In his third year of teaching, Erskine determined that creativity, both his own and his students', was the key to achieving scholarship in either appreciating or criticizing literature. Therefore, "I must practice the subject I taught, and my students must practice it too," he insisted.[24] He deviated from the requirement of written essays on assigned reading, a typical practice at the time. Instead, he began asking students in literature courses to write their own poems, short stories, and one-act plays. Some of the plays were then produced before the Literary Club, with a makeshift "stage" in an area in front of the fireplace in the student lounge. The exercise in creative writing, Erskine concluded, served a dual purpose: "To make scholars of my students, and to make writers of them."[25]

For his familiarity with almost all Amherst students and for his ability to connect literature to young lives, Erskine was widely known by the collegians as a dynamic lecturer and mentally stimulating discussant. His student George Whicher later recalled "the provocative opinions of literature and life hurled at our defenseless heads by John Erskine" and acknowledged that Erskine's "influence and inspiration" set him on his own path as a writer and English teacher.[26] In addition to his involvement with extracurricular choral productions and student plays, Erskine was actively involved in Greek life as faculty advisor to Delta Upsilon fraternity.

By the start of his fourth year at Amherst, Erskine had authored two additional books since the publication of his dissertation and was promoted to associate professor. In 1905, Longmans, Green and Company published *Selections from Spenser's The Faerie Queen*, "Edited with notes and introduction by John Erskine." Erskine's lengthy introduction to Edmund Spenser's epic Elizabethan poem included a detailed study of Spenser's historical and cultural setting, a full biography, and a critical examination of his poetic methods and influences. Erskine also added an instructional advice section, "Helps to Teachers," a glossary of hundreds of words and terms, a time line of Spenser's life and works, and extensive explanatory footnotes to help readers understand actions and consequences.[27]

A collection of Erskine's poetry, including his award-winning *Actaeon*, appeared in 1907 as *Actaeon and Other Poems*. Among its 31 poems were many he had written since coming to Amherst and some that had already been published in the *Century Magazine, East and West, Morningside*, and the *Columbia Literary Monthly*. They demonstrated a range of poetic styles and rhyme schemes, and, in poems like "Iphidamus," "Catullus," and "With Sappho's Poems," they acknowledged the author's scholarly understanding of ancient Greek and Roman poets. Other entries—"Futility," "Faith," and

"Heart's Desire"—pegged Erskine as a committed romantic. The book was reviewed in the *New York Times* by Erskine's grammar school and college friend William A. Bradley. He praised its "purity of feeling and acceptance of high poetic aims, without concession to modern vulgarizing influences." But he concluded that "Mr. Erskine has written much that is good since 'Actaeon,' but he seems for the most part to have fallen upon a more personal and minor strain." For example, he noted "Song of Friends," as "a graceful, flowing piece of verse...with a vein of personal reminiscence and admonition to the poet's fellows not to forget their splendid ideals and high ambitions in hard strife or easy achievement."[28]

Good reviews, however, did not convince Erskine that his future was secure as a poet. He had not managed to rise to the level he achieved in *Actaeon*, and he began to enjoy writing essays that allowed him to directly comment on contemporary issues in literature and education. He described his 1908 essay in the *Nation*, "The Teaching of Literature in College," as a piece about "making boys love literature as Woodberry had trained us to love it." It heartened him to appear in such a widely read journal, and he began to commit to "write as a means of reaching the largest possible audience...I dare say I never wrote again for any other purpose." He wrote prolifically by "using the moments instead of waiting for the hours"—often taking only briefly to his study to create a sentence or a paragraph before heading for another engagement.[29] His next project, also intended for wider audiences, was his first real study of American literature and culminated in his 1910 book, *Leading American Novelists*. In it, he included biographical overviews, influences, and discussions of the work of Nathaniel Hawthorne, Charles Brockton Brown, James Fenimore Cooper, William Gilmore Simms, Harriet Beecher Stowe, and Bret Hart.[30]

In the summers, Erskine returned to friends and family in New York City to write, practice piano, and visit at the old family summer home in Norwich, in central New York State. During the summer of 1907, he joined his sisters, Anna and Helen, on an Atlantic voyage and tour of England, Ireland, and Scotland. Summers away from Amherst also frequently put Erskine in the proximity of a young lady he had met in New York City during his graduate school years, Pauline Ives. A New Englander by birth and inclination, she was initially somewhat skeptical about a relationship with a college professor uncertain of his academic career route and destination or of his possible future in writing and/or music. Yet, Erskine continued to pursue her with courting letters and summer visits, insisting in correspondence from his tour of the British Isles: "You will have to say yes someday, Pauline; travel isn't going to cure me a bit."[31] Eventually, in 1910, they would be married.

Typically for faculty, summer also was an occasion for part-time employment. In 1906, Erskine was thrilled at the opportunity to return to Columbia to lecture at two three-week summer sessions. Years later, he wrote proudly at the top of the official appointment letter he had carefully saved: "My first teaching at Columbia!"[32] The $300 income added handsomely to his then $1,600 annual Amherst salary, as did payments for publication of his poetry in the *Atlantic Monthly* and the *New Century Magazine*.[33] Early in his stay at Amherst, Erskine had taken the first steps in his lifelong pursuit of public lecturing, another avenue for supplementing his faculty salary. His initial invitations were direct outgrowths of his teaching and came from a local women's club looking for educational talks about literature. Soon, he was also lecturing at nearby Mount Holyoke and was giving regular Saturday seminars to Massachusetts high school teachers. As his reputation spread, so did his ability to be a contributing citizen of Amherst College, and he found himself invited to represent the institution at various academic dedications and celebrations well beyond central Massachusetts.

* * *

Through his summers in New York City and his travel for lectures, meetings, and family occasions, Erskine was able to keep close tabs on happenings at Columbia. There, the influence of Nicholas Murray Butler, who had taken the reins as president in 1902, was reverberating through all aspects of university life and many areas of the cultural scene of New York City. With a personal office staff of ten secretaries and stenographers to shoulder various immediate administrative elements (e.g., schedules, correspondence, social functions, catalogues, speakers, and records), Butler was free to enjoy ceremonial duties, to undertake financial and facilities planning, to push for endowment growth, and to nose into academic matters. A longtime friend of then-president Theodore Roosevelt, a busy Republican politician, and a conspicuous presence on the New York social scene, Butler developed a pedigree of cultural and political connection that was well matched by his Columbia academic and teaching credentials. At age 28, in 1890, he had been named the first dean of Columbia's Faculty of Philosophy, and he quickly proved so adept at administration that seven universities offered him presidencies during the next seven years.[34]

As president of the well-endowed and greatly expanding Columbia University, Butler would prove more skilled at handling the bureaucracy than at handling individuals. By the time his predecessor in the presidency, New York mayor Seth Low, died in 1916, he and Butler were no longer on speaking terms. Butler's dealings with trustees were often difficult, and many faculty members viewed him as a domineering autocrat with little respect for academic freedom. One of his early decisions, in 1902, clearly not in the spirit of democratic governance, was to end the practice of faculty units selecting their own deans. While the move best suited Butler's businesslike commitment to bureaucratic hierarchy, it alerted faculty to the arrogant and heavy-handed side of their new president. Yet, Butler combined large visions (mostly toward continued campus growth and development) with expert administrative and social skills to earn a legacy as "the best-known university president of his era."[35]

Angry faculty resignations and terminations—some politically motivated and some resulting from petty disagreements—came to signify Butler's presidency. One of the first salvos in the long series of battles between Butler and his faculty members was a dispute with Erskine's beloved mentor George Edward Woodberry. During earlier skirmishes between Woodberry and his colleague Brander Matthews, an academic reorganization solution had landed Woodberry as head of a small Department of Comparative Literature with the support of an assistant, a lecturer, and two tutors. President Low had personally found funding for one of the tutors during his last year in office, and he extracted an agreement from the trustees that the cost would be transferred to regular university funds in subsequent years. Butler, however, determined that if Woodberry wanted to continue the second tutor, he would need to find funding for him elsewhere. As reported in the *New York Times*, the missing tutor meant "curtailment of the courses of instruction offered by this department, among which are some of the most popular courses in the university's curriculum."[36] The arrangement assured fewer course offerings in comparative literature and an expansion of the Department of English, which was headed by President Butler's close friend and frequent social companion Brander Matthews. The incident came on the heels of Butler's decision to remove Woodberry, but not others, from the university's powerful curriculum committee.

After ample published reports in the *New York Times* and the *Nation*, as well as vocal student support for Woodberry in the *Columbia Spectator*, a former student of Woodberry's, Harry H. Flagler, came to the rescue with an offer of a $3,600 donation to support a tutor for three years. Butler, however, looked the gift horse straight in the mouth. He refused Flagler's offer on the convoluted basis that Woodberry had initially stated that the position should be funded through the regular university budget. He then expelled the student author of a *Spectator* editorial that supported Woodberry, but reinstated him after extracting an apology. Next, he wrote a warning letter of rebuke to Woodberry. While on leave during the following academic year, Erskine's first year at Amherst, Woodberry resigned from Columbia.[37]

Edward MacDowell, long disgruntled that the Department of Music he was hired to initiate in 1896 could never rise in status while the arts remained underappreciated at Columbia, viewed Woodberry's treatment and resignation as the last straw. The renowned composer maintained, "Woodberry was the only spark of the ideal left at the university."[38] MacDowell's hopes for policies that favored better students in the arts and improved treatment for his own department dissolved when Butler, without warning or consultation, reduced the Department of Music to a program within a new Division of Fine Arts, a unit housed in Teachers College, which included programs in architecture, comparative literature, and kindergarten studies. "Then, the only alternative left for me was to resign," MacDowell told the *New York Times*. "The Division of Fine Arts as at present organized, is inefficient and practically useless."[39]

Although the events at Columbia must have greatly stung and disappointed Erskine, he was already enough of an academic politician to keep his own counsel. Only many years later did he venture: "I doubt if Columbia ever recovered from the mistake of letting these men go. No university can afford the reputation of being inhospitable to genius."[40] Woodberry's resignation immediately caught the attention of his former schoolmate from Phillips Exeter Academy, George A. Plimpton. An Amherst trustee, Plimpton arranged a visiting professorship at Amherst for Woodberry during spring semester, 1905. Woodberry's course on modern English literature, attended by about 80 Amherst upperclassmen and a handful of faculty auditors, was immediately popular and well discussed throughout the community. Erskine was delighted to see that Woodberry was particularly expansive and well liked in his familiar New England surroundings. He socialized happily and frequently with faculty, chatted with Erskine over coffee nearly every day, and gave additional lectures at Smith College, Mt. Holyoke College, and Johns Hopkins University. His ability to charm students and others still in full force, he received Amherst's honorary Doctor of Letters at the spring commencement.

Among Erskine's invitations to teach and speak beyond Amherst was one from President Butler to compose and read a poem at Columbia's celebration, in 1909, of the one-hundredth anniversary of Edgar Allen Poe's birthday. Erskine joined two other commemorative speakers, wealthy Virginian and popular southern author Thomas Nelson Page and Butler's own favorite literary critic and teacher Brander Matthews. The occasion proved to have been somewhat of a working interview. A few months later, after the unexpected death of one of Erskine's influential undergraduate literature professors, 45-year-old George Rice Carpenter, President Butler offered Erskine an adjunct professor position at Columbia, with a salary bump to $2,500.[41]

Erskine was somewhat disappointed when President Harris did not counter the offer. Instead, he simply counseled Erskine that if he wanted to return to his alma mater, he should do so.[42] However, the Amherst Board of Trustees was not so sanguine. Trustee chair George Plimpton, who knew about the offer from his friend and Columbia English professor William Trent, was determined to keep Erskine at Amherst. The bidding war started with his assertion that "I feel sure that you will be made full professor at Amherst and that your salary will be raised to $3,000, and then, if all works well, we propose to move the salaries up even higher than that; and I believe it is only a question of time when the conditions for doing literary work at Amherst will not be excelled anywhere in this country."[43]

Columbia would appoint Erskine initially only to the position of adjunct professor in the Department of English. However, even with Woodberry and MacDowell gone, he felt that Columbia was truly home. And with no patience for protracted bargaining between the campuses, he quickly sent his acceptance to Morningside Heights.

CHAPTER 4

GROWING PAINS AT
A NEW COLUMBIA

Among the undergraduates entering Columbia in 1909—the year Erskine bounced back to campus with the buoyant optimism of a prodigal son—was a short, stooped student with a misshapen head that testified to a botched forceps delivery. Four years older than freshmen who arrived straight from high school, he was quickly recognized as brilliant, eccentric, and brutally candid. Within only a few months, everyone on campus seemed to know or know of Randolph Bourne. By his second year, he was the editor of the *Columbia Monthly* literary journal, a post that allowed him ample opportunities to attack the ideas and practices of his primary campus nemesis, the youthful Professor Erskine. Although immediately and exceedingly popular with his younger students, Erskine struck Bourne as "a very superficial philosopher" who earned his "cordial dislike."[1]

Bourne may have been singularly sharp tongued and personal in his attacks, but he was not alone in his vocal disgruntlement concerning faculty and curriculum. A busy activist and gifted essayist, he represented a growing army of Progressive-era students, at Columbia and elsewhere, with little patience for the discussion of timeworn ethical and moral meanings in literature or other disciplines. Their preference was for teaching and learning that could shine the sober light of day on current realities—social issues, political predicaments, and contemporary injustices.

If Erskine needed evidence that campus life had changed dramatically since his own student years, he received it continually from

Figure 4.1   John Erskine, young professor, ca. 1910.

Source: Courtesy of University Archives, Columbia University in the City of New York.

Bourne and his fellow budding radicals. By 1911, they seized on the newly minted term "genteel tradition" to describe the irrelevant and old-fashioned idealism they found in the practices and teachings of Erskine and many of his colleagues.[2] Detached inquiry, whether scientific or speculative in method, was for these students a boorish distraction from the more essential exposure of current human conditions and the call to action and service. Bourne would later describe himself and his fellow restless young intellectuals as "pro-democratic, pro-hyphenate, pro-Negro, anti-Puritan, anti-English Americans."[3]

*   *   *

Erskine, although having some doubts about his ability and future as a practicing poet, had just begun to demonstrate to himself that through publishing and public lecturing he could be both a man of the ivory tower and a man of action. However, he was caught unprepared when students and others raised the bar for what counted as "action." As the twentieth century moved into a second decade of revered pragmatism, it was no longer enough to advance from literary appreciation and study to literary practice and dissemination. Nor was it enough to join the crusade to employ education and expertise as instruments of progressive outreach and service.[4] Contemporary demands, especially among politically populist and socially progressive reformers, went further, aiming to expose social and economic wrongs and reverse outdated practices in education, government, and industry. Policy change, protective regulation, human rights, social betterment, worker solidarity, and free speech were viewed as essential to the cause. Columbia University, although tightly and proudly linked to the New York cultural and intellectual scene, was not particularly involved in the social or political action of its surrounding community. As Randolph Bourne warned: "The world is a very different sort of place from what our carefully deodorized and idealized education would have us believe."[5]

Bourne and several of his friends defected from the informal literary club, "Boar's Head Society," which Erskine had initiated and which had quickly attracted a number of young men destined for notoriety in various aspects of literature and scholarship, including Bourne, Lloyd Morris, and Alfred Knopf. One student, Irwin Edman, recalled it as "a lively group whose members' talents and interests ranged widely, but who were all concerned with poetry, many of them with writing it."[6]

Erskine viewed the twice-monthly meetings as opportunities for conversational vitality where "the discussion always began with books and writing" but often moved to "arguing about life, about current social and economic questions."[7] Bourne, however, decided the group was somewhat precious with its "patronage of the English faculty, their presence at the meetings, their little pseudo-Sunday-School classes which form themselves after the serious speech of the evening is over and discuss all things with their mentors for many hours."[8] He started his own small group called the Academy.

Bourne began drawing wider attention when one of his essays appeared in the *Atlantic Monthly*. He then resigned as editor of *Columbia Monthly* to focus on publication beyond campus. His essays in national media were usually opinionated and sometimes cynical. One of the most devastating, published shortly after he graduated and when he was writing regularly for the *New Republic*, was "The Professor," a nasty attack on Erskine—not named, but far more unveiled than even thinly veiled. In it, Bourne admitted to the popularity of Erskine's courses and his willingness to allow free discussion of controversial issues in the classroom. But, he labeled the professor "a mournful relic of irrevocable days," and "a devout Episcopalian [who] deplores the callousness of the present generation towards the immemorial beauty of ritual and dogma." The essay concluded with a vision of Erskine in his study: "His deep and measured voice flows pleasantly on in anecdotes of the Authors' Club, or reminiscences of the golden past...This is the literary life, grave, respected, serene. All else is hectic rush, modern ideas a futile Babel."[9]

Bourne was likely motivated by a lengthy and laudatory article about Erskine's work at Columbia that had appeared in the Sunday *New York Times* several months earlier and included a nearly quarter-page photograph of the young professor. In it, the poet Joyce Kilmer had named Erskine as principally responsible for a "poetic renaissance" of new and good writing among Columbia students.[10] According to one of Bourne's biographers, he "resented the implication that Erskine had anything to do with his or anyone else's success."[11] More than three decades later—well after Bourne died at age 32 during the 1918 influenza epidemic—Erskine was complimentary about his critical student's literary ability and sanguine about his scathing *New Republic* article. After all, the professor had always enjoyed far more student praise than criticism, and he had undoubtedly learned from Bourne the probability that even a superb teacher might not reach all students. But, still convinced that at least some of the blame was Bourne's, he puzzled: "I wondered why he felt called upon to be an indefatigable checker-up of other men's short comings."[12]

Fortunately, Erskine had an enormous following among undergraduate students who found his lectures on poetry, literature, and life fascinating. While he often encouraged and gently prodded the younger students, he approached graduate students with greater degrees of stern and candid guidance. Therefore, when Carl Zigrosser complained about the nature of graduate work in comparative literature, Erskine took a tough love stance about "your pronouncement against graduate work, which seemed to me, if you'll forgive my saying so, to betray a dangerous ignorance of what graduate work is like. I've been through it...So have all the people from whom you receive ideas; and they owe their inspiration to the fact that their minds are trained as well as to their initial temperaments. Be as radical as you choose, but don't be too intellectually indolent to learn the facts!"[13]

* * *

The vocal and diverse student culture marked only one of many changes that had occurred during Erskine's absence from Columbia. The combined undergraduate and graduate population, more than 6,000, had nearly doubled since the turn of the century. While approximately 75 percent were from New York, students represented every state and many foreign countries. Columbia and Johns Hopkins were the only American universities with larger graduate than undergraduate populations. Football was out, banned in 1905 as too brutal and distracting. Crew and baseball were on the rise. Continuing education and adult evening classes had arrived. The first dormitory had opened. Other new buildings included the stately Hamilton Hall, with its high Palladian windows and Ionic entry columns, and the elegant brick-and-marble St. Paul's Chapel. An enormous bronze Athena statue had been unveiled in 1903 and installed in front of the granite-domed, neoclassic Low Library as a welcoming "Alma Mater." The original small clutch of lonely buildings on Morningside Heights had grown into a campus now taking shape as a classic quadrangle. Ivy was beginning to grow, and the trees seemed more substantial.

President Nicholas Murray Butler, determined that both he and Columbia University would be important and iconic institutions of national prominence, had quickly demonstrated the ability to manage explosive growth and complex bureaucracy. He reigned over the Morningside Heights campus with what one biographer characterized as an "insatiable desire for power and recognition," and he quickly earned a national reputation as an adept politician and a successful administrator who enjoyed hobnobbing with the elite and the famous of his time.[14] He had his academic preferences, among them a plan to allow undergraduate completion in three years and another to allow a "professional option" of entering a Columbia professional school after only two years as an undergraduate.[15] But, as more of an institution builder than an academic scholar, he did not make a priority of pushing curricular ideas. As a builder, however, he wanted a faculty well sprinkled with big names, and the additions in that direction since Erskine's undergraduate days were evident. John Dewey, already heir to William James in pragmatic thought and a national name in philosophy and education, arrived from the University of Chicago in 1905 to join the Department of Philosophy. His eminent colleague in the department, Frederick J. E. Woodbridge, had come from the University of Minnesota in 1902 as a widely known scholar in the study of classical Greek philosophers; he quickly gained renown throughout campus for spellbinding lectures and Socratic dialogues. Charles Beard had joined the Department of History in 1904, and was well on his way to national renown for economic and public policy interpretations of American history. Harlan Fiske Stone, appointed to the law faculty in 1902, would later become the US attorney general and then chief justice of the Supreme Court.

John Erskine thrived in a heady atmosphere marked by stimulating lunch conversations with academic notables at the Faculty Club and literary discussions with his English Department colleagues. The department offices shared Hamilton Hall with undergraduate classrooms where Erskine held forth with lectures he prepared for as carefully as he would for a piano concert. His teaching assignments, initially limited to undergraduate courses, included English Composition, English Lyric of the Sixteenth and Seventeenth Centuries, Materials of Poetry, and Problems in the Criticism of Poetry. Soon after Erskine's faculty appointment, the Department of English and the Department of Comparative Literature managed a nervous, but ultimately successful, merger. Ashley Thorndike, a noted Shakespearean scholar who had come from Wesleyan University to join the faculty in 1906, was named the new department's "executive officer," a title that President Butler had deemed most fitting for all department heads, effectively reminding them that they were administrators first and scholars only secondarily.

Interactions among and between faculty and administrators often demonstrated that campus turbulence would not be the exclusive purview of the students. This was particularly true in the English Department and throughout the Faculty of Philosophy, which was the umbrella for a dozen departments in arts and humanities disciplines. The few calm years since the Woodberry and MacDowell resignations ended when, on a warm June afternoon in 1910, Professor Harry Thurston Peck's name appeared in a bold headline of the New York *Evening World*. One of Columbia's most illustrious faculty members, Peck was being sued by his former stenographer for breach of promise. Choice selections from his steamy love letters to her appeared in print. A brilliant and nationally recognized scholar of Greek and Latin and founder of *The Bookman* literary journal, Peck was also somewhat of a dandy and very much a lady's man after, and by reputation before, his divorce in 1908.[16] He married a former student in 1909—but only after seeming to promise himself to his former stenographer. President Butler, although pals with Peck since their Columbia undergraduate years together, decided the professor must be guilty and immediately called for his resignation. No investigation. No intermediate suspension. Although Peck refused to resign, claiming he was the subject of "blackmail, backed up by perjury and forgery,"[17] most faculty either fell in line behind Butler or kept quiet. They reasoned that Columbia's reputation deserved priority above all other considerations. Damage from publicity spread by papers from Baltimore to Boston easily justified quick action. In agreement with Butler's swift decision, Erskine concluded: "The publication of this correspondence was a fantastic revelation of bad taste, bad judgment, weak character and sick brain." He determined that Peck's "usefulness as a teacher was ended."[18] After a summer of much campus discussion and argument, as well as reluctance on the part of some decision makers, President Butler prodded the trustees into terminating Peck's appointment.

The matter might have ended there were it not for the objections of Erskine's English Department colleague, Joel Spingarn. A fine teacher and a prolific and widely known scholar in comparative literature, the 35-year-old Spingarn also had a keen sense of social justice and humane treatment. He was well known for his earlier outrage at the treatment of his mentor, Woodberry, and for his vocal objections to the recent merger of the English and Comparative Literature departments. Since that time, he had refused to participate in many departmental administrative tasks and had generally pulled away from campus citizenship, much to the consternation of department head Ashley Thorndike. However, Peck's dismissal provoked Spingarn to action, and he angered Thorndike, Butler, and others when he proposed that the faculty go on record with a sense of appreciation to their fired colleague. His fairly benign resolution asked: "That the Faculty of Philosophy place on record its sense of the academic services of Harry Thurston Peck, who was connected with the University for twenty-two years and was a member of this Faculty from the date of its organization."[19] The faculty tabled the proposal. A month later, President Butler informed Spingarn that his professorship would be removed due to budgetary considerations. Six weeks after that, the trustees voted to terminate Spingarn's connection with Columbia.

Few professors voiced any objections. Certainly not Erskine, who greatly exaggerated the proposed resolution in appreciation of Peck as: "He [Spingarn] invited his colleagues to make a formal protest on Peck's behalf."[20] Clearly, a stack of animosities were at work against Spingarn, including his department work habits and his defenses of Woodberry and Peck. One analyst added: "It probably didn't help that he was Jewish."[21] Erskine waited for many years before he ventured that Spingarn's downfall may have gone beyond the Peck issue: "I know that Thorndike disliked Spingarn and was eager to get rid of him...He was on guard against original or creative natures."[22] In 1914, a broken and bankrupt Peck committed suicide. Spingarn vented against Butler and the acquiescence of his faculty colleagues in a lengthy poem about the Peck case published in the *International* literary journal. It concluded:

> For another poisoned his honor, and all the rest stood still;
> Seven hundred rats obeyed the fox's will;
> Another cast him out, another struck him dead,
> But never a word of protest the seven hundred said.[23]

* * *

Erskine's star with President Butler consistently rose as his scholarly and teaching reputations, as well as his internal political skills, advanced. In 1913, Butler flattered him with an appointment to present the honorary degree recipients at commencement. The following year, Butler went further and selected him as "University Orator," the faculty speaker at commencement. The president also often tapped Erskine for membership on university committees—from a group considering student exchanges among various campuses to one reexamining the issue of intercollegiate football—and Erskine took on all such tasks with eager goodwill.[24] Relations between Erskine, Butler, and even the Columbia trustees further blossomed through their mutual involvements in the Episcopalian Church, particularly Trinity Parish and its expanding Upper West Side chapels and schools. Erskine was appointed to the Trinity vestry in 1916, the same year he was promoted to full professor at Columbia. There, he joined a group of white males from old New York families and new industrial wealth, including chairman of the Columbia trustees, William B. Parsons.

Growing recognition for Erskine also extended back to the Amherst campus where the new president, brilliant educator and controversial administrator Alexander Meiklejohn, began a campaign to attract him to return. Between 1912 and 1915, Erskine was blunt in his refusals, insisting that Meiklejohn put too little value on scholarship and had not dealt successfully with some of the troublesome Amherst faculty. Meiklejohn, recognizing that he needed to attract top faculty to Amherst, continued a spirited correspondence with Erskine over several years to seek advice about hiring other faculty. He tried to lure notable literature professor Stuart Sherman away from the University of Illinois with a hefty raise to $5,000, but Sherman declined after consulting Erskine and deciding Amherst lacked a "critical mass of good men to keep one another company."[25]

Apparently Erskine was not perceived favorably by all of his Columbia colleagues, although this easily may have escaped his notice. For example, Amherst trustee Talcott Williams, who had been appointed the first director of the Pulitzer School of Journalism at Columbia, warned President Meiklejohn: "Erskine has not done as well at Columbia as he did at Amherst, and the English Department here does not take kindly to his methods. Exactly why, I don't know, but I think it is that he leads his students to read instead of drilling them in writing. At all events, there is some friction."[26]

Williams may have been influenced by Erskine's ongoing objections to the proposed transfer of some English Department courses to the journalism area. Or, he may have received his information from English Department "executive officer" Ashley Thorndike, who gave Erskine the impression that he was jealous of his younger colleague.[27] In 1913, Thorndike presented President Butler with a department budget that pointedly included no salary increase for Erskine. Butler minced no words in reminding him that this was an unwarranted oversight:

> I find the judgment of many of his colleagues to be that Professor Erskine is one of the chief ornaments of the University and is likely to make for himself a conspicuous place in American letters. He has a standing invitation to a full professorship at Amherst College, and I have recently learned that there is a likelihood of his being invited to a chair at Princeton. Since Professor Erskine adds to his scholarship and his strong personality the gift of literary productivity with distinction, is it not important that no situation should be allowed to develop in which it would be either easy or possible for him to detach himself from Columbia?[28]

The English Department comprised a varied group of colleagues who ranged from Erskine's own earlier professors to newer additions. Professor William P. Trent was particularly generous to his former student. Shortly after arriving, Erskine was able to jump-start his Columbia scholarly agenda with the publication of *Leading American Novelists*, a book included in a series edited by Trent for Henry Holt and Company.[29] Erskine stayed on good, or at least cordial, terms with all his English Department colleagues, but his friendly inter-action with Brander Matthews was perhaps most surprising. Still a prolific essayist and critic, Matthews was happily comfortable as part of the English Department old guard. A conservative human-ist, generally considered a snobbish and entrenched relic by the new brand of undergraduates, he retained close social relationships with President Butler and a number of Columbia's trustees. His enor-mous circle of celebrity friendships also extended to key politicians, including Theodore Roosevelt and Henry Cabot Lodge; to writers and publishers, including Rudyard Kipling, Mark Twain, Henry Holt, and George Putnam; and, perhaps most warmly, to his former student and a leading voice among African American intellectuals, James Weldon Johnson.[30] Most of Matthews's teaching comprised the drama courses he had offered for many years and that fit neatly with his love of New York theatre, opening nights, cast parties, and drama criticism. Lionel Trilling, a student during Matthews's years and later a member of the faculty, coolly described him as "a man of club lounges and theatre greenrooms. He held his university post with some irony and gave the same amusing lectures from the same set of notes year after year."[31]

*   *   *

Given his continuing fond allegiance to Woodberry, Erskine might have favored a dismissive posture toward the man who had caused his mentor so much pain and, in great part, Woodberry's resignation. Yet, Brander Matthews was an example of something Erskine had come to admire, and perhaps envy, as he sought to define the part of his life that would become a man of action. That example revealed Matthews as an individual who could easily circulate not only in the world of academic intellectuals in uptown Manhattan, but also in the realm of the city's downtown urbane literati. As a man of clubs and clubby ways, he became somewhat of a role model for the young English professor who aspired to the bon vivant life but initially had little off-campus involvement beyond family and church-related interests.[32] Matthews was instrumental in founding three New York literary and drama clubs: the Players, the Authors' Club, and the Kinsmen. At various times, he served as president of the Modern Language Association, the National Institute of Arts and Letters, and the American Academy of Arts and Letters. Erskine would eventually follow in many of those footsteps.

Polishing his natural talent as a networker and a negotiator around the potholes of departmental politics, Erskine struck up a friendly, although never socially chummy, relationship with Matthews. He also managed to continue an equally friendly relationship with William P. Trent, even after Trent and Matthews were no longer on speaking terms due to their opposing views of the political strife in Europe. That troubled relationship served Erskine well when George H. Putnam asked Trent to coedit with Matthews a new publishing project he had in mind, *The Cambridge History of American Literature*. Trent agreed only on the condition that Matthews would not be editorially involved. Instead, he invited three associate editors into the venture: Erskine and two academic luminaries, Professor Stuart Sherman of the University of Illinois and Carl Van Doren of Columbia. When they set about work in 1914 on the four-volume project, Erskine found himself in rarified company with his fellow editors and with notable chapter editors and writers from universities throughout the country.[33]

Erskine's professional network, his reputation, and his enjoyment of the New York intellectual scene continued to expand throughout the years prior to World War I. His personal life had bloomed happily since his marriage to Pauline Ives in 1910 and the birth of their son, Graham, a year later. They lived in a succession of Upper West Side apartments, finally settling with their toddler in an apartment building that also housed Erskine's parents, his sisters and a brother, and an aunt. Pauline, from a high Episcopalian, upper-crust Connecticut family, had both a brother and a sister in New York City. Readily available family babysitters greatly supported the growing cosmopolitan lifestyle that Erskine began to enjoy. He began occasionally playing the piano again, although not with any serious practice, and he dabbled in composing for Columbia Glee Club. In the summers, the family decamped to the Jersey Shore.[34] In 1916, the Erskine family welcomed a daughter, Anna. Erskine, very much enjoying his professional and family lives, wrote a romantic poem to Pauline on Valentine's Day each year. He continued to write and publish poetry in literary journals and poetry magazines, and a collection of his poems was published as *The Shadowed Hour* in 1917. For it, he selected dreamy verse about love and beauty, lost youth, war, and immortality, and he dedicated the volume: "To Pauline."[35]

*　*　*

One of the most fortunate and defining circumstances of Erskine's scholarly career occurred with the publication of an essay he originally presented before the Phi Beta Kappa Society of Amherst College in the spring of 1913. It appeared as "The Moral Obligation to Be Intelligent" in the *Hibbert Journal*, a well-regarded liberal Christian review headquartered in London and concerned with theology, philosophy, and religion. The president of Duffield and Company publishing house read it and asked Erskine to consider a book of essays anchored by the *Hibbert* piece. Erskine quickly produced a small collection of four essays, which Duffield published in 1915, titled for the lead chapter, *The Moral Obligation to Be Intelligent.*

Peppered with references to works of British authors and acknowledging a great deal of ancient-Greek influence, the title essay lamented what Erskine viewed as a dichotomy between moral goodness and intellectual cleverness. He found the former favored in British literature, and in Anglo-Saxon ethics in general; while only some Greek and French literature were more likely to recognize the latter as a virtue. Intelligence, to Erskine, should be elevated to the status of moral imperative. With a strong whiff of academic arguments about development of character versus development of intellect, he maintained: "Between this rising host that follow intelligence, and the old camp that put their trust in a stout heart, a firm will, and a strong hand, the fight is on." To explain in more lively terms, he noted individual preferences "divided into those who wish to be men—whatever that means—and those who wish to be intelligent men, and those, who unconscious of blasphemy or humor, prefer not to be intelligent, but to do the will of God."[36]

The reception to Erskine's first essay collection, with a few exceptions, was favorable. The harshest criticism came from a reviewer for the *Boston Transcript*, who noted the lead essay as "a pleasant and well-written, but hardly valuable, address." A *Springfield [MA] Republican* reviewer, however, saw in the book: "Fresh viewpoints of life, literature and service...Wit, originality and a stimulating style."[37]

One reviewer noted that Erskine had produced "a book of philosophy in the ancient and honorable sense." However, another found that he called for meeting contemporary circumstances with a "charge against the old Anglo-Saxon way of viewing life...[which] assumed that a choice must be made between goodness and intelligence."[38] Erskine himself, considering the book somewhat of a turning point that might set him on a path beyond poetry, claimed: "For the first time I felt I was saying something in a way of my own, something that was essential in me."[39]

On campus, the timing apparently was ideal, and the book struck a chord in among students. Lionel Trilling later recalled: "The great word in the [Columbia undergraduate] College was INTELLIGENCE...An eminent teacher of ours, John Erskine, provided a kind of slogan by the title he gave to an essay of his which, chiefly through its title, gained a kind of fame...I did not count myself among those who were intelligent...But eventually I was seduced into bucking to be intelligent by the assumption which was prepotent [*sic*] in Columbia College—that intelligence was connected with literature, that it was advanced by literature."[40]

With growing confidence for experimentation and a love of new challenges, Erskine also tried his hand at drama early in his Columbia career. His one-act play, "Hearts Enduring," considered issues of longing and reality and was first performed at Columbia in January, 1914. Erskine explained that it was a response to the predictability of much drama "when we are bored with waiting for the action and the dialogue to catch up with us." Instead, "it was my intention to make a drama with such economy of material that the imagination of the audience would be fully occupied from beginning to end."[41] The brief drama, spare in sets and movement, later appeared in some edited collections and was performed from time to time by local and student companies.

Most students found Erskine's teaching of literature more accessible than his written prose. And, notwithstanding the radical followers of Randolph Bourne, it was as a remarkable teacher that he was best known on the Columbia campus. Perhaps influenced by responses from Bourne and others who attacked outdated literary instruction, he fairly quickly became "genuinely receptive to all forms of contemporary art…astonishingly flexible [and] able to identify himself completely with any writer whose work he undertook to discuss."[42] The recent spread of literary culture to the middle class, indicated by a surge in public poetry readings and magazine publication of verse, favored Erskine's poetry instruction. He was savvy in recognizing that students, in and out of class, were reading and discussing contemporary poets—Robert Frost, Vachel Lindsay, Amy Lowell, Walt Whitman, and Ezra Pound—and he managed to expand his courses accordingly. Student interest also led him to teaching in American literature, which he first piloted as a summer course. According to Frank Ernest Hill, who would eventually make his own way as a poet and literary scholar, that course stood out as "the best course that I could imagine being given…the most brilliant performances I ever attended as a student."[43]

At a time when the lecture was still the most prominent tool in the instructional kit, Erskine excelled. He was a large, energetic, and imposing presence in even a cavernous lecture hall, where his deep voice and steady modulation set students guessing about the origin of his accent. "Kind of a South of England sound," concluded Horace Coon who added, "but nobody can deny its charm. Few who ever heard him say 'layzhure' ever again said 'lees-yure.'" He used no notes and spoke in a conversational tone, but he followed an organized set of ideas that resulted in "stating his thesis so lucidly that even the stupidest boy could understand it and think himself pretty clever for catching on."[44]

Erskine's characteristic style was particularly refreshing for students accustomed to his closest disciplinary colleague in literature, Professor Jefferson Butler Fletcher, who had arrived from Harvard to replace the departed Woodberry. Although a superb scholar in a number of literary areas, Fletcher carefully read every word of his detailed written notes, and, even in more casual settings, he would not speak extemporaneously. Yet, his studied approach was not truly unusual in its day, and Erskine favorably contrasted in classroom demeanor.[45]

A student who later joined the Columbia faculty, Irwin Edman, recalled that even Erskine's classrooms had their uncomfortable moments: "One felt about him something of the prima donna lecturer; it was evidenced by the pointed silence that would occur while some unfortunate late-comer found his way to his seat. It was clear, too, from the way in which, not infrequently, Shakespeare or Marlow or Castiglione would be the springboards for little bravura lectures by our teacher on the importance of love or of being a cultivated gentleman, the latter one of his favorite themes." Yet, Edman concluded that his professor's efforts to promote a love of literature and literary abilities in his students were invaluable assets to the undergraduates. "Other teachers might make literature seem a set of documents to be investigated; no one quite knew why. Erskine made it an art to be lived and loved."[46]

To assure adequate preparation on the part of his students, Erskine often required them to write a brief essay—graded, but not with great weight—on works to be discussed in class. This promoted a foundational understanding of a literary work and/or its author, so that Erskine's lectures could quickly move on to suggest less evident ideas and meanings. Lloyd Morris, an undergraduate learning to become the expert literary critic he later would be, summarized his professor's best teaching:

> He always drew from the book or play or poem under discussion implications which you had failed to detect; as he stated them, they were not only obvious, but so logical as to crystallize its essential import...He succeeded in making the habit of free reflection highly contagious. He had the faculty of opening up long vistas, of guiding your vision to distant horizons; and without seeming to do so, he disciplined your

imagination...It was Erskine's constant references to the Greeks that first sent Morris to Plato and Aristotle. This offered him the most exciting intellectual adventure he had yet had.[47]

Oscar Hammerstein II, who attended Erskine's classes in 1916 and was particularly affected by his poetry reading, extolled: "One day John read a poem. It came to me as a shock that poetry was intended to mean something. Whatever I've done in the theater I really owe to the way he read that poem."[48]

Predictably, not all students agreed. Corey Ford, eventually a prolific author and a well-known American humorist, later described Erskine as "a pompous Tennysonian figure who seemed to me totally devoid of humor, and who read aloud the compositions of the class in a sonorous voice, which usually put me to sleep." Ford earned an F when he submitted a composition to Erskine which parodied a much-praised theme submitted earlier by another student. Undaunted, he later submitted his essay to *Life* magazine and recalled, "It was my first published article, and I had the satisfaction of waving the check under Erskine's nose."[49]

*   *   *

The heavy authoritarianism of President Butler and his trustees, as well as faculty eccentricities and political maneuvering, combined with disagreements over developments in Europe to provide continuing opportunities for acrimony across the Columbia campus. Erskine, however, could not be goaded into joining the fray. As the years and the months prior to US entry into World War I grew shorter, and pro- and antiwar political rhetoric grew louder, Erskine found that "for a while, all thinking was confused...The events occurred too fast for the majority of us to understand them; we found it hard to throw overboard our traditional respect and friendship for Germany, and harder still to abandon the faith in diplomacy and arbitration which our intellectuals had for years been planting in us."[50]

A nervous waiting game concerning the war in Europe was on, and the odds in favor of US involvement continued to grow. In the meantime, Erskine simply plowed ahead with his lectures, his students, his Boar's Head literary group, his friendships with President Butler and key trustees, his writing, and his enjoyable times at the Faculty Club and the Authors' Club. In early 1917, he proposed to his

Department of English colleagues a new linked sequence of courses entailing reading and discussing ancient classics, but most were "hostile to the idea."[51] Nevertheless, when chairman Thorndike reported to President Butler plans for Erskine's 1918 course responsibilities in the English Department, he noted that in addition to undergraduate composition and courses on seventeenth-century literature, "he will give the new course planned for college juniors and seniors on Greek and Roman literature."[52] By that time, however, US involvement in the Great War had become a reality. The Great Books would have to wait.

CHAPTER 5

WORLD WAR I AND
THE FRENCH SEDUCTION

Nicholas Murray Butler, once and future pacifist, changed his mind (or at least its outward manifestations) as it became apparent that the United States would enter the Great War. So did Frederick Keppel, dean of Columbia College. Even John Dewey seemed to shift a bit.[1] At campuses throughout the country, peace enthusiasts and preparedness objectors flip-flopped to embrace what Gerald Graff labeled "the widespread acceptance among American professors of the Wilsonian view of the war as a holy crusade."[2] To favor military intervention was now to desire peace. William James cogently concluded: "Every up-to-date dictionary should say that 'peace' and 'war' mean the same thing, now *in posse,* now *in actu.*"[3] No matter how bloody or tragic, a war laced with democratic ideals, patriotic pride, and honor imperatives was the right and necessary thing.

At Columbia, neutrality became as unwelcomed as pacifism, and Columbia professors who adopted it were highly suspect at best, fired at worst. Star anthropology professor Franz Boas survived in the suspect category, although reprimanded by one busybody trustee for teaching "anthropology as construed from the German standpoint."[4] Terminations swept up a well-known psychology professor with 16 years at Columbia, James McKeen Cattell, and a young English department assistant professor, Henry Wadsworth Longfellow Dana, grandson of the poet.

Additional firings and requested resignations without due process eventually frustrated preeminent historian Charles Beard, who

supported the pro-war fervor but insisted on the rights of his colleagues to hold varying views. He shocked the wider academic community and left a gaping hole in Columbia's scholarly reputation when
he resigned in 1917, explaining: "The university is really under the
control of a small and active group of trustees who have no standing in
the world of education, who are reactionary and visionless in politics,
narrow and medieval in religion. Their conduct betrays a profound
misconception of the true function of a university in the advancement
of learning."[5] Beard's resignation set off large campus protest rallies
and pronouncements among many students and even a few faculty
members who objected to the politically motivated dismissals of some
of their favorite professors and colleagues. Will Durant, a recent PhD
graduate who was working as a Columbia extension instructor at the
time, found his contract terminated after he gave a speech in support
of Beard. Several journalism students were expelled for publishing
antiwar articles and journals.[6]

John Erskine, however, remained too politically cagey, or perhaps
too genuinely uncertain of where he stood, to join the fray in most of
the heated campus issues. When US involvement in the war became
inevitable, President Butler asked him to address, with Butler and
another faculty member, a university-wide assembly of students gathered to hear about the response on campus. Erskine, however, did
not echo Butler's strident advice concerning duty to country; nor did
he join with professor Frank Giddings who "urged us to get into the
fighting and kill as many Germans as we could." Instead, he simply
reminded that scholars, whatever their opinions, needed to maintain
humane and tolerant values.[7]

Erskine had sometimes spoken in defense of academic freedom. He
had gone public with his defense of artistic freedom when he signed
a petition protesting the official censorship and prohibition on sales
of Theodore Dreiser's 1915 semiautobiographical novel, *The Genius*.
However, he did not view these scholarly and intellectual freedoms as
the most prevalent concerns in all cases of sudden faculty removals.
This was particularly evident in the case of Henry Dana, who was
friendly with Erskine for a half-dozen years before being fired for
his association with pacifist organizations. Erskine, by this time one
of a circle of faculty members who enjoyed President Butler's hearty
camaraderie, agreed with the dismissal. He reminded Dana during
the investigation that ended in his termination: "From our conversation in the faculty club, I understood that you did not want to resign

and that you did agree to disassociate yourself from propaganda hostile to the government... You should have conducted yourself in these difficult times as you knew Columbia expected you to, or you should have resigned." When President Meiklejohn wrote from Amherst expressing his surprise at news of the dismissals of Dana and Cattell, Erskine scoffed: "I am personally convinced that the University is better off without Cattell and Dana."[8]

Dana later asserted that, thinking Erskine still a friend, he had tried to communicate with him shortly after his dismissal, but his letters were returned unopened. However, when word of that reached Erskine, he denied receiving the letters.[9] Eventually, when his need to protect his own position and Columbia's reputation had passed, Erskine retreated from his earlier narratives on the Dana case. In his 1947 memoir, he finally supported Dana and blamed the Columbia trustees who "made a mountain out of a molehill" and "overstepped their authority and their good sense and in the end made themselves ridiculous."[10]

*　*　*

As faculty members and students alike began emptying the nation's campuses for training camps and battle sites, the war debates and their consequences subsided. Those on the faculty who remained were busy filling the gaps created by multiple leaves of absence among their colleagues and developing courses emphasizing war issues and patriotic themes. Large and noticeable bands of students on campus were in uniformed volunteer groups or in preinduction military units of the Student Army Training Corps, which slowed the drain of tuition revenues by keeping students in college while preparing for active duty. The passage of the Espionage Act muffled dissident voices, leaving them "isolated on the campus, lacking that sense of comradeship which one gets in a mass organization... Men and women opposed to the war now appeared like scattered ineffectual molecules."[11]

The excitement of finally joining the fray was especially palpable in New York, with the transportation and financial industries vividly demonstrating a country changed by the wartime economy. It reached the Erskine family when John's brother Robert, by then a Manhattan lawyer, decided to enlist and when John Erskine was visited on campus in November, 1917, by a representative from the Young Men's Christian Association (YMCA). He wondered if Erskine would consider joining in educational work for the soldiers being under-taken in cooperation between the YMCA and the army. The offer to contribute to military support efforts in France was one the professor simply could not refuse. Finally, he was to get a chance at an interlude as a genuine man of action, and he could be part of the Great War as a civilian, building on his academic background. Analyst Joan Shelley Rubin noted that the opportunity fit perfectly with Erskine's linger-ing desire to move beyond a strictly scholarly approach to shedding the restraints of gentility. Now he could actively respond to the "lure of undomesticated experience in his own life."[12]

Although his father had died two years earlier, his mother's health was precarious, and his family with Pauline included a toddler and a six-year-old, Erskine was more enthusiastic than concerned as he pre-pared to sail for France. He had studied the language, the history, and the literature of France, but his only overseas journey had been a sum-mer trip to the British Isles with his sisters Helen and Anna during his Amherst years. After arranging for several colleagues to take over his teaching, he formally applied for a leave of absence to start January 1, 1918, with a promise to return to Columbia in September for the fall opening. President Butler was happy to agree and provided him with letters of introduction to his own contacts in France.[13]

As it had in the Civil War and the Spanish American War, the YMCA sent support personnel to World War I venues to help the American Expeditionary Forces (AEF) with troop welfare activities such as entertainment, education, leave preparations, and communi-cation. Erskine's first assignment, nowhere near the bold action he might have longed for, was as general support personnel in a French *foyer du soldat*. Called "huts" by the Americans, the *foyers* were opera-tions well behind the front staffed by French and American civilians to provide troops in the field with a place to write, read, drink hot chocolate and coffee, purchase supplies from the canteen, hear an occasional instructional lecture, and listen to phonograph music. Erskine balked at the idea of hut work when he arrived in Paris and received his orders. Anson Phelps Stokes, the energetic secretary of Yale University who was undertaking planning for YMCA educational work to be started during demobilization, had recruited Erskine with a description of looming academic needs. But Erskine's January arrival in Paris was too early for the coming educational work. That was still in a developmental stage without yet a formal proposal. Even the issue of whether educational activities should be undertaken by the YMCA, the army, or in combination was not resolved. Ultimately, Erskine gamely accepted the challenge of assisting in hut operations, and, after several days touring Paris, headed east for the front at Haudainville, a village neighboring Verdun.

At the *foyer* in Haudainville and later at a nearby *foyer* in Sommedieue, Erskine's primary job was to work with French counterparts in general helpfulness to battle weary soldiers. He wrote home to his mother that an essential duty for the American YMCA worker at each *foyer* was to teach English to the French and "to represent our friendly feelings toward France," because "the average American soldier, fine as he is, seems pretty crude over here."[14] Erskine was determined to put his own stamp on *foyer* activities, spreading a bit of education and culture to circumstances that were best known only for relaxation and entertainment. To that end, he organized phonograph concerts and poetry readings, and he appointed himself librarian of the *foyers'* small collections of books. However, on supply runs and errands to the nearby trenches, he witnessed the reality of battle with its relentless artillery, cold, pain, death, and mud.

Erskine's *foyer* work, although somewhat suited to his desire to sample the real activity of war, was temporary. It lasted only until the YMCA educational plans were established enough to generate agreement in principle. By April, 1918, when the author of those plans, Anson Phelps Stokes, returned to the United States, Erskine relocated to Paris as acting director of the Educational Department, YMCA, AEF. His first order of business was to review Stokes's plan for the work of the Educational Department, and his first priority was to adjust the organization so that the YMCA would not have primary authority, but would share or cede authority to the US War Department.[15]

His next step was to alert President Butler to his intention to stay longer than originally anticipated, requiring an extended leave of absence. Butler was not surprised, since Erskine had already written, "It is hard from this angle to think of any work so immediately important as this that we are doing, but perhaps if I were in New York at the moment I should see the greater need at Columbia." Perhaps even more telling of his intention to stay in France well beyond what he originally contemplated was: "I confess to a most enthusiastic admiration of the French and of practically everything French, though I have not quite understood their complicated politics."[16] Although his family encouraged him to come home when it appeared an armistice was in the making, Erskine had not had his fill of France or the excitement of wartime participation. In July, his leave was granted for the 1918–1919 academic year. Erskine made plans to sail home for a brief autumn visit with his family and then to return to France and put demobilization education into action.

*   *   *

As the November, 1918, armistice drew closer, it became apparent to all involved in the Great War that the demobilization of several million AEF troops would be a long task that demanded nearly as much careful planning as their mobilization. Transportation availability back across the Atlantic would be bottlenecked by too few ships for too many soldiers. And since there was at least some chance that fighting might start up again, demobilization needed to be slow and strategic. That approach also would fit best with the very real problem of suddenly adding 2 million job seekers to the US labor market.

Erskine, already aspiring to a large part in demobilization efforts, promoted a measured approach and pace: "Even if the soldiers could be brought back in three months, would it be proper to bring them back so quickly? There are two million of them; the country has been reorganized since they left; there is perhaps no place for them ready, except in the affections of their families. Almost all of them need to earn their living and many need to learn how to earn it; it hardly seems fair to throw them into an altered society without providing them with the opportunity to find their place in it."[17]

Estimating that the troops' long way home would take more than a year and noting that the Canadian forces in Europe were already forming a network of "colleges in khaki," Anson Phelps Stokes had pleaded for primary attention to education work in his initial report to the YMCA on demobilization needs. In order to "prevent the long period of demobilization from being a period of demoralization," he proposed an educational plan of enormous scope and reach. "The education available must consequently provide instruction in the elements of reading and writing the English language at one extreme, and at the other, meet the needs of the student of law or engineering who has given up his professional studies to enter the Army." He suggested an organization that would include: American liaisons with nearly every European university and technical school to pave the way for troops who wanted to study in those institutions; elementary and secondary instruction delivered in schools set up within the scores of army posts throughout England and France; and correspondence and extension courses for those who could not get to an educational institution. The plan was quickly approved "in general" by AEF leader, General John J. Pershing.[18]

As John Erskine set about putting the plan into action after Stokes's departure from Europe, he sought to adjust it to quickly changing realities and to his own new understandings of the soldiers fighting in Europe. He determined that it was not likely that a large network of European universities and technical schools could provide for all troops interested; nor could all soldiers receive necessary furloughs, qualify to attend, or afford the tuition. However, Erskine initially felt that the existing posts and huts were appropriate not only for elementary and secondary school-level work, but might also be the sites of higher level noncredit work if they were provided with adequate textbooks, good libraries, visiting lecturers, and systematic correspondence courses. Further, he began to push for greater limits on YMCA autonomy in the educational endeavor, making it a secondary partner in a primarily army undertaking. His candid observation to army and YMCA officials was that "many hut Secretaries and divisional Directors frankly believe that the canteen, supplemented with religious programs, should be the whole enterprise of the Y.M.C.A."[19] Eventually, he convinced the YMCA to transfer his own position to one of "temporary duty with the U.S. Army."[20]

Since his upbringing and experience had shielded him from knowledge of the many truly uneducated US citizens, Erskine was amazed to discover illiteracy. He noted this particularly among "southern mountaineers" and "illiterate negroes who desire to write home to their people, and who would fit themselves for better citizenship." He was convinced that literacy training, along with basic American citizenship courses, would be beneficial and could include troops from other countries and continents as well. In addition to spoken and written English, other curricular areas that he felt would fit soldiers' needs and preferences—whether at the secondary or undergraduate level—included French language, French and British history, French art, French and American geography, mathematics, and American social and economic problems.[21]

The YMCA educational efforts soon morphed into the Army Educational Commission, located in Paris and still closely cooperating with the YMCA, with Erskine as its chairman. He was joined at the commission headquarters at 76 rue du Faubourg Saint-Honoré by Frank Spaulding, superintendent of Cleveland Public Schools who would take charge of elementary and secondary education; Kenyon Butterfield, president of Massachusetts Agricultural College who would guide agricultural and mechanical education; and Algernon Coleman, professor of Romance languages at the University of Chicago who acted as the commission's executive secretary. General Robert Irwin Rees, who had directed the Student Army Training Corps, was the military commander over the commission. At varying times, these men interacted with university authorities in France and England, appealed for books and textbooks for post libraries, recruited and hired lecturers and instructors, developed curriculums, negotiated for soldier furloughs, arranged for credit transfers with US universities, and coordinated with other groups in Paris like the American Library Association and the American University Union.

*   *   *

Amid the rush of planning and implementing for large-scale demobilization needs that might last only a year, Erskine and his colleagues determined that something more was needed—something beyond the continuing education based in the *foyers* and posts and more accessible than the existing French and British institutions of higher education. That something was an AEF university in France. While at home in the fall, Erskine had met musician and conductor Walter Damrosch and learned about his AEF Bandmasters' School in Chaumont. He had also encouraged the work of an old friend from his Columbia student years, George Hellman, in founding and directing the AEF Art Training Centre near Paris. In addition, 11 Canadian "Khaki Colleges" were getting underway as new undergraduate institutions for Canadian troops in England. Why not develop a full institution of higher education somewhere in France?[22]

While finding spots for about 6,000 soldiers in French universities and 2,000 in British universities—including the Sorbonne and Oxford—as well as developing traveling lecture series and educational programs at posts, Erskine and his colleagues set about establishing a new campus-based institution in France.[23] They were particularly encouraged by the attitude of General Pershing toward educational work for the demobilizing American troops. "I count on the Educational Commission to provide opportunities for any kind of study the men want," he insisted. "Teach them Greek if they ask for it, though I dare say they won't. If a man has been a house painter and intends to go on with that work, send him home a better painter than when he enlisted."[24]

Erskine and General Robert Rees, the military director of educational programs, considered a number of large field hospital facilities in central France as possible sites for a fully functioning university campus. They eventually settled on the hospital in Beaune, just south of Dijon, for the main university facilities, with an agricultural school farther north at Allerey. Colonel Ira Reeves was appointed military commander of the AEF University, and Erskine was appointed its educational director. Together, they developed their institution in a matter of weeks in early 1919. In doing so, Erskine "learned from the Army the main principles of administration—to keep rules and regulations few and clear—never to let lines of authority get crossed—always to communicate through channels." Accordingly, General Order Number 6, on February 21, 1919, listed 13 elements that described the organization of the university through departments and committees responsible to a University Council; called for positions such as registrars, librarians, and teaching faculty; and explained the network of meetings and reports necessary for accountability.[25]

The frantic early days of getting the university under way for spring semester meant dealing with both the physical plant and the academic infrastructure, and the experience was exhilarating, if exhausting, for Erskine and his colleagues. They created and furnished classrooms, barracks, mess halls, and more. They requisitioned items from the army by the freight car and truck load: A hangar and assorted engines and machines for the engineering school; slides and microscopes for the medical science school; instruments for the school of music; and paper and pencils for everyone. Just before the students arrived, the men in charge renamed the roads that crossed the sprawling hospital grounds for American colleges (e.g., Williams, Amherst, and Swarthmore) and the perpendicular avenues after the names of great universities (e.g., Harvard, Cambridge, and Sorbonne).

After some fretting about admissions requirements, the founders agreed there was no time for any testing or secondary school reporting. Instead, prospective students could simply state their preparation (high school graduation) and attend classes in any of the 12 colleges they desired: Agriculture, Fine Arts, Applied Arts, Correspondence, Education, Engineering, Journalism, Law, Letters, Medical Science,

Music, and Science. Depending on their preferences and aspirations, students could sign up for subjects that "ranged from automobile repairing to Greek grammar, from sign painting to dentistry." Erskine was particularly proud to note that one busy soldier was attending "a course in Medieval history, a course in hog-feeding and a course at the art school in landscape painting."[26] Writing to an African American corporal who wondered about classes for black military men, Erskine insisted that the admission requirements were the same for all and "the opportunities which the university at Beaune offers are the same for the colored men as for the white." However, he admitted elsewhere that "their presence will undoubtedly create a problem, but there is no reason why we should fear problems, I suppose."[27]

The deans of the various colleges and the faculty were recruited mainly from among American college and university faculty who had recently served in the military or performed civilian duties in Europe. The more than 500 instructors represented institutions such as Stanford University, University of Nebraska, University of Cincinnati, University of Indiana, Delaware College, University of Wisconsin, Columbia University, University of Minnesota, and scores of other institutions. Their constant contact in shared community created a network of valuable academic contacts for one another.

The students were required to take at least three courses, each meeting Monday through Friday, as well as a Saturday morning citizenship class. They also needed to participate in evening study hours. The citizens of the town of Beaune, initially somewhat overwhelmed by the influx of thousands of soldier students, grew more gracious as the semester proceeded. They even outfitted the huge, old, fourteenth-century country home of the dukes of Burgundy as a club and meeting facility for all students. Concerned that many of the students would need to draw upon their attainments at Beaune for college transfer or career opportunities when they returned home, university officials published a two-volume catalog of course descriptions, faculty (with credentials), and students. Copies of the set were sent to registrars in every known college and university in the United States to demonstrate the academic stature of the university at Beaune, and Erskine was particularly pleased that it was "the only university catalog, so far as I know, ever printed by an Army in the field."[28]

About halfway through the term, more than 9,000 students had enrolled in more than 200 courses. Those who needed to leave because their units were ordered home received certificates detailing their courses and grades, as did those who stayed the entire term. These were presented to US colleges that determined transfer credit. As the student numbers stopped growing, and then began to shrink, Erskine noticed: "Immediately after the war the shortage of transports had seemed very great, but now the number of available boats was apparently increasing, and no soldier wanted to stay away from his family longer than necessary."[29] The great academic experiment, with Erskine at its helm, was destined to be as temporary as it was successful.

By the end of May, the farewells among faculty and staff had begun. A delegation of French ministers arrived to hold a ceremony of thanks and honor. Erskine, along with General Rees and Colonel Reeves, was awarded the Legion of Honor, a designation that would give him great pride throughout his life. He then left Beaune for Paris, where he spent June taking in ceremonial duties, attending some opera, and writing reports and ledger entries concerning the AEF University. He sailed home from France in July, now aware that his most meaningful professional activities would be educational contributions encompassing a wide spectrum of individuals and experiences and requiring significant action as well as talented intellect. The experience in France had been frantic, exhausting, and joyful. Although it lasted only a year and a half, he would forever consider it to hold far greater significance in his life than its duration indicated. Years later, he would wistfully conclude that Beaune "was a dreamlike experience."[30]

A CANON FOR THE REST OF US

Contrary to numerous reports, the Columbia University curriculum for a two-year program of reading Great Books was not one of those fortuitous innovations developed in war and later spread to important peacetime applications (e.g., the Civil War invention of a nasal chloroform inhaler or the World War II development of freeze drying). Yet, the rumor long persisted that John Erskine first experimented at the AEF University with an educational program made up of selected classic works and then returned to install it at Columbia—and the rest is history. Reminiscences by Mark Van Doren and Jacques Barzun fueled the myth, but got it wrong, prompting a continuation of mistaken assumptions.[1] After Scott Buchanan, who with Stringfellow Barr founded the Great Books curriculum at St. John's College, made the same mistake in an article, Erskine wrote him to chide: "I was amused to see the legend of the AEF University in Beaune growing steadily, and how like all legends it gets badly twisted...We had no selected reading list at Beaune."[2]

Although the university in France did not pilot a course in Great Books, Erskine's experience there, so democratic and energetic, had an enormous impact on his rationale for including a Great Books program in the college curriculum. Before US involvement in the Great War, he had an idea for increasing the reading and discussion of fine literature among Columbia boys—giving them all a course in common that might even spark academic interactions outside the classroom. After he returned from France, his rationale for the notion expanded to include the democratic intent of bringing educational emblems of the highbrow elite to a far larger audience that now sought higher learning opportunities.

Upon receiving the Butler Medal for contributions to education, Erskine gave the 1919 opening convocation address at Columbia. He noted that from the war experience "three conclusions seemed invariable—that the war was but a preparatory safeguarding of the world so that the real problems might be grappled with; that these problems would be solved only by the well-trained; and that if the world is to be democratic, good training should be made accessible to all men and women." He insisted that all who served, from soldiers in trenches to administrators like himself, believed that upon return they "should have a decent place in the world, and should be equipped not only to occupy that place, but also to grow out from it into the enjoyment of life as a whole. They believed, that is, in a complete education."[3]

The young man brought up in gentility had finally experienced a world far different from the confines of Weehawken, Amherst, and Upper West Side. Clearly referencing his own situation, he had long wondered: "Why should not a poet like Woodberry be a man of action, competent in daily affairs?"[4] In *The Moral Obligation to Be Intelligent*, he had maintained that his suggested synthesis of poetry and action would require elevating intelligence to a virtue, perhaps even above character. His war service provided convincing evidence that he could indeed apply intelligence to action with important outcomes, and upon his return to Columbia, he brought a new worldview to shaping that action.

Erskine's thoughts upon returning from France were particularly prescient in terms of developments that would soon envelop American higher education. Two major elements paved the way for change. First, the postwar economic and emotional impulse to extend upper-crust cultural trappings to the middle-class supported individual hopes—including those of growing numbers of women—for social uplift through college degrees. And, the collegiate embrace of professional fields added new options for career training. College enrollment nationwide swelled from 597,857 undergraduates in the 1919–20 academic year to 1,053,955 in the 1927–28 academic year.[5] David O. Levine noted: "The American college and university of the 1920s emphasized professional training and social status...Self confident, students expected higher education to fulfill the democratic promise of modern America."[6]

The timing for a Great Books undergraduate program was an excellent match for these new postwar educational directions. It could appeal to middle-class youths seeking the polish of upper-crust knowledge, even including those who arrived at college with career aims in mind. A seemingly ivory tower idea aimed at nearly any student, it was well suited to the reality noted in a 1922 *New Republic* editorial: "The college became one of those democratic institutions whose function seemed to be to give exclusiveness to the masses."[7] Further, it didn't hurt that the Great Books largely referred to Western classics at a time of postwar puffery—and college course development— about the importance of Western civilization.

* * *

If college and university study in Great Books was an idea whose time had come, it was also an idea that had been coming for some time. As the industrial age ushered in advances in papermaking, printing, and binding, books of all kinds became less expensive and more available. Self-help advice about what and how to read followed not far behind. Noah Porter led the charge when, in his tenth year of the presidency of Yale College, he authored *Books and Reading: Or What Books Shall I Read and How Shall I Read Them?* British writer Sir John Lubbock, concerned with the education of working adults, talked about the need for a list of best books when he addressed London's Working Men's College in 1887. Eventually he published a pamphlet entitled "The Hundred Best Books" for use in British libraries and mechanics institutes. He included the Bible and the Koran, as well as selections by Plato, Aristotle, Homer, Virgil, Shakespeare, Dante, Molière, Darwin, Emerson, Goethe, Dickens, and other ancient and modern literary classics. Harvard professor Charles Eliot Norton brought out a series of "selected portions of the best literature" for children in 1901, and Harvard president Charles W. Eliot soon after selected a 50-volume "five-foot shelf," *The Harvard Classics*, that promised enough fine literature to provide a liberal education in 15 minutes a day.[8] In 1901, Professor Charles Mills Gayley introduced a survey course about important books at the University of California, Berkeley. The series of one-hour lectures on ancient and modern classics attracted many students and large numbers of visitors from the community.[9]

Closer to home, Columbia professor Brander Matthews contributed advice on reading fiction to the 1900 edited volume *Counsel Upon the Reading of Books*. The following year, Erskine's most influential professor, George Woodberry, wrote the introduction to a book published by the Grolier Club, *One Hundred Books Famous in English Literature, With Facsimiles of the Title Pages.* In this, he used the label Great Books and insisted that they should be read and enjoyed for their contribution to understanding "the perpetual mind of the race," without criticism or personal viewpoints.[10]

Since thoughts about reading good books largely emanated from academic scholars, these professors undoubtedly were passing at least some of their preferences on to their own students. However, classroom exposure to fine literature became less of a certainty as the elective system grew in popularity throughout American higher education just before and after the turn of the century. This supplied college students with attractive alternatives to courses that might require difficult reading in ancient styles and/or languages. In addition, many literature professors still favored analysis of literary methods and/or literary criticism over reading for appreciation and understanding. Thus, the idea of Great Books as collegiate reading, even in a time of growing book listing and reading advice, was unlikely to appeal to all students or all faculty.

Perhaps most significant to Erskine as he pondered a possible reading course for Columbia students was the conviction about literature that he had embraced from his mentor Woodberry. Lamenting that literary studies typically took instruction, rather than enjoyment, as their end, Woodberry insisted: "It is perhaps better to consider the process rather than the ends. Literature is a key to one's own heart...outside of direct experience and observation literature is the principal means of obtaining knowledge of human life."[11] Erskine and scores of other Woodberry followers became convinced that the primary value of literary study occurred not by analyzing style or form, but by allowing literary works to inform and enlarge readers' own experiences. In his 1907 volume, *The Appreciation of Literature*, Woodberry recommended much of the salient infrastructure that eventually found its way into Erskine's Great Books course rationale. He noted that reading should not concern "how much the readers can know about the work, the author and the age, but whether he truly responds to the poem, romance or essay, and finds there an expansion of his consciousness of life." And he recommended that readers "should take the greatest masters first."[12] Only in the area of selection, where Woodberry favored individual choice of works and personal preference in place of reading, would Erskine find it necessary to deviate from his mentor in contemplating a Great Books course at Columbia.

Even during his earliest teaching at Amherst, Erskine had steered away from criticism or discussion of literary methods. Instead, with echoes of Woodberry, he wanted students simply to read lots of good books and to be encouraged to find something interesting in them:

> They [students] read of their own choice stories, no matter how crude, that present life with the greatest zest and energy...Should not the first principle of teaching literature be to discover what prevents the life-loving youth from seeing the life stored up in those other books, as yet dead for him? Should not the second principle be to remove that obstacle?...A college course in literature should provide for two things—the actual contact of the student's mind with as many books as possible, and the filling in of any gaps in his sympathy with what he reads. Almost all the great books were intended for the average man; the author contemplated an immediate relationship with his audience...The business of the teacher, then, is to supply an historical or imaginative approach to the book; beyond that, it should appeal for itself.[13]

Many early twentieth-century professors, at Columbia and elsewhere, agreed with Erskine's concerns, although not necessarily with his ideas for dealing with them. They lamented that college students lacked a reading knowledge of classic literature, essential history, and foundational philosophic and scientific works. Just prior to US involvement in World War I, Erskine started to pull together his views about educational content needs, pedagogical preferences, and curricular organization into ideas about approaches to tackle multiple issues. While familiarity with and enjoyment of a great deal of fine literature were aims of the program Erskine began to work into a proposal, they were also means for dealing with broader educational concerns. For example, literature course offerings were typically discrete, chronological studies divvied up into various historical periods and/or categories (i.e., drama, poetry, criticism), and faculty specialization allowed for teaching in one or two of those areas. But Erskine wanted study that did not adopt as its orienting framework the context of historical timing. Instead, the book and what it said to the contemporary reader would surface as the units of analysis.

Discrete and specialized literature courses had added to lack of curricular coherence in undergraduate programs that opted for increased course election and decreased prescription. At Columbia prior to World War I, only about one-third of the undergraduate courses were prescribed, and "the rationale of their interconnection was ill-defined, and the whole mode of study too tight and departmentalized...The conception of basic preparation was dull and unimaginative."[14] However, the only proposal offered to address the disconnection among courses was a suggestion in 1910 from the university's Committee on Instruction that "greater emphasis should be laid upon the continuous study of single subjects through sequential courses; it is both desirable and practicable to establish a new system of honors, based upon such continuous study, which will present a strong incentive to more independent and thorough reading in chosen branches of learning."[15] Apparently, the suggestion for alleviating the chaos of free election through emphasis on single-subject study was to be reserved for the new honors program.

Erskine, reluctant to throw out the elective baby with the bathwater, recognized that increased choice attracted students who longed for greater independence in shaping their studies. Students free to study subjects of natural interest to them might learn more. Nevertheless, he decided that "the advantages of the elective system have been somewhat offset by the loss of intellectual tradition from college life...The college boy no longer takes up a subject as though his neighbors knew all about it, but rather as though it were a little discovery or whim of his own." Erskine saw that in his own undergraduate years and at Amherst, student-body size and institutional requirements supported a great deal of student interaction outside the classroom about coursework undertaken in common. He was determined to find a way to recapture some of the community intellectual spirit, even within a large population of undergraduates, from a time when "what they knew of the classics, of mathematics, of history they knew together; not only their sports, their dormitories, their meals, but also the adventures of the mind, were experiences to be shared by all, and the college gave them the ability to think and talk in one intellectual world."[16] Further, by sharing their literary learning, students would learn that "the humility of spirit that makes comradeship possible is necessary to any pursuit of truth."[17]

*   *   *

In the spring of 1916, Erskine made his proposal to the Faculty of Philosophy, to be reviewed by the Committee on Instruction. Calling for widespread change, it was immediately controversial. The idea suggested a two-year sequence of reading great works (books, plays, and poetry) or selections each week as a requirement for all juniors and seniors who were not preparing for professional degrees. It was the "general student" in his last two undergraduate years who Erskine viewed as "dangerously isolated in his intellectual pursuits." His idea was to "restore the social aspects of scholarship" and provide them with "important ideas in common."[18] The students would meet in weekly discussion (no lecture) sections facilitated by two faculty members from two different departments. Someone from English might be paired with someone from romance languages, fine arts, history, or philosophy. Erskine was clear in the benefits he sought for students: "The advantage of knowing the contents of great books and of discussing them intimately and the advantage to a large group of men of knowing the same books and of reading them at the same time."[19]

"Nobody who knows what a college faculty is like will jump to the conclusion that my proposal was greeted with applause," recalled Erskine. "The faculty rejoinders were rather warm."[20] His colleagues voiced a number of objections. These included the idea that all the reading would be in translations from Greek, Latin, or Hebrew, which would seriously cloud the authors' original intents and meanings. Additionally, the weekly assignment, even with two-hour discussion periods, did not give enough time for serious and in-depth consideration of each work. Perhaps most disturbing to some faculty members was what Joan Shelley Rubin identified as the proposal's "frontal attack on the ethos of specialization" or what Jacques Barzun defined as the program's "disregard [for] the academic cutting up of thought into subjects."[21] The idea was to allow students to share their own perspectives without considering the critiques and interpretations of scholarly inquiry.

Erskine's ongoing adeptness in making friends at or near the top served him well in keeping the proposal alive amidst vocal objections. President Butler, for example, liked literature and liked Erskine. Their relationship gained political clout for Erskine with deans and senior faculty. Erskine could also call upon what other faculty members recognized as his own "ingenuous persuasiveness."[22] However, one colleague wrote to Dean Frederick Keppel to "express my entire disapproval of the plan," explaining:

An ambitious program like this can lead only to a smattering of knowledge, and not to a real understanding of any one author. It is proposed, for instance, to instruct the student in Dante, Aristo, Rabelais, Tasso, Cervantes, Shakespere [sic], Calderon and Corneille in a single half-year, during which time he is to complete an equally elaborate list in history and another in philosophy, to say nothing of other academic activities in his Senior year in the curriculum and elsewhere. When is he to eat and sleep?...I feel that the results of any such plan will be most unfortunate for true scholarship in Columbia College, that if that institution is to make a choice, it should stand for exact knowledge of a few things rather than for superficial acquaintance with many things.[23]

Dean Keppel hosted an informal meeting at the Faculty Club to allow for candid discussion of the proposal, including those who were not on the Committee on Instruction. Erskine deflected arguments by insisting that the aim was first round exposure to great literature, not scholarly investigation of the writing, the authors, the intent, or the meaning. The problem among undergraduates "was not their lack of scholarship, but their reluctance to read great books. The audiences who thronged the ancient theatre to enjoy a new work by Aeschylus or Sophocles were not classical scholars; they were merely the human beings for whom the play was written."[24] He insisted that "when the great books were first published, they were popular, which was the first step toward their permanent fame, and the public who first liked them read them quickly, perhaps overnight, without waiting to hear scholarly lectures about them."[25]

However, according to Columbia professor Moses Hadas, "Some of his colleagues were outraged that an author like Herodotus, for whom a year's graduate course was not deemed adequate, should be trampled over by undergraduates in a week."[26] Mortimer Adler interpreted the resistance of Erskine's colleagues as the difference between exploratory enjoyment and academic inquiry:

It never occurred to him [Erskine] that his special competence as a scholar in the field of English literature and especially in that of the Elizabethan period stood in the way of his general competence to read and discuss books in every field of learning—in theology, philosophy, and the exact sciences as well as in literature, history, and biography. I am sure he thought such competence belonged to every educated man, certainly to every man with an inquiring mind still trying to educate himself. He approached the great books with the amateur spirit, in the best sense of that term. His colleagues...insisted on being strictly professional about the books they taught, and that, of course, restricted them to books in their own specialized spheres of scholarly competence.[27]

The list of books initially proposed was actually three lists—one each in literature, history, and philosophy—totaling 133 works, or occasionally selections (e.g., Aristophanes, two plays; the Bible, selections). A fourth area, science, was not represented by a list of books or authors. However, the proposal noted that a science sequence would start with key ideas prior to the nineteenth century (in mathematics, astronomy, chemistry, etc.) and then move on to more contemporary topics and readings, including evolution, in the second year. In their third and fourth years, students would be required to undertake three of the four areas.[28]

The choice of works to include on the lists, although considered tentative in 1916, undoubtedly prompted a great deal of scrutiny by members of the Committee on Instruction. This, however, did not particularly bother Erskine. He had his own favorites, but there is no indication that he was ever attached to a precise canon. And, although the literature that he and his colleagues knew and found available at that time was largely Western, he understood that faculty would refine and revise any list many times. Thus, his 1916 proposal eliminated both the authority of scholars sharing the conclusions of their specialized literary investigations and the authority of a chosen canon of must-read works. His aim was to introduce students to literary and humanistic exploration in ways that would spark multiple interests and perspectives for lives of citizenship. Lionel Trilling, reflecting on his own student experiences, noted loftier objectives rooted in Erskine's belief in developing "large-minded men, committed to great ends, devoted to virtue, assured of the dignity of the human estate and dedicated to enhancing and preserving it; and that great works of the imagination could foster and even institute this large-mindedness, this magnanimity."[29]

Notably, the proposed Columbia list bore little resemblance to the list developed by Sir John Lubbock nearly three decades earlier, although that list often has been considered the taproot for such endeavors. Lubbock's list was slightly less literary, more global, and more British. Like the Columbia list, it included the Bible. But it differed by also including the Koran, the Mahabharata, the Ramayana, and the Shahnameh. Explorations of Cook and Darwin were included, as well as works by Dickens, Thackeray, Burke, and Lytton. The proposed Columbia list carried a greater number of Greek and Roman classics; more French, German, and American works; and philosophers as contemporary as William James and Georges Santayana. Shakespeare appeared on both lists.[30]

When the Committee on Instruction convened in early 1917 to reconsider and refine the Erskine proposal, the members reduced the book list to 80 works, and they exempted students who intended to study law. In February, 1917, they approved the proposal by a vote of 13 to 8.[31] Dean Keppel's *Annual Report* of 1917 announced a fall 1918 launch for the program, stating that it would "give a unified view of culture, and...make the students familiar at first hand with world masterpieces of literature, philosophy, and of history."[32]

The general campus confusion wrought by the US entry into World War I, as well as Erskine's absence, quickly deferred implementation of the new program. Two months after his arrival in France, Erskine received news of its stalled state from his colleague and friend, psychologist Herbert Lord, who wrote: "Your dear plan, wrought out with such hope, enthusiasm and promise, has come to a pause. The philosophy man, [John J.] Coss, is in national service, while [Frederick J.] Woodbridge who could and would substitute cannot do it as desired. The science man, Barry, seems to be on the ragged edge of doubt...The history man, [Carlton J.] Hayes, has misgivings. So 'til the tangle of the war, or at least for a year, has somewhat unraveled itself, the thing waits."[33] Implementation of the controversial plan, precarious in its slim margin of supporters, clearly required on-site nurturing from its originator.

* * *

When Erskine returned from France, he was more than ever up to the task of pushing his plan to fruition. Decorated with the French ribbon of Chevalier of the Legion of Honor and the US Army Distinguished Service Medal, he received an offer of the presidency of Smith College and would soon receive additional such offers. He had proved an expert educational innovator and administrator, and his confidence soared. While some at Columbia, such as President Butler, were delighted to welcome another star to the faculty galaxy, others were doubtless a bit envious. The majority, however, had increased respect for accomplishments that now went beyond their colleague's well-recognized excellence in teaching and writing.

Still, Erskine needed to begin at the beginning, reintroducing rather than simply reviving his idea for Great Books in the curriculum. Now in its favor was its context among a citizenry that saw special goodness in knowing about all things Western. A Great Books sequence could be encouraged for "its capacity to provide familiar touchstones (self-reliance, character, Western civilization) in a changing world," while solidifying tradition in ways that might "dispel the threat of class conflict and social disarray."[34]

Additionally, two other courses paved the way by flying in the face of enthusiasm for electives and specialized training. A "war aims" course taught to all Student Army Training Corps students at Columbia and elsewhere had successfully surveyed Western ideology and the Allied cause. Frederick Woodbridge, the eminent philosopher and Columbia dean of Graduate Faculties who had designed the course, turned his post-armistice attention to a new course for freshmen, Introduction to Contemporary Civilization (CC). Along with the newly appointed Columbia College dean Herbert Hawkes,[35] and others, he pushed for a required yearlong survey of recent and current cultural, social, economic, and political issues in American life. Their idea, according to Jacques Barzun, was "to teach the new generation the ideals and the history of Western Civilization, in hopes that when they were leaders of opinion and makers of policy they might avoid the ghastly mistakes that had brought the Continent to self-destruction in total war."[36] The proposal was immediately embraced by the faculty Committee on Instruction. CC began in September, 1919, with 15 discussion sections meeting for an hour in the morning, 5 times a week. It soon grew into a two-year program that included historical and philosophical contexts.[37] CC, along with the Great Books program, later labeled "the other half of the core," eventually would earn Columbia's place as the leading spirit in the American general education movement.[38]

Perhaps weary from the 1916 struggle for a sequence in Great Books, and perhaps equally weary from the monumental work in initiating the AEF University, Erskine favored a fairly low-key approach when he proposed a two-year reading course to start in 1920. He did not strategize or politic to win favor for his proposal among his colleagues. He did not emphasize high-level support, although Mortimer Adler later claimed that President Butler's intervention did eventually occur.[39] Ultimately,

Erskine simply asked the Committee on Instruction for permission to teach the new course. He recalled that after a lengthy, but inconclusive discussion about defining a Great Book, "the Committee abandoned the task and told me to go ahead in my own way. The permission was granted in a tone which seemed to say, 'And may God have mercy on your soul!'"[40] Most disappointing to Erskine, his two-year sequence was limited to an elective for third- and fourth-year students in the Honors program who might seek a "general" course along with their "specialized" honors areas of study. Erskine explained: "Most of my colleagues were still hostile to the idea, and they tried to protect the students—and themselves—from it by decreeing that my course should be open only to the specially qualified, who would take it as an extra, or as they like to say, as 'honors.'"[41] The course was somewhat veiled under the official name General Honors.

Erskine's colleagues also wanted a hand in blessing the list of books, eventually agreeing on "some 50 or 60, from Homer to William James, masterpieces in all fields—literature, economics, science, philosophy, history."[42] The original list, which was modified nearly monthly once the course started, contained the works of 51 authors. It varied from the 1916 approved list by eliminating the organizational typology of literature, philosophy, and history and by substantially paring down the number of books.[43] However, the malleability of the "list" proved more important than exactly what was on the list.[44] One analyst later explained: "It was never the purpose at Columbia to inculcate any sort of philosophy or world view through its selection of books, a selection which has always remained open ended, hence more flexible than the tendency elsewhere to seize upon 'the' greatest books and then set them in stone."[45] Mortimer Adler noted that the number of books in the initial program helped dispel the notion of an authoritative canon: "One of the usually unnoticed virtues of Erskine's original list was that it avoided the canonical number 'one hundred' which had become connected in the popular mind with the making of such lists."[46]

Erskine had used the label "great books" in his 1908 essay in the *Nation* on teaching literature, and Woodberry had used it in 1902 in his introduction to the list suggested by the Grolier Club.[47] Neither they nor others using the phrase at that time felt a need to define the term or to use it exclusively. Erskine also sometimes referred to "important books" or "masterpieces." There seemed to be some agreement that the phrase generally referred to classics. Only later, as Great Books was institutionalized (and capitalized) as organized endeavors, did definition seem necessary. Erskine finally decided: "A great book is one that has meaning, and continues to have meaning, for a variety of people over a long period of time. The world choses its great books by a social process."[48] Stringfellow Barr, the first president of St. John's College in its Great Books format, agreed with Erskine: "One of the chief reasons for calling the very good books 'great' is that they are apparently able to bring the intellectual process to life and have done so repeatedly in many historic contexts, although not in identical ways. They are in dialogue with every generation that wants to talk with them, since they talk much better than most books do."[49]

Although Erskine's seminar course was officially titled General Honors, Erskine never used that label. He long remained disconcerted that while his own intent was to broaden access to cultural emblems once reserved for the elite, his colleagues insisted on keeping the seminar minimal and meritorious by limiting it to honors students in their upper-class years. Mortimer Adler recalled that Erskine introduced the new course to a meeting of curious students as a study in "the classics of Western civilization." Another early student in the course, Clifton Fadiman, called it the "course in the classics." In a letter to Fadiman, Erskine referred to the seminar as the "so-called Honors Course." In his 1948 memoir on teaching, he mentioned only the "Great Books course," never General Honors.[50]

The first Wednesday of fall semester 1920, at 7:30 p.m. in Columbia's Hamilton Hall, a section of students gathered for a two-hour discussion of the *Iliad* in the initial meeting of General Honors. Erskine and his English Department colleague Raymond Weaver were the co-instructors. Of their 24 students, 23 returned for the second year of the sequence. As enrollment soon demanded more sections, the instructors also included Joseph Wood Krutch, Mark Van Doren, Mortimer Adler (whose first involvement was as a student in the class), and others. Although never formally required, "General Honors became a must course for the brightest College students of the mid-1920s."[51] Over the next five years, total enrollment in the two years of the course climbed to as many as 114 students.[52]

Among those students were an unusual number of future luminaries, such as: Henry Morton Robinson, Clifton Fadiman, Lionel Trilling, Whittaker Chambers, Jacques Barzun, and Joseph Mankiewicz. Other less recognizable names joining them were: future

Truman economic advisor Leon Keyserling, future head of the College Entrance Examination Board Frank Bowles and future McGraw-Hill president Eliot Bell.

The logistics of General Honors alone were revolutionary. Instead of meeting three or more times a week for the traditional 50 minutes, "Sessions [were] conducted weekly for two hours on Wednesday evening," according to Mark Van Doren. "Seminar rooms were used so that the students could sit informally around a long table and smoke; and at the end of this table were two teachers, not one, so that benefit might be derived from differences between their views of Aristotle, Euripides, St. Augustine, Dante, Rabelais, Montaigne, Shakespeare, Molière, Voltaire, Goethe, or whoever else was being encountered through one of his masterpieces."[53]

The timing of the new and innovative course was particularly well suited to the postwar sense of liberation from institutionalized tradition and collective direction, as well as the rise of a middle-class culture that aspired to acquire high-class materials, if not status. American higher education in the decade after the Great War experienced an unprecedented surge in student numbers, as well as in curriculum change and new degree programs. Jacques Barzun, who was among that huge flock of students, explained:

> Second generation Americans showed their deep thirst for all the learning that their parents had missed and that the upper classes had presumably kept to themselves. The new-risen took to it with ease, and the upper classes apparently did not want to hoard it. Some of the demobilized soldiers made their way to college to resume an interrupted education or went there to start one, and this injection of mature minds also gave those years on campus an unusual vibrancy.[54]

As experienced faculty members partnered with younger colleagues for the sections, a general culture of friendly Socratic discussion permeated the seminars. Barzun recalled that a session "always began with a question addressed to a particular student: 'Mr. So-and-So, do you agree with Plato that society is in need of specially designated and trained guardians?'"[55] Typically, there was little formal coordination between the two instructors, but a fair amount of peer learning and alternating questions and follow-up arguments.

Mortimer Adler, who first partnered with Erskine for teaching a General Honors seminar, later remarked: "I tried, not too successfully, to imitate his idiosyncratic, and therefore inimitable, style of questioning." He next partnered with Mark Van Doren who started the first class meeting with, "What is the ruling passion in the *Iliad*?" He would then ask nearly every student around the table to answer. Adler quickly learned that the opening question was often the most important pedagogical tool, especially "one that not only opens the discussion, but also generates other questions that will reach out in a number of different directions to sustain a coherent discussion for two hours."[56]

Erskine's style in the seminars was to offer little in the way of his own ideas, but to bring students to their understandings with questions and brief comments that might be cagey, thought provoking, or "gotcha." He was especially adept at encouraging students to reexamine their firm opinions or tightly held assertions. When a student insisted that all literature was economically determined, Erskine asked for an example. "Sir Walter Scott," the student named. "He wrote his last novels to pay his debts." Erskine, who counted Scott among a handful of the greatest writers, simply lowered his usually forceful voice and mildly countered: "I would have thought that the sense of honor had something to do with it."[57] While Erskine held fast to his belief that students' own ideas about the reading were most relevant to their discovery and enjoyment of Great Books, his seminars were lessons in the art of questioning and the value of entertaining alternative explanations.

Faculty interest in teaching and student registrations grew as word of mouth carried about the stimulating conversations and interesting reading. An enthusiastic Leon Keyserling wrote to his father in Beaufort, South Carolina: "Our General Honors course is progressing wonderfully...Meeting at seven-thirty, we often stay until ten or later. I've never had so interesting a course, nor so instructive. We do a lot of reading, about 500 pages each week, and all of excellent material, usually one classic, one biography of the author, and one secondary work or criticism...The three profs in my general honors section are from the departments of Philosophy, English, and Ancient Classics, a good department, and unusually good men. It's pretty near impossible—tho' I've tried—to keep regular hours, as to retiring, etc. Tonight for example, after the honors meeting, two other fellows and I started a rather heated discussion as to what constituted the tragic flaw of most great men, real and in literature."[58]

Clifton Fadiman, who insisted "I do not think I would ever have learned how to read" without the General Honors course, later tried to analyze what made Erskine a "great teacher" and to explain "the influence he wielded over his students, even over those who didn't care greatly about literature." He decided that Erskine's "enormous respect (not merely liking) for his subject matter" set the stage, while his expectations of his students completed the scene. "He challenged us...He called upon us for a kind of mental exercise that is ordinarily devoted to mastering such 'hard' subjects as philosophy and the sciences. Erskine made us work."[59]

Although the original idea was a nod to pedagogy that was individualistic and open to spontaneity, within a few years the faculty began discussions—perhaps inevitable—about more formal structure and consistency among the sections. In 1924, they gathered the list of books, along with suggested supplementary readings and discussion questions, into a slim volume titled *Outline of Readings in Important Books*. The "Preface" carefully explained, "It is not to be understood that this list of reading has been approved by the faculty of Columbia College as a selection of the fifty or sixty best books of the world...The choice of this list has been governed largely by the needs of students of Columbia College." Among the 10 to 12 widely ranging discussion questions listed for each book were: "To what are the Greeks loyal [in the *Iliad*]?"; "What is Thucydides' attitude toward oracles and supernatural causes?"; "If you like Balzac, what kind of pleasure do you find in his books?"[60]

*　*　*

After about five years, when a core General Honors teaching group of a dozen or more regulars had gathered, the faculty members involved began meeting weekly at the Faculty Club for lunch and interaction about the course. Much discussion centered on changes to Erskine's list of 52 works. Mortimer Adler recalled: "Discussion of how to modify Erskine's original list went on week after week and promised to be as fruitless as faculty meetings generally are when curriculum reform is under discussion and the representatives of each department plead for the inclusion of more courses in their area and reduction of courses in other areas."[61] Eventually, Adler drafted a compromise list of 176 works. The faculty group pared it down to 76 and voted to use it as the official revised version. The interesting idea had moved from malleable experiment to institutional program—with all the consequences that implied.

Additional changes related to the General Honors course included, in 1927, the practice of students and instructors meeting earlier for dinner at the new dormitory, "John Jay," where casual discussions began. After dinner, sections retired to their seminar rooms for the regular sessions.[62] The same year, Scott Buchanan, a recent Harvard PhD and Rhodes Scholar, was serving as assistant director at the People's Institute, a community lecture series endeavor of Cooper Union. He told his friend Mortimer Adler about plans for expanded geographical reach through seminar groups at locations of the New York City library system, and Adler suggested he model the curriculum on Erskine's General Honors. The Great Books quickly became popular continuing education, with Columbia faculty and students among the seminar instructors.[63]

Erskine did little to assert ownership over the General Honors reading course or to direct its future as it grew, although he enjoyed guiding his own sections, partnering with younger faculty, and watching students awaken to fine literature. And undoubtedly, he enjoyed observing that the outcomes he had in mind were happening. Students were discussing the readings outside the classroom, and the books were bridging cultural divides. Lionel Trilling, who graduated in 1925, observed the impact of General Honors on development of a "Columbia mystique" that succeeded in "showing young men how they might escape from the limitations of their middle-class or their lower-middle-class upbringings by putting before them great models of thought, feeling, and imagination."[64]

Erskine's interest in involvement with English Department policies and practices seemed to wane after General Honors took off, either because of his growing impatience with inevitable department politics or because he was simply too engrossed in other career and personal interests. He was, after all, a man with a huge reservoir of talent and energy. He kept a busy writing schedule in the first several years after returning from France, with essays regularly appearing in the *Nation*, the *Bookman*, the *New Republic*, and elsewhere. He published five books between 1920 and 1925. He lectured beyond Columbia frequently and was active in the Poetry Society of America (where he was elected president in 1922), the American Council of Learned Societies (where he was secretary from 1921 to 1924), the Authors' Club (where he served as president from 1920 to 1923), the National Institute of Arts and Letters, the Modern Language Association, and Trinity church.[65]

On campus, he reinvigorated the student society, Boar's Head, which frequently met in his apartment. In addition to his seminar sections in Great Books, as well as his regular poetry and general literature courses, he developed two new courses. For undergraduates, he began a course in writing poetry and fiction, and it quickly became well known for its annual public readings of undergraduate literary efforts. He then created a lecture course for master of arts candidates, "Materials of Poetry." For it, he later recalled that he "decided to lecture on as many of the world masterpieces in poetry as I could crowd into two hours a week from October to June...My scheme was to show how actual events and actual people had been transmuted into myth or fable by popular imagination and by the genius of great and perhaps long-forgotten artists." When the course quickly attracted scores of students, Erskine felt it became perceived as "something of a scandal" among his faculty colleagues. But to him, it paved new inroads in interpreting literary works by closing the distances between history, myth, and literature.[66]

His poetry lectures might be crowded in large halls, but as one student recalled: "Professor Erskine speaks casually, as though he had just been lunching with the man he is talking about...The author is seen to be a mortal...always living, dramatic, and never a textbook dummy."[67] Student accolades went public when the undergraduate daily newspaper, the *Spectator*, published student evaluations of nearly 100 courses. Of Erskine's course "Literary Practice from Sidney to Milton," the paper noted: "This course is particularly fortunate in its subject matter and instructor. Prof. Erskine's lectures make any of his courses worthwhile. There is much diversity of opinion as to whether it is a snap course. Several essays are required, covering most of the reading before it is taken up in class, but these are marked very leniently."[68]

* * *

Erskine's mother died in 1920, his brother and his three sisters continued to live in New York, and he saw them frequently. Upon his return from France, he moved with his wife Pauline and two children to a rented apartment close to Columbia at 39 Claremont Avenue. He also purchased an old farm house in Wilton, Connecticut, as a family summer home (see figure 6.1). A large colonial-style, stone structure, its state of neglect allowed for a relatively small purchase price but also demanded immediate renovation and repair.

Figure 6.1   "Nod Hill," Erskine's country house, Wilton, CT.
Source: Courtesy of Robert J. Toy, photographer.

Finally, John Erskine the professor was fully restyled as John Erskine the man of action. By initiating the Great Books program at Columbia, he brought to life his observations and thoughts about the needs of students on their way to full citizenship and his concerns about the general state of teaching and learning in higher education. He had successfully tested his position as "a realist who felt that some knowledge was better than none at all; that students who lacked Greek should not thereby be prevented from knowing Homer; that Dante and Molière are in many ways as valuable to the American mind as Shakespeare; and that, although true to Pope, 'A little knowledge is a dangerous thing' can be an adage destructive of all intellectual curiosity."[69]

Like the AEF University, the General Honors program proved a more powerful force than even Erskine may have hoped. Mortimer Adler proclaimed it "a college in itself—the whole of a liberal education, or certainly the core of it." He particularly applauded "the discussions which Erskine conducted in the manner of highly civilized conversations about important themes and in a spirit of inquiry . . . and still further, the conversations that the students themselves had with one another in between times, both about the books being read and about matters touched on in the seminars."[70]

Erskine, however, was content to put the continuance of General Honors in the hands of others. Teaching the seminars was his special expertise and enjoyment. Joining committee deliberations about curricular adjustments could only be frustrating. In the postwar spirit of optimism about innovation and change, Erskine had a full life with plenty of new ideas and activities to pursue. The Great Books idea had achieved a life of its own.

CHAPTER 7

CELEBRITY ATTRACTION

While he couldn't know it at the time, Erskine became the benefi-
ciary of a life-changing coincidence only a few months after his return
from France. In November, 1919, he shouldered his way to the upper
level of a Fifth Avenue bus and discovered there an acquaintance from
three years earlier, Ernest Hutcheson. A celebrated piano virtuoso,
born in Australia and schooled in Germany, Hutcheson had come to
the United States in 1914. He was on the bus joking with his wife just
days after he had made musical history by performing with the New
York Symphony three piano concertos in a single concert. Erskine had
first briefly encountered him in 1916 at the Chautauqua Institute,
where Hutcheson directed music and Erskine taught some summer
courses in literature. The chance meeting suddenly gave Erskine the
impetus—perhaps the imperative—to decide once and for all if he
would renew his lapsed endeavors at serious piano playing. "I knew
I must play again," he determined that day. "If I wanted to play,
what excuse had I for not playing? Was I afraid? Why postpone an
ideal?" He decided to commit to the task of regaining, perhaps sur-
passing, his earlier musical ability. He would begin to work on his
own and play in informal groups, honing his skill enough to deserve
a renowned teacher—Ernest Hutcheson.[1]

With recent lecture fees, he purchased a Steinway grand. He began
practicing regularly—at least two hours a day; sometimes more—and
he performed with university colleagues in a chamber music group.
He later recalled that his determined return to piano practice was
"to the extreme annoyance of my wife Pauline." Some of this dissen-
sion he credited to his practice at the Wilton farmhouse on a "simply

God-awful" old upright; but it is just as likely that Pauline was being sensitive to the neighbors during late night practices at the New York apartment.[2] After several years of practice and enjoyable play with local groups, and with an eye toward more and better public performance, Erskine was finally ready to put himself in the expert hands of Ernest Hutcheson. His weekly private lessons were supplemented with weekly evening performance occasions among all Hutcheson's students, where group criticism about technique and interpretation could be devastating.

Erskine's decision to redirect priorities and energies—initially toward music, but soon to include new areas in writing and in education—was consistent with the postwar mood that swept into the 1920s throughout the country. That mood, a spirited and individualistic modernism that favored the optimistic embrace over the exclusionary cold shoulder, soon seeped into art, literature, commerce, technological innovation, and entertainment. It welcomed experimentation and possibilities, ushering in what Jacques Barzun saw as a national embrace of all things contemporary. With it came greater tolerance for everything from women's rights and free-form art to sexual banter and atonal music. In human relationships, "informality had become the fashion and it simplified encounters; for etiquette is a barrier, the casual style an invitation. The soft collar, the short skirt, the slip-on shoe accompanied a new feeling of camaraderie between the sexes."[3]

Erskine and other urbane intellectuals closely monitored the popular dramatic and literary elements that marked a shift in the arts scene. Among them were the clever comedies of manners by writers like Noel Coward and Somerset Maugham; the light verse and humorous essays of Robert Benchley, Max Beerbohm, and Dorothy Parker; silly and satirical limericks; and short, often shallow, stories in monthly magazines. Taken together, these illustrated a decade that was "fond of seeing the highbrow mind at play...It was relaxing and 'humanizing.' "[4]

The new national mood also was ripe for another advance that would eventually have significant consequences for Erskine and others who might seek large audiences. In the spring of 1920, with wartime security limits on public use of wireless radio lifted, Dr. Frank Conrad of the Westinghouse Company in Pittsburgh decided to test various generations of radio transmitting equipment by talking over the airwaves to employees at a handful of listening posts. When he finally tired of using his voice, he decided to play records on a phonograph instead. After widespread feedback from ham radio operators who happened on his transmissions, he instituted regular hours and mentioned the names of the local merchants who donated his records. Eventually, with help from the top at Westinghouse, the operation in Conrad's garage was replaced with a broadcasting station with call letters KDKA. Entertainment and commercial uses of radio, a technology initially envisioned for locational and emergency broadcasting, immediately boomed. Within a few years, motion pictures with synchronized audio dialogue, "talkies," would clinch the prominence of entertainment in the postwar years and its place in commercial advances, technological innovation, and celebrity recognition.[5]

* * *

In the immediate years after his return from France, Erskine went about his academic activities—especially writing and publishing—as if he had some precognition about a new future and sensed a need to tie up loose ends and restate his case before moving on. His first published volume of the period attended to final thoughts related to the war years. He collected together several essays and addresses written while he was serving as an educator in France, bookended them with an address to an educational association in 1917 and another delivered at Columbia in 1919, and brought out *Democracy and Ideals* in 1920. In it he called for a common definition and advancement of American ideals, better understood in light of knowledge gained from the recent war. He also addressed access and equity in higher education, determining: "I should admire only the scholar, whether in the narrow paths of science or in the open fields of letters, who sought truth with his whole heart, who shared it with the greatest number of his fellows whom he could reach...Truth is for all men, but some are less prepared for it than others. The task of preparing the more ignorant is a necessary task; in the eyes of scholarship, however, it is sometimes considered less dignified than the companionship of the learned."[6] While the volume was widely viewed as nicely patriotic, close readings exposed it as somewhat didactic and arrogant. The *New York Evening Post* reviewer concluded: "Where Dr. Erskine does not impress the reader as fumbling, he irritates him by his assertion of debatable theses as if they were axioms."[7]

Next, in the 1920 volume *The Kinds of Poetry*, Erskine reiterated his ideas about reading and teaching poetry in a collection of four essays. Three of these had been published in various venues during his earlier years at Columbia. The essays called for poetry study of a less formal nature than typical in college courses—a personal and spiritual approach (in the mode of Edward Woodberry), rather than a historical, technical, or biographical undertaking. And, they favored a broad definition of poetry well beyond verse, one that could include dialogue and prose. The volume also allowed Erskine to repeat his own impressions of various poets: Tennyson was wonderful, but Frost was not; Edgar Lee Masters was very good indeed, but Amy Lowell was uneven.[8]

As if convinced that printed reminders of all his accomplishments were now due, Erskine soon reacquainted readers with his best poetry over the previous 15 years in *Collected Poems: 1907–1922*. The book contained works collected from two previous volumes and a dozen different periodicals, from the *Atlantic Monthly* and *Harper's Magazine* to the *Texas Review* and *La Revue de Bourgogne*. Critics applauded the romantic and thoughtful collection for "emotional intensity and intellectual force" and its "rare sensitiveness to beauty."[9]

A fourth Erskine collection appeared in 1923. This one, *The Literary Discipline*, gathered essays previously published in the *North American Review* and the *Bookman*. With a dedication to George Edward Woodberry, the author introduced the volume as "studies in the discipline which literature imposes on those who cultivate it as an art" and emphasized its concern that "language as a medium of expression has certain limitations which the writer must respect, and that the psychology of his audience limits him also in what he may say, if he would gain a wide hearing and keep it."[10] His appeal was for assessing and enjoying literature as art, not as information, and he insisted that only through the artistic lens could readers distinguish the truly enduring works that matter over time. True to the postwar relaxation of restrictions on appropriate literary topics for public consumption, Erskine included the question of depictions of sex in literature. The volume's first essay, "Decency in Literature," was summarized by one reviewer as a call for "literary decorum" that insisted: "Sex is a proper subject for literature so long as it is represented as a general force in life..., but sexual actions are indecent when they cease to illustrate the general fact of sex and are studied for their own sake."[11] The book was widely reviewed with nearly unanimous approval. Only his Columbia colleague, Joseph Wood Krutch, wrote a truly dismissive critique, insisting that "if rules exist in the realm of literature, Mr. Erskine does not know what they are."[12]

This proliferation of collected and bound recent work apparently convinced Erskine that no scribble or utterance should be ignored for possible publication. Accordingly, he decided to nudge into print something very different, an allegory he had written "some time ago" titled *The Enchanted Garden*. Recasting the theme of ideal beauty that had guided much of his poetry and would eventually steer many of his novels, the story focused on a fictional princess who represented the ideal in appearance and spirit. Various visitors in the princess's garden symbolized hopelessness, skepticism, and other ideas that interacted in an effort to illustrate the interplay of realism, illusion, and disillusion. The slender book was published in 300 copies by the Torch Press, a small printing house in Iowa that specialized in limited editions. Each copy was numbered and signed by the author. Erskine's former student Lloyd Morris, now a well-regarded literary critic who could always be counted on for enthusiastic newspaper and magazine reviews of his professor's published work, received copy number seven inscribed "with happy memories of a long friendship." Erskine would soon seek Morris's feedback on the manuscript for his first major novel.[13]

Turning his attention to new verse only after most of his earlier efforts were printed and bound, in early 1925 Erskine brought out a volume that contained his most recent work, *Sonata and Other Poems*. In it, he reiterated the themes of beauty and artistry that recurred with great regularity in his writing. Beauty, in everything from the human form to fine arts and literature, was to be Erskine's great priority and puzzlement. He would never define it, but he became impatient when others found greater importance in intellect or knowledge. The title poem of his new collection told the story of a lovely young woman who posed nude for a great painter, but later became a well-regarded painter herself. Her paintings, however, were not of beautiful things, but of ordinary landscapes—mere "wallpaper" according to the disappointed artist who had once appreciated the beauty of her nude body.[14] A humorous verse in the collection, "The Poetic Bus Driver," told of a New York bus driver who found his route filled with poetry and music. A fun and whimsical Erskine introduced these lines:

Art for Art's sake—Allegro agitato
To Eighty-fifth Street; presto, then until

The bridge at Ninety-sixth, horn obligato;
A pause, and then adagio up the hill;
Then scherzo to One Hundredth with a will.[15]

Writing late at night, generally following his piano practice and straddling several hours just before and after midnight, Erskine also used the half-dozen years after the war to write essays and literary criticism. Three or more articles appeared each year in widely read periodicals. His primary areas of concern were the state of American literature and the state of American higher education. Concerning the latter, he was able to broadcast notions about higher education that he only began to touch upon when he argued that an ancient classical work could benefit the education of any Columbia boy, even on a first reading in translation. His postwar ideas, first mentioned in *Democracy and Ideals*, scanned a far broader horizon to include students of all genders, ages, and circumstances and to embrace learning from almost any medium. He accused the selective universities of stifling his new vision by narrowing aims and hoarding knowledge:

> The schools and colleges are resolved to keep out the crowds, and the few institutions—a university or two, an occasional lecture system, a correspondence school here and there—which try to meet the need, all the greater because so few are trying, are dismissed with a phrase; they are "intellectual department stores" or "degree factories." They encourage that bad thing, "mass education." When you consider it, there is no reason why a university should not be an "intellectual department store"—that is, a place where the community can get any kind of instruction it needs.[16]

The less selective institutions accessed by less prepared students often failed to understand that "to assume a boy has a mind is the quickest way to develop a mind in him." Instead, they tended "to assume that he hasn't a mind but needs some training in mediocre information."[17] Erskine recommended expanding colleges and universities to more areas of learning and more learners—not unlike the big tent of knowledge and skill building at the AEF University in France, where he proudly noted: "Now a farmer from Iowa could take a course on Renaissance painting and find a whole world he never knew existed."[18]

In his most widely distributed article on higher education, Erskine summarized a viewpoint that was not likely shared by his Columbia colleagues: "Personally, I should like to see every citizen, of whatever age, finding the instruction or the aid he desires in the nearest university. If he wishes to be an engineer or a painter or a blacksmith, I should like to see him turn to the university for training. No doubt, as our universities learn to serve the community with more and more completeness we shall begin to think of carpentering and of plumbing as academic subjects."[19] Although it may have been disconcerting in elite institutions, Erskine's concept was not altogether shocking. A growing middle-class aspiration for the patina of culture and the promise of professional and vocational careers had already begun to pull commercially minded colleges and universities in the direction of Erskine's vision. David O. Levine later observed: "After World War I, institutions of higher learning were no longer content to educate; they now set out to train, accredit, and impart social status to their students."[20]

Erskine's writing about literature largely focused on his observations of the teaching of literature, and his criticisms undoubtedly would not have pleased some of his own colleagues. He charged that the utilitarian sentiment had invaded even the fine arts, which had a purpose of giving students "one more kind of insurance against embarrassment in polite society."[21] Literature, he insisted, should be seen as art; and, as art it should touch the individual spirit rather than simply add to the store of knowledge about form, authorship, style, and historical context. Instead, however, "when we begin to teach children to write, we do not ask them to write beautifully; enough if they write intelligibly. When we teach them to read, we do not ask them to notice beauty in the book; enough if they can tell us 'what the book is about.'"[22]

Since prescription was the enemy of art, Erskine offered no cure for neglecting art in literature. If pressed, however, he undoubtedly would have suggested his own light guidance in General Honors seminars that led students to recognize the artistry of the works they read, rather than to acquire the knowledge of themes, times, and places.

Somewhat surprisingly, considering that his own career in writing commercially successful novels would soon blossom, he also railed against writing and learning to write for purposes of selling books and articles. He insisted that contemporary popular literature demonstrated "a tendency toward journalism instead of art." Pointing to F. Scott Fitzgerald and other writers "who bring us news of the Younger Generation," he warned: "They now enjoy our gratitude for the news, but in that kind of popularity there are always the seeds of neglect and obscurity."[23] His argument centered on the idea that too much of what passed as fiction was not art, but commentary on the current scene, and good reviews happened simply because reviewers agreed with the commentary. The American public was becoming so accustomed to informational narrative from novels that they began to ask of them "the level of service that should be rendered by histories, essays and sociological reports...we expect little else of the fiction we read, and if the book happens to be important for artistic reasons we may overlook its merits."[24] Apparently, the professor who came back from the war—or perhaps just the professor who had now matured past his fortieth year—was far more prone to public candor, even at the risk of controversy or antagonism.

*   *   *

Erskine undoubtedly experienced significant inner turmoil during the immediate postwar years. His English Department colleagues had only grudgingly approved the launch of his idea for a course in Great Books, and then only after paring it down to General Honors; few of them agreed with his ideas about student access and curricular reach in higher education. His published essays, more and more candid concerning his unfavorable views of recent literature and its teaching, could easily annoy his fellow scholars, many of whom were already skeptical about his professorial chops due to the popularity of his courses. Ultimately, his best Columbia friends were his students and graduates, as well as a few colleagues from other departments who he met at the Faculty Club. His piano playing was a welcome outlet, but hardly appreciated by his immediate family, and, along with his writing, it left him little time for his wife and two growing children or for his nearby extended family of three sisters, a brother, and a sister-in-law. A perceptive student in his Erskine's General Honors seminar, Henry Morton Robinson, noted: "Those who knew him between the 40th and 45th years of his life realized that he was undergoing a severe emotional crisis, induced partly by creative needs that no burden of academic work could crush or allay. Mind you, he was at the very peak of his physical and emotional energy; it was only a question of time before this energy would erupt."[25]

Initially, much of that energy was devoted to the family country house at Wilton, Connecticut. Situated at the summit of Nod Hill, about 40 miles from New York City, the old stone house had come with "an abandoned farm of more acreage than I needed or wanted, but at least I had here a summer home for my children and, as it turned out, the nucleus of a rather large place which could have been an all-year round residence."[26] The first order of business was the addition of plumbing. Erskine then busied himself with small projects and plans for the extensive renovations that would have to wait for financial improvements. The plumbing alone had required a small loan. His hopes were high, and on February 14, 1921, he titled his annual Valentine poem to his wife, "Valentine for the First Year of Wilton," and wrote it as a dreamy description of seasons changing in the rolling countryside.[27]

By coincidence, a number of well-known musicians lived in Wilton or spent summers there, including several who toured with string quartets. Erskine was soon accompanying cello and bass players in casual music making at their homes, generally in the evening and followed by drinks and talk about music. With musical neighbors Marie Rosanoff and Sascha Jacobsen, he gave annual benefit concerts at the Wilton Public Library. At Columbia, he gave occasional performances with a small group of faculty and others who specialized in Brahms and Beethoven and managed to include violin, flute, clarinet, and piano. Later, he admitted: "My love of music was a love of performance. Perhaps love of performance is the essence of my nature."[28] For his first public symphonic concert, at Columbia and including players from the New York Philharmonic Orchestra, he practiced a Schumann concerto five to six hours a day during the summer of 1924.[29]

In his second decade on the Columbia faculty, Erskine also took great pleasure in tracking the careers of recent graduates who still kept in touch, visited him with news, and sought his advice. He urged one of his earliest Columbia students, Alfred A. Knopf (class of 1912) to pursue his ideas about a career in publishing, and he encouraged PhD graduate (1914) Emory Holloway to continue his Walt Whitman research, which eventually led to a Pulitzer Prize in biography for Holloway. Henry Morton Robinson, who attended Erskine's General Honors seminar, regularly stayed in touch as he forged his own career as a well-regarded poet and an author of popular novels.[30] In the case of his postwar graduate student, Harold

Sproul, Erskine involved himself as well with Sproul's first employers at the University of Minnesota. When, after two years on the English Department faculty, Sproul was not reappointed for a third, Erskine immediately wrote to department chair J. M. Thomas for an explanation about the removal of a young teacher he considered highly expert in knowledge and technique. When the response was not satisfactory, Erskine got the last word, writing to Thomas: "I am growing used to the sort of trouble a boy gets into who has personality and the artistic temperament. The meek and the mediocre are destined to inherit the departments of English, but I am doing what I can here to encourage just such fellows and to aid them in the development of their teaching ability."[31]

Perhaps Erskine's most ardent admirer among recent Columbia alumni, Hugo Guiler, had graduated in 1920 and taken employment in New York's growing banking industry. So frequently did Guiler gush about his favorite professor to the girlfriend he would eventually marry, that she concluded: "He [Guiler] is masterful, he is strong. I have learned the source of his moral strength. It comes of John Erskine's teaching...Then Hugo gave me Erskine's books to read. I have felt like one stepping into a new world—a world of independence and security. Some of Hugo's bravado has penetrated my own spirit."[32] Guiler's future wife, Anaïs Nin, at 19 years old already an avid diarist, immediately identified Erskine as someone whose writing and teaching achieved the synthesis she sought for herself among intellectual agility, emotional passion, and active experience. Guiler and Nin had long conversations about Erskine's teaching and his poetry, writing that they defined as including all prose, as did Erskine. Soon, Guiler invited Nin to a local lecture by Erskine, and he did not disappoint in person. For Nin he was the "embodiment of a Divine Ideal, and Hugo and I were brought closer to each other by the ties of common worship."[33]

By her twenty-first birthday in early 1924, Anaïs Nin had married Hugo Guiler and was struggling haltingly with her own writing while her husband was forging forward with his banking career. Erskine assured his former student that he would be happy to take a look at Nin's early work, which left Nin both thrilled and nervous, insisting, "I just dread the day he will read my book, and I wonder whether he will denounce me publicly as a defiler of the pure English language." Several months later, Nin met "the talented Mr. Erskine" face-to-face for the first time at a lunch in New York City and found that he "intimidated me so much that I could neither talk nor eat."

However, she wasn't too intimidated to detect a hint of arrogance in Erskine: "He lacks the genius…of bringing out the best in other people. He perpetually drops others' ideas to follow another of his own." Therefore, Nin decided it was too early to show Erskine her own work and sat silent while her husband "filled Erskine's ears with talk about my book." Although Erskine listened politely as the fawning husband extolled his wife's creative promise, "the result was that Erskine talked of his work, which was certainly the work of a genius…He told us the story of the book he is writing now and was, generally speaking, and above everything else, terribly *clever* and terribly *human*."[34]

* * *

Even the indefatigable Erskine—described by Henry Morton Robinson as a "huge mast of a man" with "enormous energies"—was getting tired after four whirlwind postwar years of nonstop writing, teaching, public lecturing, piano practicing, performing, and undertaking myriad family and social obligations. Additionally, his relationship with his wife had begun to falter under the pressure of both his limited time at home and his personal desire for a life cut loose from the Victorian restrictions of his earlier upbringing. Pauline, from a very straightlaced and disciplined family, did not share his readiness for spontaneity and new experiences. She was happy to raise children, garden, decorate, attend to neighbors and family, and watch every penny spent. Erskine was granted a Sabbatical leave from Columbia for the fall semester, 1925, during which he would take his family to Europe and perhaps rejuvenate his spirit and his relationships.

Erskine planned to clear the decks on his writing commitments before his European trip by tackling a manuscript on John Milton for a series of volumes produced by the Bobbs-Merrill Company on "How to Know an Author." The series had been under way since 1915 and had included academic books combining biography and anthology on Dante, Robert Browning, Robert Burns, Thomas Carlyle, Daniel Defoe, Matthew Arnold, and others. As Erskine began reviewing information for a Milton volume, however, he also began to lose interest. He found more joy in collecting new historical and fictional legends for his Materials of Poetry course, which covered the evolution of ideas for verse and fiction "from actual events to the great stories which imagination made out of them."[35] A footnote in a volume that dealt with the legend of Troy sent him on a search for references to Helen and her exploits. Her legendary beauty, as well as her passion and her embrace of living life riskily and fully, undergirded ideas that had interested Erskine for some time. And it is likely that he identified in Helen his own sense of rebellion against the genteel regard for personal restraint. As he researched throughout 1924, he began to imagine contemporary conversations that might have taken place when Helen and her husband, Menelaos, returned to Sparta. The possibilities were somewhat of a natural extension of the arguments he made in *The Literary Discipline* about the preeminence of enduring themes: "If the object of literature is still, as it was for the great writers, to portray human nature, then the only new thing the artist will look for is a greater success in his art. Human nature is old and unchangeable: he will hope to make a better portrait than has yet been made—better, at any rate, for his own people and his own age."[36]

Writing notes about the conversations he envisioned among Helen and her family, generally in a vernacular that was contemporary and smart, Erskine began to produce the makings of a short novel. In it, Helen arrived home from Troy as an admirable and intelligent free spirit who need not repent for the passion of her liberating, if adulterous, ways. When he contacted his editors at Bobbs-Merrill about dropping the Milton book, they were happy to do so as they had decided to discontinue the series about authors. They agreed to take a look at an alternative work he called *The Argument of Helen* instead, and they soon signed a contract with him that included a royalty advance of $253.63. Erskine began revising his efforts into an acceptable manuscript during the winter of 1925, and by spring he was sending 30 or 40 pages at a time to Bobbs-Merrill. The editors were immediately enthusiastic and pushed him for completion. Laurance Chambers, the Bobbs-Merrill vice president who would guide many Erskine novels to come, wrote: "I don't need to tell you how anxious we are to get the balance of the manuscript and be able to start setting type . . . Each fresh installment makes us more enthusiastic."[37] By working feverishly, Erskine was able to send off the final portion in late June. He explained that it was typed in red because he had run out of black ribbon and added: "Here's the last of her, thanks God!"[38] Shortly after, he realized that many of his friends were stymied about the possible meaning of the proposed title, *The Argument of Helen*; but, he had not particularly preferred another working title,

The Intimate Helen. He asked that the title be changed to *The Private Life of Helen of Troy.*

When advance copies went out to generate publicity buzz from various scholars, the praise for Erskine's novel was voluminous and immediate. Harvard professor Bliss Perry extolled: "It is a delicious book, and I am singing its praises," and Princeton professor Henry van Dyke glowed: "Erskine's book is a wonderfully brilliant satire...amazingly witty."[39] Laurance Chambers decided it should be marketed at $2.50 a copy, rather than the usual $2.00 price for a hardback novel at that time. He wrote Erskine that "such artistic a thing deserves a more attractive format than would be possible with a $2.00 retail price. I do not believe that cultivated people will hesitate to pay $2.50 for it. And it is not for morons. What do you think about that?" What Erskine thought about it was typical of the astute professor with an expert grasp of irony and humor: "I fear that the very people who will appreciate the book may not have so much money as some of the morons. Your letter assumes that the cultivated are rich and the morons are poor. I didn't know that so much innocence ever survived in the publishing business!"[40]

* * *

As the Erskine family sailed for Europe in early September, the professor realized that his first novel, packed with racy innuendos and contemporary patter, could easily deflate his scholarly reputation. But, with the Columbia campus many miles away for the coming months, he quickly decided that writing about Helen "gave me more satisfaction than anything else I had ever done...There was more of myself in it than in all my previous writing put together."[41]

Travel in Italy and France—including a nostalgic visit to Beaune—with Pauline, 14-year-old Graham, and 9-year-old Anna was a welcome distraction. Eventually, in Paris, he found copies of his book at Brentano's and bought a half dozen for European friends. Back home, the excitement about its publication had already taken hold. Readers enjoyed its stance against moralism and its creative premise that Helen's daughter, Hermione, had covered for Helen's Trojan love journey with Paris by claiming she had been in Egypt with friends. Once home, however, Helen spoke only too candidly about her adventures to Menelaos, Hermione, and others, determined not to apologize for conduct led by passion and enjoyment. The story unfolded as an extended dialogue in which Helen controlled the forces of logic in rather ordinary family issues and arguments. And, to keep the dialogue moving, Erskine turned to keen one-liners during various debates and soliloquies:

When her daughter Hermione proclaimed she was "in love" with Orestes, a skeptical Helen rejoined: "Yes, child, in love—but not very far in."

Hector objected that Helen was: "Always determined to be frank. Who wants her to be frank? You'd think she was yielding to public demand."

Husbandly Menelaos insisted to Helen: "I wish you'd learn that a man may be profoundly occupied even standing still and gazing out a door."[42]

Erskine was determined that his readers should be interested in "not Helen's infidelities, but her beauty, her extraordinary sanity, her wit, her generosity, her zest for living...The bourgeois moralist will insist that such virtues are incompatible with such goings-on, and he is reluctant to have his attention called to them. Perhaps they are inconsistent, but a sincere view of life must notice them."[43] By setting his story in the context of historical sequel and animating it with contemporary terms and language, Erskine had employed a fresh genre that seemed to be just what the public wanted—the same public that enjoyed drawing-room comedy in their plays and inventive wit in their light verse. Stage drama and poetry, as well as ancient Greek mythology, could topple off the pedestal of high culture and into the reach of mass audiences when laced with humor and concerned with widely recognized human conditions.

Although he did not always believe his reviewers understood what he really meant to say in his first novel, especially regarding their emphases on wit and satire, Erskine was thrilled with the nearly unanimously positive reception and huge sales. "The reviews of *Helen* have surprised me by laying so much stress on the humor of the book," he wrote to Laurance Chambers at Bobbs-Merrill. "I thought someone would be interested in the implication of the ideas."[44] The usual Erskine focus on questions of love, beauty, truth, and morality came through to reviewers as a bit clouded by the compelling writing— spirited dialogue that was always lively, often funny, and sometimes sexually candid. The *New York Times* reviewer, who claimed that the book's distinguishing features were "humor, wisdom and beauty," applauded it as both a satire and a romance where "each page

Figure 7.1 John Erskine, ca. 1920.

Source: Courtesy of University Archives, Columbia University in the City of New York.

scintillates with a lively and restrained humor based on the unchanging foibles of mankind, as apt to this day as to Helen's."[45] Rare negative reviews found Helen simply not likeable or believable, including one that noted her dialogue seemed that of "a modern woman who is rehearsing a part in a Greek play for some college entertainment."[46] Nearly all reviewers, and probably most readers, noticed that Professor Erskine perceived love as both wonderful and disappointing, passion as an enchanting and irresistible state that inevitably evolved into bitter disillusion or friendly harmony, morality as less important than moral clarity about risks and consequences, and truthfulness as kin to sincerity and goodness. He also admired women and was pretty certain that men would never understand them. His ideas struck a chord. Between Thanksgiving and the last day of 1925, approximately 14,000 copies had sold.[47]

After touring southern France and parts of Italy, the Erskine family arrived in Paris just before Christmas, 1925. Hugh Guiler and Anaïs Nin had moved there a year earlier and were delighted to invite the Erskines to visit their apartment. Nin, still nervous about her youthfulness and her status as a would-be writer, was visibly jumpy when "John Erskine arrived with his wife, his young boy and his little girl...Everything conspired to increase my distress. The character of Mrs. Erskine—I can never talk before those who do not understand. One cold, unsympathetic look paralyzes me completely." Still, she was thrilled that Erskine liked their small library, showed "a sincere interest" in her journals, and advised her to adopt "his method of writing without criticizing each page (as he thought I had) so as not to grow self-conscious—but to continue on and on until the end."[48] Only in retrospect did she consider the visit a success. The Erskine family stopped by again on Christmas day, with gifts of two of Erskine's books of poetry. Later, Nin spent a day shopping in Paris with Mrs. Erskine. The families got together again in early January for a trip to Chartres and a week later for a dinner.

Erskine encouraged Nin's writing, critiquing her work and offering to help her get published one day. He found her writing, largely autobiographical, sometimes too shy and reticent, and he urged her to be more daring. But he labeled much of her work "exquisite" and "penetrating." Nin filled five pages in her diary with dramatic thoughts, sometimes fantasies, of Erskine. His feedback left her "eager to work, eager to grow up to Erskine's intelligence so that I can appreciate more deeply one of the most talented men alive today." Under his

spell, she found, "My whole life is clear now. I work every day towards
that development which is to bring me nearer to Erskine and all that
he represents...To write every day—that will be the first rule of my
life from now on...He [Erskine] proved that by writing only three-
quarters of an hour a day, one could write a book a year."[49]

Nin and her husband apparently spoke of Erskine often, speculating about his personal life and concluding: "Though he has never
said anything, we have seen signs that make it clear his marriage and
his home life conflict with his ideals and his philosophy." According
to Nin, her husband felt this was further verified in his one-on-one
conversations with his former teacher, as well as in his recent novel.[50]

When the Erskine family departed from Gare St.-Lazare in mid-
January to make their way to the ship that would carry them back
to the United States, John Erskine clearly understood that his life
would change dramatically when best-selling novelist was added to
his accomplishments. Already, through Laurance Chambers, he knew
that negotiations were under way for dramatic rights to his novel and
that a lecture agent was urging him to sign up and go on tour. The
Century monthly had asked him to commit to regular essays in each
issue, and a women's magazine had approached him about a series of
brief articles. He admitted that the success of *Helen* "convinced me
that I can reach my audience through the page," and he acted immediately on that conviction. He arrived home from Europe with the
draft manuscript for a second novel and the outline for a third.[51]

CHAPTER 8

FAME AND LOATHING ON
MORNINGSIDE HEIGHTS

When Erskine and his family arrived back in New York, it was immediately apparent that *The Private Life of Helen of Troy* would be the book that launched a thousand new opportunities. Now Erskine had a popular platform—name recognition that could sweep him into numerous endeavors well beyond the confines of academic thought and duty. Public speaking, live radio concerts, newspaper columns, magazine fiction, and dramatic scripts were just the beginning of the outlets for the talents and ideas that marked his new commercial success.

Complementing his wildly successful first novel in paving his route to popular prominence was Erskine's willingness to appear wherever the public gathered and to be photographed and quoted whenever needed. His impressive physical presence—pale blue eyes, broad-shouldered frame, slightly salted hair, and towering height (6 feet, 2 inches)—made him a crowd and camera favorite. Also compelling were his distinctive low and clear voice at a time of increasing radio reach and his strong and candid opinions—willingly shared—at a time of expanding public clamor for celebrity viewpoints. The New York press eagerly reported his return from Europe, and he fueled their news angles with claims that he had known nothing of the popularity of the book published during his absence. The *New York World* headline on the subject read, "John Erskine Returns to Find Himself a Wit."[1]

Throughout the spring semester, 1926, Erskine also kept up a busy schedule of teaching interspersed with frequent public-speaking engagements and interviews about his first and future novels. He also began a regular series of articles in the *Delineator* magazine, starting with one titled "Explaining Helen" and moving on to "Chivalry: Ever Old, Ever New" and "There's Fun in Famous Books." Next, he launched a monthly series of ideas and advice for *Century* magazine, with titles such as "Liberty to Live by," "Changing the Past," and "Modesty." He became a frequent guest on radio, first as an interviewee and later as a piano performer and quiz-show participant. Although he proved adept and enthusiastic at marketing his own work, he demurred at the suggestion of commercialism by referring to himself as "an unintentionally popular novelist."[2]

His colleagues, some still idealizing the concept of monastic studiousness for faculty, were undoubtedly taken aback. Many would agree with Professor Oscar Campbell who referred to Erskine's first novel as "a witty but indecorous satire."[3] In earlier decades, the lecture circuit had long been a common promotional pathway for restyling scholarly intellectuals as public intellectuals, widely cultivated by the likes of Louis Aggasiz, Ralph Waldo Emerson, and William James. However, taking advantage of ideas and advances generally not available to earlier scholars—especially in journalism, publishing, photography, and radio—Erskine was able to push beyond "public" notoriety for academic professionals and cross over to real "celebrity." He was arguably the first American professor to manage that. But the idea of a "celebrity professor" was new and not altogether comfortable for his fellow scholars back in the ivory tower.

Erskine decided to put off a book tour for at least a year, insisting to publisher Laurance Chambers at Bobbs-Merrill that "I shall confine myself rather strictly to my university work and my writing." He did, however, promise to ask for a leave of absence to undertake a coast-to-coast tour after a year or so.[4] He also needed to attend to follow-up issues on *The Private Life of Helen of Troy*, including negotiations for motion picture rights and a collaboration with Winthrop Ames on a stage version that Ethel Barrymore had expressed interest in considering. And, he was working with his former publisher, Duffield, to acquire rights that would allow Bobbs-Merrill to bring out new editions of some of his earlier works. Finally, he put himself in the able hands of his longtime friend and old Columbia classmate Melville Cane. Cane, a lawyer and literary agent, was able to negotiate far better returns for Erskine's future work with Bobbs-Merrill and would be with him for the next 25 years.[5]

The relationship between Erskine and Chambers quickly moved from professional interaction to close friendship. Chambers was an enthusiastic cheerleader for Erskine's ideas and manuscripts. He even corresponded with Pauline Erskine, sending her copies of books he thought she might enjoy. Erskine frequently, and always enthusiastically, suggested new authors to Chambers, including some of his former students. For example, he urged that Chambers favorably review a manuscript by James Dabbs, a former student who was by then teaching at Coker College in South Carolina, labeling it "a rather original study of the psychology of the reader of poetry" and noting that "if you care to publish it, I've promised Dabbs to write an introduction." When Bobbs-Merrill determined the book had little sales potential, Erskine tried one more time: "The book is important..., and I am sure will be used by teachers of poetry here and there in the country."[6]

Happily for Erskine, his friendships with his new literary agent and his publisher enabled him to make money and access it in ways that were not always common business practices. Within six months of returning from Europe, he received a $9,341 royalty check from his first book. Soon after, motion picture rights sold to First National Pictures for $30,000. Erskine's share, half that amount, translated to approximately $161,000 in 2011 dollars.[7] A popular silent film version, starring Maria Corda, was released in 1927. Because Erskine had needed funds earlier to pay a note on his country home and make other purchases, he had already borrowed on the amounts now being produced. In the coming years, when he needed to pay taxes or otherwise spend, he simply asked Chambers for advance money and launched into more writing.

The expanded resources dramatically changed the lives of Erskine family members—materially and beyond. John Erskine, somewhat to the disappointment of his more restrained wife, discovered that he enjoyed making and spending money. He began collecting art and became an active stock market trader, especially in steel, railroads, copper, and commodities. At Nod Way Farm, he contracted for major remodeling work. A new study quickly grew into a separate stone house with a library, a large music studio with two pianos, a kitchen, and bedrooms. The main house was expanded and its siding converted from all wood to stone and shingle. A tennis court was added, and Erskine enjoyed playing with his children. The old hay barn on the property got a new floor and a fine Victrola phonograph. Neighborhood dances at the Erskine barn were regular entertainment throughout the summers, with the "neighbors" coming from as far away as Bridgeport until the annual season-end masquerade. One regular attendee recalled that the dance tradition occurred because "the Erskines were very protective of their children" and wanted them close to home at "well chaperoned formal dances in the barn."[8]

*　*　*

In early July, 1926, Erskine sent Chambers the last of five portions of his second novel: *Galahad: Enough of His Life to Explain His Reputation.* He characterized it as taking "a very different tone from *Helen,* and there is little place in it for the frivolity I poured over that lady."

Chambers, giddy with delight at what he read, telegrammed Erskine at Nod Way Farm immediately: "*Helen* was divine, but *Galahad* is a knock out...He has the strength of ten best sellers. Congratulations from the happiest and proudest publisher alive."[9] Regardless of the direction indicated by the title, Erskine's story focused on three women: The flawless Guinevere; Galahad's mother, Elaine; and another very young Elaine. Erskine insisted that the idea of the novel was to provoke questions about life, morality, and reputations. Galahad was the fine son of fine parents, who happened to have passion but not marriage. "Only to a very conventional mind are they disturbing," he charged. "Galahad entered this world in an irregular and not very admirable way, but he became a great saint. I can't see what was gained for his sainthood by winking at his origin. Equally, I can't see that to recognize the facts about his birth is to take the bloom off his name as a saint." The author decided to set the record straight by humanizing the characters involved with contemporary ideas and language.[10]

Again, reviewers were impressed with the Erskine style and story. The *New York Herald Tribune* critic found it steeped in "much shrewd knowledge of human nature and philosophic erudition displayed easily and gracefully; wisdom feathered by wit flies straight to the mark." A year-end literary retrospective in the *New York Times* concluded that readers "who reveled in the first book, and their number was legion, will find in "Galahad" a little less shrewdness and a little less humor, but a better story." And reviewer Elmer Davis chuckled in print that "John Erskine takes his proper place as one of the principal fomenters of happiness in marriage and pillars of the sanctity of the home. For nothing is better calculated to make the Average Man married to the Average Woman contented with his lot than this appalling demonstration of what it must have been like to live with Helen or Guinevere."[11]

In the growing arena of women's magazines, Erskine's work was particularly favored. Of *Galahad*, the fiction editor of *Woman's Home Companion* gushed: "Here is America's coming of age. Here is profundity and brilliance and sheer creative power and finally a ripe understanding. I wanted to get out and shout when I finished it."[12] Not surprisingly, this segment of the publishing industry would become the most lucrative market for Erskine's future short story fiction and serialized novels.

In matters of book sales, Erskine could be counted on to take an active role. He frequently suggested to Chambers ideas for contacts who might be interested in foreign translations, serializations, and dramatic rights, and he pushed Chambers to redouble marketing efforts when sales began to lag. Disappointed when the Book-of-the-Month Club jury passed over *Galahad* in favor of *The Orphan Angel* by Elinor Wylie, Erskine fumed that the jury members lacked "the detachment or the disinterestedness, all of them, which should be presupposed in an enterprise such as this." He then reported to Chambers that he had told the Book-of-the-Month Club president that "if they really thought *Galahad* not so good as *Orphan Angel*, my contempt for their judgment was so thorough going that I didn't want my name mentioned on any paper that was connected with their enterprise."[13] Chambers may have felt he needed to head off any disgruntlement concerning the possibility of a Pulitzer Prize for *Galahad*. He was quick to inform Erskine that a member of the Pulitzer committee noted to him: "You will understand that the Erskine books, able as they are, hardly come under the definition of novel we have to bear in mind in the award. Otherwise, they'd win."[14]

The critics were far less taken with the last of Erskine's trilogy of modernized mythology novels, *Adam and Eve, Though He Knew Better*. In it, a hapless Adam became entangled in the original love triangle, with two women who represented two distinct and familiar contemporary female types. One, the beautiful and intelligent Lilith, was so ideal as to be desirable but scary. The other, the nurturing housekeeper Eve, was so capable as to be necessary but scary. Although words like "amusing" and "satiric" peppered the reviews, some writers identified the book as an extended dialogue with little action. Others seemed irritated that Erskine refused to resolve the conundrum of marital frustration between the enchantment of Lilith and the reality of Eve.

The New York reviewers tended to be the most sanguine critics of Erskine's work, but they may have been at least somewhat influenced by the bias that came with critiquing each other's books on a regular basis. Several observers of the final book in the trilogy conjectured that the Erskine genre had run its course. One reminded that the "potentialities of his method are approaching exhaustion," while another noted that "sophisticated dialog is likely to pall when served in unrelieved doses."[15] Nevertheless, *Adam and Eve* was quickly a publishing hit. It arrived in print just a few months after *Helen* retired from two years among the 20 top books on weekly best-seller lists, and its commercial success expanded with its serialization in *Collier's* magazine. Motion picture rights and various foreign rights sold quickly, bringing Erskine's 1927 income from his writing to $71,320.[16]

Erskine's most virulent detractor was New York's Rabbi Stephen Wise, a cofounder of the NAACP and the Free Synagogue. Always hyperalert to the possibility of a smut factor, Rabbi Wise publically attacked Erskine's books as "notoriously salacious." *The Private Life of Helen of Troy*, in particular, had substituted "the unmoral Hellenic sanctions for the ethical Hebraic-Christian sanctities...He [Erskine] glorifies Helen's casting aside of moral standards and makes his book the tragedy of an unsatisfying and insufficient husband." He told the press and his congregation: "I don't know of a book which has appeared within decades comparable in its power for evil to *Helen of Troy*, unless it be *Galahad*."[17] Undoubtedly, Rabbi Wise provided substantial publicity for Erskine's work.

*   *   *

Opinions by and about Erskine seemed to be everywhere during the second half of the 1920s decade. His books were discussed, and his comments were sought. Requests for interviews and lecture appearances ballooned. Radio came calling, and he lectured over the airwaves about his books and the ideas behind them.[18] He was often approached by strangers, especially women. Broadway actress and future California politician Helen Gahagan, for example, tele-grammed him: "I have long been anxious to meet you. Would you give me the opportunity by coming to my house to a small after the-atre party next Wednesday evening?"[19]

Erskine had no intent of allowing his fiction writing and its asso-ciated demands detract from his two to four hours of daily piano practice. He played piano with friends and at benefit concerts—most notably one at Steinway Hall that reversed roles by putting writers on stage and seasoned performers in reviewers' roles for the local press. Erskine's performance for that MacDowell Colony benefit was accom-panied by his sister Rhoda, who he had often insisted was the truly superior musician in the family. George Gershwin's review noted that he had found it "a bit difficult for the fourth finger of either hand always to hit the note it was aimed for," but admitted "there were many moments and some sustained moods of real beauty...I don't know how he would negotiate the 'St. Louis Blues,' but in Mozart he seemed quite at home. A college professor must have a lot of spare time in order to acquire a technique and tone such as Mr. Erskine displayed yesterday."[20] By 1928, Erskine also had appeared as a piano soloist with the Baltimore Symphony Orchestra and had toured with the New York Symphony Orchestra.

In the summers, Erskine generally spent at least one week as a lec-turer at the Chautauqua Institute in western New York. He was able to continue his musical associations there, since his piano teacher, Ernest Hutcheson, was in residence for summer instruction, and renowned musician Albert Stoessel conducted concerts. Much to Erskine's delight, those two friends and associates "let me try out piano concertos before the large amphitheater audience, and each summer I practiced chamber music with the Musical Art Quartet."[21] Also a welcome summer visitor at the MacDowell Colony, Erskine had joined its board of directors in 1920. The Peterborough, New Hampshire, retreat site was formed by Mrs. Edward MacDowell in honor of her husband, Erskine's great musical inspiration Edward MacDowell. Inaugurated with a memorial concert in an outdoor amphitheater in 1910, the MacDowell Colony formed a community where "artists of every kind could find leisure and quiet during the summer months to pursue their creative work, whether in music or in painting or in sculpture or in literature."[22]

Just as he had earlier found he loved public performance, Erskine now discovered he loved public recognition and approval. He quickly realized that controversial statements provoked attention, and he used them often in garnering publicity for his comments on marriage, contemporary youth, prohibition, and literature—the areas that journalists most frequently asked him to address. His stance on prohibition and on censorship was strictly libertarian, and he was happy to speak out on the issues. He helped form a group of 40 leading authors into the Committee for the Suppression of Irresponsible Censorship, with members including Ida M. Tarbell, Mary Roberts Rhinehart, Edgar Lee Masters, and William Allen White. Its aim was to "call attention to the dangers from bigotry and blind prejudice that threaten to stifle the intellectual life of the country" and to demonstrate "to the public by specific examples the absurd situations which censorship legislation already in force creates in the name of law."[23] His personal statements on censorship relied on clever phrasing and twists of logic:

> I would remind you that when John Milton wanted to print "Paradise Lost"—which is so good few people read it—the censor held it up for an interminable time until it could be thoroughly studied...The censor who warns me against a play excites my interest in it, however good I am, and he must have developed an extraordinary interest in it himself before he set out to advertise it...Censorship also seems to me a singularly childish attempt on the part of a well-meaning society to dam up the ocean. I am going to be protected for two hours, when I go to the theatre, against the subjects which really interest me. I should like to see how you can make any impression on me that way. I will find the subjects elsewhere. I oughtn't to see nudity on the stage. Very well, then, close the doors of the Metropolitan Museum against me too. I oughtn't to be interested in sex. Very well, I'd like to see you stop our interest in that. You know I am telling the truth there. We all know it.[24]

Prohibition, Erskine proclaimed, was simply at odds with the Christian faith. He explained in a speech to a Rotarian convention: "The idea was originally that no virtue could be credited to any of us unless practiced by free will and choice. Christ has a good deal of contempt for those who lead 'good' lives not by choice and for which they deserve no credit. The objection to prohibition...it takes away the freedom of will."[25]

As the New York press continued to report Erskine speeches and interviews, newspaper headlines blared with items such as: "Erskine

Outraged on Attacks Against Classics," "Modern Parent Handicaps Child, Erskine Asserts," "Dr. Erskine on Democracy," "Erskine Asserts a Dry Cannot be a Christian," "Nobel Prize Award Hailed by Erskine," and "Professor Erskine in Hospital." The last of these reports stemmed from a throat infection and concluded happily: "Last night he had no temperature."[26]

While Erskine's published words were key to his growing wealth and fame, they could also sometimes embarrass his family members. His wife, Pauline, certainly would have been mortified to see in a 1926 edition of *New York Evening Graphic* a bold headline in inch-high type that quoted his statement: "I Blame Wives' Physical Decline For Husbands' Seeking New Loves." The subhead further explained, "Wife Losing Vigor at 40 Disappoints Husband in Prime." Although appearing in a sensationalist tabloid, and very possibly embellished or slipped out of context, the quotations stung:

> What do I think makes for unhappiness in marriage? Of course, I think the physical relation has very great effect on happiness. This is what makes the man between forty and fifty often go his own way—find new companions, neglect his wife and family. I feel that for a woman of forty, much of the physical splendor of life is a thing of the past. Men between forty and fifty [Erskine was 47] are often in the flower of their manhood—at the prime of their lives. Their physical desires are at that time at their height and often they are disappointed in the reaction of their wives...Money too often creates discord. But even women of the idle rich, who spend their lives in doing nothing more serious than bridge and golf, still lose their vitality around forty.[27]

The marital relationship themes in his novels, his focus on questions of ideal beauty and types of love, his enjoyment of public adulation, and his commitment to action combined to point in one direction: His sense of romance with his wife was gone. Anaïs Nin was certain that Pauline Erskine was cognizant of the situation: "She understood him, knew his failings (susceptibility to flattery); knew he sought romance and could no longer connect it with her; saw clearly his problems, a desire for all knowledge and experience, a pagan thirst for living, so incompatible with loyalty."[28] Yet, like Eve in his novel, Pauline was the expert organizer in his life who made the arrangements for the children, kept the social calendar, undertook the household tasks, and tended to the relationships with his sisters and brother. She prepared, maintained, planned, and managed with the stoicism and discipline of the Victorian upper-class social status that had formed her early years. And, like Adam in his novel, Erskine soon found his enchanting Lilith.

At 39, Adeline Lobdell Atwater was not nearly as young as the Lilith of Erskine's book when they met in the fall of 1926. She was tall and striking—lovely, but by no means beautiful. She was an active and artistic working woman with strong opinions, an ex-husband, a steady job, and two young daughters who lived with her parents in Chicago. Nonetheless, Erskine soon took to calling her "Lilith" and referring to her as such to his closest friends. They first met at a dinner where Erskine was one of the speakers, and, according to Atwater, "The emotional explosion was terrific. On both sides of the battle line, it was involuntary combustion at first sight."[29]

Born in Chicago and educated at several seminaries and the Art Institute of Chicago, Atwater moved to Washington, DC, with her husband. She became active in the struggle for women's suffrage and served as chairman of the District of Columbia branch of the National Woman's Party (NWP). In 1919, she represented Illinois on the National Advisory Council of the NWP. She divorced Henry Atwater in 1920, moved to Chicago for a year, and then settled in New York City to manage the New Gallery, specializing in modern art.

After 1926, Erskine and his Lilith saw each other frequently, and friends often extended them invitations as a couple. At times, Atwater also acted as Erskine's social secretary, responding to requests from his friends and associates for appointments.[30] With his apartment in Manhattan and his family often at Nod Way Farm without him, arrangements for the affair were not difficult. Atwater explained the relationship: "He was a misunderstood man with a nagging wife, who cared nothing for him—and I did. Our longing and passion could only be right. From the beginning, it had been ordained."[31] Later, she looked back to sum up their years of much togetherness:

> For five years, I was an introvert, an apostate to my kind. I turned away from those who lived outwardly, from those who seek life away from themselves, and with him, lived the infinite life of the soul, where great adventures, after all, take place. Within the measureless boundaries of our own inner depths, we dreamed of noble things. One never talked with him without a feeling and sense of exhilaration.[32]

Erskine had begun to write *Adam and Eve, Though He Knew Better* when he met Adeline, and the scores of letters he wrote her over the next five years always addressed her as "Lilith."[33] He soon escorted her to Manhattan functions and occasionally traveled with her. He described her to Anaïs Nin as a beautiful writer who loved music, explaining, "Temptation never bothered me before because it came in such vulgar forms. But when I found my ideal..."[34] He also understood that he was likely to drift and vacillate about the affair, just as Adam had done in his novel. Even though the book ended with Adam finally leaving Lilith to return to Eve, Erskine wasn't so certain that the story ended there. "I rather suspect he returned to Lilith later," he conjectured, "and perhaps after a while went back to Eve, and so vibrated between the two forever."[35]

* * *

Somehow, amidst his bon vivant social enjoyments, his precariously bifurcated personal life, his serious piano practice and performance, and his busy production of published writing, Erskine still managed to teach his large and legendary literature classes, review student work, and dazzle the young men in his seminars on Great Books. However, his commitment to Columbia—now a secondary source of income and attention—clearly waned. In particular, most of his English Department colleagues viewed his new accomplishments and reputation with attitudes ranging from skepticism to disdain.

The discord came to a head when, two years after returning from his Sabbatical, Erskine wanted a leave of absence to undertake a three-month nationwide lecture tour. Since his department colleagues were not likely to support the leave, he circumvented them by appealing directly to President Butler and the board of trustees. Appreciative of his reputational value to Columbia, the upper-level decision makers immediately approved. This undoubtedly further estranged him from the other English professors, with whom he already sensed little common ground due to "the conflicting theories we held about education." In that vein, Erskine charged that his colleagues were content to turn graduate students into "docile and stationary folk, who would remember what they had been told, and repeat it to their pupils, and never, never disturb the peace with a new idea." Further, he maintained, "In their opinion I had ended my usefulness by becoming a novelist." Claiming exploitation by people who enjoyed the revenue from the enormous numbers of students in his literature classes, Erskine calculated that his largest course produced tuition dollars annually equivalent to almost twice his $7,500 salary.[36]

The lecture tour in the early months of 1928 would provide welcome respite from the complications of a wife and family, an extra-marital affair, two residences, teaching and advising responsibilities, local lectures, obligatory guest appearances, piano practice, and piano performances. Erskine recently had added to his packed schedule by accepting a position on the board of directors of the Juilliard Musical Foundation, a role he had begun to immensely enjoy but could continue by letter and telegram while on tour. And, as an efficient writer who could call upon quick and productive focus by working for just an hour—sometimes only a few minutes—at a time, he had no need to slow his writing while traveling. He managed to submit three of his monthly essays to *Century*, during the cross-country trip.

Erskine prepared for his 17-state tour as doggedly and precisely as he had for piano performances, but built in the flexibility of having on hand alternative discussions of different novels and essays depending on audience preferences. The Louis J. Alber Agency, which had contracted with him for the tour and made all arrangements, advertised that he would speak on the ideas behind his three novels and the philosophies he brought to the ideas for the stories. His most notable modification along the way happened when someone at a stop in the South asked if he would play something on the piano that was in a corner of the stage. He did, and used the music to illustrate his points. From then on, he combined lectures and piano solos in performances that drew large audiences and enthusiastic reviews.[37]

The tour, largely by train, began in Brooklyn. It then headed south through a number of Confederate states; west through Oklahoma and Texas; on to the Pacific Coast states, through Montana and the Plains States, and back to the East Coast via the Midwest. The lectures, often two or three a day, were under the aegis of local entities that ranged from colleges to Parent-Teacher Associations and from book stores to women's clubs. Their locations ranged from downtown Chicago and Seattle to small towns like Athens, Alabama, and Durant, Oklahoma.[38] Erskine had never visited the most southern states or anywhere west of the Mississippi River, so he found himself intrigued with the Civil War resentments still alive in the South, the wealth and vastness of Texas, the Spanish influence throughout the Southwest, and the tinsel of Hollywood. He was delighted to reconnect with a number of old friends and former students along the way. Los Angeles was his favorite stop. There he stayed at the home of his former schoolmate William de Mille and his wife Clara whose hillside mansion provided panoramic views of the city and the ocean, as well as the hospitality of good conversation and Hollywood insider chat.

Returning to New York in late April, Erskine was tired, but at least somewhat refreshed by his absence from the Columbia campus—and perhaps by the time out from his complicated personal life. He knew for certain that he could not simply backpedal to his old life on campus or at home, but real change—even with the obstacle of limited financial resources now removed—was a challenge he was reluctant to face head on.

*   *   *

The question of next steps in his personal life was at least temporarily answered for Erskine when his son Graham expressed an interest in attending art school at the Sorbonne in Paris. Why send him off alone? Why not have Pauline and their daughter Anna accompany Graham in Paris during that year, living in a rented apartment with a governess for 13-year-old Anna? With his family on another continent, his time management issues and extramarital complications were at least marginally simplified—but only slightly. At the same time, Erskine was approached to become the first president of the Juilliard School of Music. He decided he wanted the job, but only on the condition that the full responsibilities of the position could be deferred for six or eight months, during which he wanted to be free for trips to Paris and for completing some immediate writing commitments.

Late in the summer of 1928, after sending his publisher a volume of new and old essays to be published as *The Delight of Great Books*, Erskine and his family boarded the SS Paris to launch Graham on his college experience. Erskine would help get his family settled before returning to professional duties in New York City, not the least of which now included initiating the amalgamation of the Juilliard Graduate School and the Institute of Musical Art into the new Juilliard School of Music. Anaïs Nin and Hugh Guiler, who had visited the Erskines at Nod Way Farm a year earlier, welcomed the family back to Paris. Nin played tennis with Graham and apartment hunted with Pauline, while Erskine took time off each day to write.

Figure 8.1 The Erskine family aboard the SS Paris, ca. 1930: l to r, Anna, John, Pauline, Graham.

Source: Courtesy of Library of Congress, George Grantham Bain Collection.

Nin, always awed by Erskine's accomplishments, now became fully intrigued by him:

> At the Folies Bergère I realized that he is very susceptible to women's beauty. He is also difficult to live with, willful, a little overcritical. He has the admirable power of concentration, works anywhere, leaves an unfinished page in the typewriter at night and can go right on with it when he returns to it in the morning. I like his big voice, his manner of speaking, the swiftness and subtlety of his mind, his wit...I find out that he is slightly hypocritical about women, slightly proper Anglo-Saxon malgré lui [in spite of himself]. When I get rational, intelligent, reasonable, then he comes up with the old hackneyed "conduct affecting the life of others," "kindness," and other sentimentalities. I don't know any more what to think of the human mind if Erskine contradicts himself."[39]

Erskine told Nin about his affair with Adeline Atwater, and she decided: "They love each other...I envy Lilith his companionship." She also interpreted the stress of his multiple commitments: "He sacrifices his life to his children and remains fond of Pauline because she is so fine. He has remorse." When Erskine returned to New York after his wife and children settled in a Paris apartment, Nin observed that "Pauline sees and says things plainly. But both of them are thick-skinned at times...Pauline knew about Lilith. She knew John was returning to New York to see her. She suffers and I feel sorry for her." Yet, Nin offered to provide alibis for Erskine when he returned to Paris just before Christmas, since Adeline Atwater was conveniently visiting France at the same time.[40] Erskine skipped Christmas day with the family, while a disappointed Pauline and children "weathered the day as well as could be expected," and left for a week in St. Moritz soon after.[41]

In May, near the end of Graham's year at the Sorbonne, Erskine returned to Paris for the third time in a year. It was only a matter of time, and not much of it, before John Erskine and Anaïs Nin moved beyond the limits of flirtatious confidantes. Certainly Nin loved the role of seductress. One of her biographers observed that "no matter who they were or what the circumstances, inspiring and pleasing men made her feel powerful and in control."[42] She yearned for a physical relationship with Erskine and recorded in her diary with great drama their first stolen kiss—"strong, possessive, absolute...His tongue in my mouth seemed like his very own flesh penetrating me." The flirtation went on with surreptitious touches and meaningful glances during various social occasions between Nin and her husband and the Erskine family. But when the opportunity for privacy occurred, Erskine found himself physically unable to consummate the relationship beyond groping that "caressed all of my body, sought my breasts, and my most secret, most sensitive part." He decided that his failure with Nin stemmed from greater guilt than he'd anticipated that her husband was his former student. Nin had some remorse concerning Lilith. Neither mentioned Pauline.[43] Days later, the Erskine family sailed back to New York. Nin's editor later determined: "It was her first transgression, but it is very important because it became the pattern of her life."[44] Nin began to obsess about Erskine as soon as he left Paris:

> John took away my contentment. I never get anything back in exchange! Nonsense. I got a formal letter, which included the thanks for my kindness. Kindness, hell...My illness (missing John) comes back unexpectedly when I think I'm cured. It rather baffles me. I don't find anything to replace our talks—those long talks about his problems and Lilith—and I wonder rather wickedly why John liked to talk to *me* about these things instead of his other women friends."[45]

Soon, however, Nin decided that her experience with Erskine, however brief, was a worthwhile endeavor that made for invaluable memories: "It was wonderful. So is my getting over it. It's curious how I now have a feeling that holding John's love for a few minutes is the only experience I couldn't endure missing...There is only one Hugh and only one John. For me, there are no other men worth knowing."[46]

* * *

Erskine returned to New York to find his book *The Delight of Great Books* well received by reviewers. A guide to reading in general, as well as to specific literary achievements such as *The Tempest, Romeo and Juliet, Paradise Lost,* and *Moby Dick,* the book reiterated the philosophy he developed in his Columbia proposal for "great books" and the ideas he set forth in his General Honors seminars. In his preface, he announced to readers that great literature need not be reserved for school and college work. After all, the authors "wrote to be read by the general public, and they assumed in their readers an experience of life and an interest in human nature, nothing more." With arguments reminiscent of his early appeals to his Columbia colleagues, he exhorted the general public to "not be awed by their greatness" and "sample as many of the great books as we can." He then advised readers that if they got stuck in their attempts to understand something in a book, "the impulse is to go for help to other books, to works of criticism. It is much more profitable to go directly to life."[47]

At Bobbs-Merrill, Laurance Chambers was eager to bring out Erskine's next two novels. These, *Sincerity* and *Uncle Sam*, were to be the first two in what Erskine planned as an "American trilogy," far different than his first three novels in contemporary settings on US soil. However, while working on new and different book manuscripts, Erskine also wrote short fiction for the lucrative popular magazine market—stories that returned to the formula used in his best-selling novels. Appearing in *Cosmopolitan* were "The Last Voyage of Odysseus," "Afterthoughts of Lady Godiva," "The Private Life of Pocahontas," "But What About Mrs. Paul Revere?," and "The Candor of Don Juan."

Although he was writing with speed and determination, it appeared that Erskine would head into the years of the Great Depression with his literary career already peaked and his bank account overcommitted. *Sincerity*, a tale of a marriage and infidelity that questioned whether sincere people could be moral in an immoral environment, was published in 1929. Even Erskine admitted the reviews and sales were not encouraging. The *Outlook* critic called it "a dull and tractlike tale of three people" and found Erskine's style "tedious." While the *New Republic* reviewer found that "the prose is well used and sometimes rich," but "applied to characters who seem little more than puppets."[48]

Erskine insisted to his publisher that the reviews "say that the book is disappointing because it isn't like the others. Of course I was doing my best to make it different, but I did think there was a little irony in it, even considerable humor."[49] Net sales of *Sincerity*, at $42,000, were only about 20 percent of the net for Erskine's first novel.[50]

In addition, the distinctive genre Erskine had brought to his first trilogy was easy to imitate. Other authors began to pen similar fiction, such as one offered to Bobbs-Merrill that Laurance Chambers characterized as "the most obvious, self-confessed imitation imaginable of your manner in your first four novels...called *Don Juan*,

The Amazing Lover."[51] While that news did not particularly bother Erskine, he was seriously unhappy about the news that after examining his manuscript for *Uncle Sam*, his inventive biography of that character, the editors at *Collier's* wanted to opt out of their contract for serializing. Editor William Chenery wrote him that it "would be gravely disappointing to the audience which read your 'Adam and Eve.' The publication of a disappointing serial would be as bad for you as for us." Erskine, refusing to budge on the contract, replied, "Instead of being ashamed of the story, I am proud of it. I even believe it is better than those you usually publish."[52]

While Erskine knew he was waging an uphill battle to recapture the success of his first novels, he decided he would simply continue to write books, short stories, and articles. His name alone assured publication somewhere, and maybe something would become another big hit. At the same time, he had another professional change of direction to keep him busy—the new Juilliard School of Music.

CHAPTER 9

RAISING JUILLIARD

"I continued like a juggler to keep my three plates, teaching, writing, and music, in the air," Erskine wrote of his ever-accelerating professional pace during the second half of the 1920s decade.[1] His music plate in particular began to overflow after his appearances with the New York Symphony, the Baltimore Symphony, and the New York Musical Art Quartet in 1927 and 1928. When he was out of town lecturing or attending conferences, local amateur orchestras often asked if he would appear as a soloist. He typically agreed to donate as much time as possible, concluding: "Apparently the spectacle of a novelist at the piano risking his neck on a difficult piece of music had some drawing power with audiences. In quite a number of places, I was invited to repeat the concert the following afternoon or the following evening whenever the demand for tickets outran the capacity of the hall."[2] When he played with the large Baltimore Symphony (e.g., 34 violins, 12 violas, and 8 cellos), several hundred of the nearly 3,500 in attendance had to find standing room.[3] Eventually, he estimated that he had appeared as a guest artist with more than 200 amateur orchestras throughout the country, typically in small-town playhouses or school auditoriums. His repertoire favorites were pieces by Schumann, Mozart, Cesar Franck, and Edward MacDowell.

Erskine's musical interests had quickly led to friendships with notable musicians such as his piano mentor Ernest Hutcheson, conductor Walter Damrosch who had founded the American Expeditionary Forces Bandmasters' School in France, violinist and conductor Albert Stoessel, and others who populated the New York musical art scene. He frequently attended musical theater, the Metropolitan Opera, symphonies, and Columbia student musical performances. When the trustees of the Juilliard Musical Foundation, established by the bequest of Augustus Juilliard, formed a board of directors to initiate educational activities that might meet the terms of the bequest, it was not surprising that Erskine's name should be mentioned as a potential member.[4] However, when Ernest Hutcheson told him that he had recommended his famous student for the board, Erskine knew little about the ideas and controversies that had circulated for several years about the potential uses of the Juilliard fortune.

*   *   *

Wealthy, self-made textile merchant Augustus D. Juilliard, born in 1836 and raised in Ohio, was a fan of museums and music who regularly attended New York's Metropolitan Opera Company where he was a box holder and board member. When he died in 1919, his wife was already deceased. They had no children, although a nephew, Frederic Juilliard, had lived with them for some time. Frederic and two bank presidents were named in the will as the trustees of the Juilliard Musical Foundation. Juilliard's bequest left an estimated $14 million to musical interests, although the exact nature of those interests was stated in rather vague terms and left for the trustees to specify. *The Etude* magazine noted that "the administration of the gift is provided for along lines of great simplicity and elasticity" and quoted the terms stated in the will for the work of the Foundation:

> To aid all worthy students of music in securing complete and adequate musical education either at appropriate institutions now in existence or hereafter to be created, or from appropriate instructors in this country or abroad; to arrange for and to give, without profit to it, musical entertainments, concerts, and recitals of a character appropriate for the education and entertainment of the general public in the musical arts, and to aid the Metropolitan Opera Company, in the city of New York, for the purpose of assisting it in the production of operas.[5]

Juilliard's commitment to music education and performance occurred at a time of thriving music conservatories of great repute in Europe (e.g., Leipzig, Berlin, Paris, Vienna), while the US music schools struggled to keep pace. Most impressive in that struggle were the Peabody Institute (Baltimore), the Oberlin Conservatory of Music (Ohio), and the Cleveland Institute of Music, as well as the Institute of Musical Art, the Manhattan School of Music, and the David Mannes Music School in New York City. Just how these schools might figure in any plans to carry out the terms of the will concerning music education and the public appreciation was unclear. These questions, along with the issue of how and when to assist the Metropolitan Opera Company, generated considerable debate and confusion among Foundation trustees during the five years following Juilliard's death.[6]

The secretary to the trustees of the Juilliard Musical Foundation, Eugene A. Noble, took a particularly active role in guiding trustee deliberations. Noble was a Methodist minister who served as president of Goucher College for three years (1908–1911). He was then named president of Dickinson College, but its trustees requested his resignation after two and a half years for his failure to improve the institution's dire financial circumstances. He was eager to see the Juilliard money make a large and material impression on the music world. The first actual Foundation endowments, extravagantly generous, supported individual music teachers at up to $100 an hour. Critics and musicians, especially supporters of the Metropolitan Opera and the existing music schools, wondered why the funding did not target existing institutions instead. Dr. Frank Damrosch, who had partnered with benefactor James Loeb to found the Institute of Musical Art in 1905, received a note from his partner: "Unless Dr. Noble is a complete numskull, he ought to recognize that more can be accomplished by supporting the Institute of Musical Art, that is, by giving it a handsome endowment, than by distributing the income of the Juilliard Foundation in driblets!"[7]

On the other hand, John Erskine later noted that some exploratory proposals did occur between the Juilliard Musical Foundation trustees (through Noble) and the Metropolitan Opera and also with the Institute of Musical Art. However, he maintained that both entities were at that time unwilling to agree to the levels of control that would be exercised over their institutions by the Juilliard trustees if they should accept funding.[8] Finally, in 1924, the Juilliard Foundation bought the huge 7-story, 50-room Vanderbilt guest home in midtown Manhattan. It would house Foundation offices, Eugene Noble's lavish living quarters, and a newly formed music education endeavor providing endowed instruction to advanced students in piano, violin, cello, voice, and composition: The Juilliard Graduate School.[9] Two additional new music schools also were recently under way elsewhere: The Eastman School of Music in Rochester, New York, and the Curtis Institute of Music in Philadelphia. The field of well-endowed music education was becoming very crowded indeed.

The Juilliard Graduate School had little trouble attracting tuition-free pupils and well-paid, notable instructors to what was essentially a conglomerate of individual student-teacher tutorials, rather than a coherent school. However, it also attracted controversy when squabbles about Noble's heavy-handed control of decision making became public and when critics began asking why so little had been done for music in the five years since Augustus Juilliard's bequest. At the same time, the well-regarded Institute of Musical Art found itself in an increasingly perilous situation in the competition for funds and talent. By 1926, the two entities reached an agreement that would benefit both. A new Juilliard School of Music would combine the Juilliard Graduate School and the much larger, but not as well endowed, Institute of Musical Art. Frank Damrosch, originally named Franz after his godfather Franz Liszt, was particularly crushed that the school he had managed into substantial prominence would now disappear under the Juilliard umbrella, and he successfully fought to keep the Institute of Musical Art name for that unit of the Juilliard School for many years.[10] The Foundation trustees also reorganized management with a new group of nine directors—three each from the two newly joined instructional units and three from the general public.

Erskine, joining the latter trio, attended the first meeting of Juilliard School directors in late 1926. The directors agreed to search for an individual who would serve as president of the Juilliard School and who would appoint a dean of the Graduate School, while Frank Damrosch would remain the Institute of Musical Art dean. At a subsequent meeting, after two college presidents had turned down invitations to be considered for the Juilliard presidency, Erskine agreed to chair a three-member administrative subcommittee that would manage the amalgamated school during its first year and presidential search. This move allowed the new directors to buy time in finding a candidate other than Frank Damrosch, who seemed a logical choice but was not supported by either Frederic Juilliard or Eugene Noble. While Noble himself wanted the job and was still officially the secretary to the Foundation trustees, he was not well regarded by the directors and was no longer in a formal position involving the Juilliard Graduate School. Erskine, with an office at Columbia in Hamilton Hall, moved into a second office among the Graduate School space in the former Vanderbilt house. He delighted in his new responsibilities and "was having the time of my life in those early months" as he busily commuted between one office lined by bookshelves and student papers and another accented by oak paneling and a gold-leaf ceiling.[11]

*   *   *

Erskine entertained the proposal to become the first president of the Juilliard School of Music two years after joining the board of directors, later claiming some surprise at the offer: "I did not know at the time that Paul Cravath, a member of the Board, had been exchanging letters with General Pershing about my work as director of the AEF University in Beaune. I learned later that I was chosen for my experience in education as well as my knowledge of music."[12] He accepted on the condition that he would be granted necessary leave the first year to travel to France when Graham entered the Sorbonne and for several additional visits.

As a compromise choice when the board of directors realized that the appointment of either Eugene Noble or Frank Damrosch would only polarize their endeavors, Erskine had intellect, charm, ideas, executive ability, and the right contacts going for him. He also had name recognition that could only help attract publicity and perhaps even top faculty. Longtime followers of the New York music scene typically found his appointment a bit unusual, but intriguing and hopeful. The aging James Loeb, benefactor of the Institute of Musical Art, wrote to him: "I must tell you how glad I was to hear from Paul Warburg that you had consented to accept the presidency of the Juilliard School...Even though I know nothing about your eminent qualifications for the office you have now accepted, your 'Adam and Eve' would prove to me how deep is your insight into human nature."[13]

In February, 1928, President Butler granted Erskine an indefinite leave of absence from Columbia. Insisting that this personnel loss was really not a loss at all, simply a natural segue for everyone's benefit, Butler optimistically commented:

> We feel that he is not in any true sense severing his relation with Columbia University, but merely changing the form and field of his educational activity. We hope very much that ways and means will be

found to bring about close cooperation between the work of Columbia University and that of the Juilliard Foundation, since it is our earnest desire to contribute whatever we may to strengthen and develop the movement to raise the standard and broaden the field of influence of the fine arts in American education and American life...Professor Erskine's rare combination of intellectual gifts and accomplishments makes him the ideal executive to set so important an undertaking on the right path.[14]

At Columbia and elsewhere there was regret about Erskine's departure among some colleagues, but enthusiasm among others. While some of his friends, possibly including his wife, had thought he could one day be an appropriate successor to President Butler, others decided that his celebrity novelist status had irreparably estranged him from the academic firmament. The velocity of his rising campus stardom, which at one time seemed to promise at least a department chairman or dean position, had been curtailed drastically by his commercial success. However, Jacques Barzun, teaching history and earning his PhD at Columbia during that time, insisted that Erskine's departure was simply a matter of a better fit: "He was not pushed out in any way. His interests were in music and creative work rather than in administrative demands...At the time it seemed a good solution all around for him to move to Juilliard."[15]

Erskine wasted no time in publically defining his objectives for music in general and for the Juilliard School. As he wanted for even seemingly "highbrow" literature, he preferred that music move toward popular acceptance among wide audiences with varied tastes. He did not feel that enjoyment required special understanding, only accessibility and exposure. Juilliard's responsibility would be not only to produce fine musicians, but also to cultivate music-loving audiences. He insisted on a dual mission that went beyond performance preparation: "The policy of the Juilliard School of Music is, of course, to train first-rate talent for performance, but quite as much to lay the foundation for audiences everywhere in the country and for musical careers which will decentralize the art of music."[16]

Although he had not yet worked out a strategy for implementation, Erskine quickly determined that Juilliard's reach would be national and promotional by influencing music well beyond the large city cultural scenes and the polishing of top talent. In one of his first major speeches after accepting the Juilliard presidency, he told Music

Industries Association conference attendees, as well as a live radio audience:

> No country is ultimately happy or prosperous unless each individual in it has an opportunity to study the art of music...Audiences everywhere are eager to enjoy the art. In certain parts of the country there are great teachers, especially since the war. The difficulty, however, is that the teachers are not in touch with the talent. Some of the gifted youngsters live in remote parts of the land and in whole sections of the country there is no adequate provision for music teaching. A problem equally urgent is the lack of contact between talent after it is trained and the audiences waiting to hear it. Both teachers and pupils show a disposition to cling to the large cities of the East and a panicky fear to launch out into those parts of the country which most need them.[17]

Just as he had contended that great ancient classic literature was meant for the enjoyment and education of students of all means and ability, Erskine insisted that fine music was meant for all citizens. And just as he had encouraged amateur writing as a route to literary appreciation and understanding, he promoted voice and instrument practice across all abilities and motivations. Viewing Juilliard students as a cadre of high talent that could eventually fan out across the country, his lofty aim was to graduate great musicians prepared to create, teach, and perform to the benefit of citizens everywhere. "This country must be musical throughout all its territory before it can call itself musically educated," he told a wire service reporter whose interview appeared in dozens of newspapers.[18] Especially disdainful of the single-minded training of virtuoso performers that too often occurred in music conservatories, he argued:

> It is up to the teacher of music to preach the gospel of music for its own sake and to run down the virtuoso as such. He must help the art of music by taking away from young pupils the desire to become glittering opera stars and to enter a field which is already overcrowded. The false gleam of becoming a virtuoso in a large city will have to be replaced by the desire to create good music in one's own locality before a proper standard of music can be attained. It is to that end that music teachers all over the country should work.[19]

Not only did the virtuoso system limit great music to large cities and wealthy audiences, it also limited opportunities to a miniscule working talent pool at the top: "Where we have young opera singers coming on, there is no opera for them to sing in; where you are training these youngsters to be orchestra players, there is no orchestra for them to play in...If you can produce composers, they will have no chance, practically, to hear their compositions." Erskine's proposed solution was state and municipal support to create local music centers throughout the country. He praised the Baltimore Civic Opera, which used tax dollars to keep ticket prices below one dollar at the time, and he suggested a tax-assisted music center in every state that would somehow include the involvement of school systems and working musicians.[20]

In addition to promoting music education broadly throughout the country, Erskine was eager to extol American artists and artistic styles at a time of great sentiment toward Europe as the sole venue of great music and musicians. After receiving several nearly incoherent letters from expatriate poet Ezra Pound, whose residence in Italy left him doubtful about the success of American music schools, Erskine responded: "You think Europe still is the best place for music, and I think that since the war the future of music is on this side of the water. At any rate, America is on this side, and I see no reason why Mr. Juilliard should be cursed out for having preferred to leave his benefaction to America and to Americans."[21]

In another letter to Pound, perhaps wary of the recipient's tendency to misinterpret, Erskine offered one of his most clear and succinct statements of the founding aims of the Juilliard School: "We are trying to give the best possible training to young Americans who wish to be artists. Our pupils are drawn from the entire country. We are also trying to raise the level of artistic appreciation throughout the country...We are also encouraging the American composer to the best of our ability by arranging for the publication of his scores and for the performance of his works. And we are sending abroad well-trained singers to acquire routine experience in the great opera houses. We are also collaborating with various musical bodies in this country to give young talent a chance to get at its audience."[22]

*   *   *

Erskine's high profile, combined with his personal magnetism and energy, worked well in creating a widespread presence for the new Juilliard School of Music. Just as the applause for his novels began to lose vigor, he added music educator to his repertoire of commentary and coverage in magazines, journals, newspapers, and radio. In addition to opinion essays in serious national magazines like the *Nation* and *Harper's*, advice columns in popular outlets like *Coronet* and *Reader's Digest* and fiction in numerous women's magazines, he now appeared regularly in periodicals such as *Musician, The Etude, Music Educators Journal,* and *Talking Machine and Radio Weekly.* He was able to quickly spread the Juilliard name, as well as his own ideas about music education. Music, he insisted, was essential to a full general education, and practicing musical arts was important to understanding music. "I would like to see the arts developed as baseball is developed," he observed. "When you go to a ball game you know that every man in the audience, and a great many girls too, has himself played baseball. They never had to take a course in baseball appreciation."[23] He was optimistic about a "new general education" that would emphasize creative artistic practices for both aspiring professionals and recreational dabblers. "It is better psychologically, morally and physically to have a creative art outlet in life," he maintained.[24]

Erskine's populist ideas about music education were immediately welcomed by a growing middlebrow public that clamored for at least a passing acquaintance with typically upper-class pastimes. Yet, his impulse for musical knowledge widespread throughout the country and across socioeconomic classes implied to many great teachers and students, at Juilliard and elsewhere, a lowering of standards and a looming depreciation of the special fame and glamor attained at large urban symphonies and opera companies. His approach could be viewed as more commercial than cultured in its attraction to the uncultivated taste of the masses, leaving one observer to conclude: "Erskine's love of literature and music was genuine and he soon proved himself a competent administrator, but he was also pretentious, self-advertising and very naïve in his belief that the attention paid to him was owing to personal achievements rather than to the money he controlled."[25]

* * *

The Juilliard presidency, of course, meant administrative leadership. To that end, several immediate issues loomed large: The appointment of a dean for the Juilliard Graduate School; the integration of the work of the Graduate School and the Institute of Musical Art in a way that went further than two units under one umbrella; and the possibility of a physical move to a more suitable facility for the combined schools. These issues would consume most of the early years of Erskine's presidency.

Undoubtedly one of the most astute early moves made by Erskine was to remove Eugene Noble from his leadership of the Graduate School and to persuade the reluctant Ernest Hutcheson to accept the position. Widely recognized as a great pianist, conductor, composer, and teacher, Hutcheson had also proved his administrative talent through the organization and management of a fine summer music school at Chautauqua. For Erskine, this was a welcome contrast to Noble who he viewed as "a man of many cultural interests and of considerable miscellaneous experiences in education, but the essence of education, the building up of a school to respond to the larger interests of society, was a secret which Heaven had concealed from him."[26]

As dean of the Graduate School, Hutcheson was organizationally above the dean of the Institute of Musical Art, Frank Damrosch. Erskine and Frank Damrosch—called Dr. Frank by Erskine—shared few common views of the Juilliard School mission. Damrosch, although he received a salary increase and a defined pension when the Institute merged with the Graduate School, was continually resentful that the school he had nursed to great prominence had needed to join with the wealthy, but uncertain Juilliard venture. He considered Erskine an amateur musician with a vocational flair for middlebrow fiction and self-promotion. However, Hutcheson and Damrosch were good friends who rarely disagreed. Hutcheson was able to calm the rocky waters occasioned by the integration of policies, curriculums, and students of the Institute of Musical Art and the Graduate School.

Equally astute was Erskine's conclusion that the two schools would never reach their potential as a single entity until they were physically merged. The Institute, located near Columbia University in Morningside Heights, was three miles uptown from the Graduate School location on East Fifty-Second Street. Hutcheson and Erskine shuttled back and forth, but students and faculty at the Institute largely ignored them until the Graduate School physically pushed into their territory. Erskine, at the end of his first year as Juilliard president, moved into the Berkshire Hotel, not far from the Graduate School. His wife and children took an Upper East Side apartment

Figure 9.1 Two Juilliard School of Music presidents, Ernest Hutcheson and John Erskine (l), ca. 1934.

Source: Courtesy of Anna Erskine Crouse and the Juilliard School.

and spent most weekends at the home in Connecticut, where Erskine sometimes visited. Although the physical separation from his family worked well for Erskine, he determined that the two Juilliard entities needed a physical merger. Not only was distance a problem, but also "the plan of the house in which the Juilliard [Graduate School] functioned had no relation whatsoever to a music school."[27]

Initially, Erskine hoped for a location that would put the Juilliard School of Music close to a rumored new Metropolitan Opera location. However, the directors of the Met decided it would stay put for a while.[28] Next, he considered some empty lots on Claremont Avenue adjacent to the Institute of Musical Art building. Before pushing for a move so close to Columbia, he consulted President Butler. Enthusiastic about more activity in the neighborhood, Butler encouraged: "By all means bring the Juilliard to Morningside Heights. There are many things which the University, already established, can do for students of music without new expense or overhead cost to the Juilliard Foundation. This will leave your school's funds free to care specifically for musical art."[29] Against the wishes of many, if not most, faculty, as well as Deans Ernest Hutcheson and Frank Damrosch, Erskine convinced the Juilliard Musical Foundation trustees to embark on a $6 million building project that would move the Graduate School to a new building at 130 Claremont Avenue. It would be an extension of the existing Institute of Musical Art building and six times its size. The Institute, accessible through a set of glass doors, would preserve a sense of autonomy by maintaining not only a separate dean from the Graduate School, but also a separate address: 120 Claremont Avenue, rather than the Graduate School's 130 designation. The design was the work of the architectural firm Shreve, Lamb and Harmon, the same group that was simultaneously designing the Empire State Building.

With its marble *foyer*, 1,000-seat auditorium, 125 new Steinway pianos, 8 dressing rooms, and elegantly furnished offices and studios, the 6-story building opened in November, 1931, 2 years into the Great Depression. Erskine's large presidential office was on the second floor overlooking a park. His private study, with concert grand piano, desk, suede chairs, and velvet drapes, was one floor above. Slowly gravitating further from his life as a husband and father, he moved his hundreds of books from the studio he had built at the Wilton house to his new Juilliard study. For the week of opening ceremonies at the new Juilliard, Leopold Stokowski conducted a student orchestra. He was paid $3,000 for the occasion—approximately $36,000 when adjusted to 2011 dollar value. Several days later, Sergei Rachmaninoff played a piano recital for invited guests. The following week, the new school introduced the opera *Jack and the Beanstalk*, with music by Russian composer Louis Gruenberg, libretto by Erskine, and performance by Juilliard students. A whimsical production, complete with a large cow that took tenor and baritone parts, it played three nights at the new Juilliard building, followed by two weeks on Broadway, and eventually capped in a production at the Chicago Opera House.[30] It later was produced regularly throughout the country in high schools and community halls as an opera for children.

Erskine and Hutcheson managed to attract fine teachers to the Graduate School to complement the faculty Damrosch had built at the Institute of Musical Art. Among them were luminaries such as pianists Olga Samaroff Stokowski and Alexander Siloti, composer and pianist Rubin Goldmark, soprano Marcella Sembrich, violinist and composer Paul Kochanski, and violinist and conductor Albert Stoessel. Erskine's sister and accomplished pianist, Rhoda Erskine, and Hutcheson's son, Harold Hutcheson, were hired to teach literature.

Like Erskine, Hutcheson was a recognizable name well beyond his own circle of friends and acquaintances. Network radio began broadcasting live symphony performances in 1926, and Hutcheson was a frequent piano soloist with the WABC orchestra and others in the coming years. Erskine sometimes played piano, but more often was interviewed, on radio. He was the featured guest on the 1931 premier of the NBC-sponsored nationwide radio program "Keys to Happiness." That early experiment in distance education offered piano instruction to Saturday-morning listeners with the aid of cardboard key and note charts they received in the mail and set above their home keyboards. The 25,000 students who tuned into the premier with Erskine grew to 40,000 the next week.[31] Later, Erskine became a regular judge for the Metropolitan Opera's "Radio Auditions" show.

*　*　*

With the two Juilliard schools finally physically joined, Erskine was relieved of regularly shuttling between them. Ernest Hutcheson and his wife, Imgart, already lived in the upper reaches of Manhattan's West Side, and Erskine decided it was time to move out of his mid-town room at the Berkshire Hotel. As someone who loved social gatherings and spent only rare weekends with his wife and family in Connecticut, he also wanted a larger and more imposing residence. Just before the completion of the new Juilliard building, he took an apartment in the building on West Eighty-First Street that also housed the Hutchesons' large apartment. His new residence was a spacious penthouse—a rooftop addition to the building constructed especially for him—with three balconies, a large great room, kitchen, dining room, study, and three bedrooms. He explained: "I have always adored space...With fifty or sixty people in the living room, there was still no sense of crowding. I like people and I like parties...Not a weekend passed that I did not have some party."[32]

Erskine's romance with Adeline Atwater, who he still called "Lilith," had continued as he took over the reins of Juilliard, and his marital situation deteriorated further. Late in 1930, he wrote to Hugh Guiler in Paris about his unhappy situation: "Practically everyone who knows us at all knows that Pauline and I are separated, and we have been discussing a divorce at great expense to the nerves of all concerned. Pauline's own family think it is the sensible thing to do in the circumstances, but she is so far opposed to it, and she uses the children as much as possible as a weapon...I certainly hope we can get the thing straightened out permanently on some basis of decent friendship. Certainly we have had no such relation for the last ten years of our married life."[33] Typical of many friends who viewed Atwater as Erskine's true partner, Guiler wrote to Erskine: "Anaïs and I send you and Lilith our very best love and are looking forward to seeing you both soon."[34]

Although Nin was still romantically fixated on Erskine, her connection with him largely amounted to fantasies played out in her diaries. For his part, Erskine recast his relationship to Nin as strictly one of friend and mentor, addressing her in letters as "dear friend," advising her on her writing, and promoting her work to editors and publishers. He introduced her to Alfred Knopf and encouraged Knopf to publish a US version of her book on D. H. Lawrence. Unsuccessfully, he also urged publication of Nin's short stories to Frank Crowninshield at *Vanity Fair* and Samuel Chotzinoff at *Gentle Reader*.[35]

Nin was alternately perplexed and irritated that the John Erskine who had demonstrated so much physical attraction to her could later write her only very formal letters that exchanged the niceties of platonic friendship. "Why he should have such power over my thoughts is a mystery to me," she pondered in early 1931. "In spite of the real John, the John in my mind is a great man, full of brilliancy and warmth and potency...Curse such dreams, such living with one's own created images."[36]

When Erskine wrote to Nin and her husband that he might be coming to France alone upon his wife Pauline's suggestion that he get away and "think things over," he suggested that the three of them take a driving trip to some parts of France he longed to see again. By this time, however, Nin was thoroughly vexed that her infatuation had failed to develop. She wanted no part in being of service to Erskine's touring plans. "Hugh and I are not going with John to visit Chateaux. Of that I am certain," she wrote in her diary. "John is out of my ken because he does not know how to express his feelings, and he is unconscious of mine."[37] Apparently, even Erskine's repositioning of the relationship into the realm of companionable pals went only so far. Twice Nin wrote him to ask for a dust jacket testimonial for her 1932 book *D.H. Lawrence: An Unprofessional Study*, and twice he failed to write back. Undeterred, she eventually grabbed several lines from a letter Erskine had written earlier to Hugh Guiler and submitted them to her publisher. They appeared on the cover with the famous Erskine name.[38]

Adeline Atwater, perhaps noticing how readily a busy person like John Erskine could manage to push forth manuscripts for books and articles, decided that she too might succeed as an author. And, as he had with Nin, Erskine used his contacts in the publishing world to help her get a start. He personally sent her first book manuscript, titled *No Matter Which Way*, to Bobbs-Merrill. Laurance Chambers gave it an in-house reading and responded that it simply was not adequate for publication.[39] Soon, however, Atwater was working on a new manuscript, touted by Erskine to Chambers as "much better than her first book... Her idea is such a striking one that I can't see how she could miss considerable sales." It was published by Bobbs-Merrill as *The Marriage of Don Quixote*—a contemporary story of adventure, romance, cads, and suckers, with no resemblance to the Cervantes tale beyond the first name (Don) of the protagonist.[40]

Erskine's five-year romance with his spirited "Lilith" ended abruptly, and perhaps predictably, when a new Lilith appeared on the scene. Erskine had promised some musical friends that he would join Sir William Hadow, editor of the *Oxford History of Music*, in cochairing the Second Anglo-American Music Education Conference in Lausanne, Switzerland, during the summer of 1931. On the SS Paris from New York to Le Havre, he was invited to lunch with the captain and several other passengers on the last day of the voyage. Among them was Helen Worden, a New York reporter and newspaper columnist. Erskine managed to have breakfast and dinner with her the next day on the train to Paris and in Paris. He saw her as soon as the Lausanne conference ended, and they returned from France together aboard the Aquitania.[41] At 35 years old and unmarried, Worden was a seasoned journalist, although she had studied drawing at the University of Colorado. She wrote various society columns for New York newspapers, primarily the *World Telegram*, as well as feature articles and guidebooks. [42]

There was, according to Anaïs Nin, some awkwardness when Erskine confessed to Worden that Adeline Atwater was waiting for him back in New York. This was followed by Erskine's own indecision, or perhaps his reluctance to confront Adeline with the truth about a new woman. Suggesting typical end-of-relationship dodges and delays, he shared with Adeline only the news of his sense of vague confusion about what he wanted in life. He explained his predicament to Anaïs Nin as, "I find it hard to say goodbye."[43] It took several months of vacillation for him to completely end the affair with his first Lilith and turn his full attention to Helen Worden. However, she was on his arm at the opening of Juilliard's vast new home only four months after they met, and she occupied that place in the coming years. Friends soon sent notes and invitations to the two of them, and they entertained as a couple. Not surprisingly, Bobbs-Merrill soon published two of Worden's New York City guidebooks.[44] Pauline Erskine and the children continued to reside at the Connecticut estate and an apartment in Manhattan. They saw less and less of John Erskine, although he sent checks when necessary and wrote letters to the children often. His infrequent visits to Connecticut were a treat for Anna and Graham, but often required extensive urging on their parts.[45]

*   *   *

With its large endowment, the Juilliard School of Music confronted the Great Depression in a condition less dire than that of many other educational institutions. Still, belt tightening became essential. Although Erskine's annual salary was more than adequate— somewhere between $15,000 and $20,000—in the early Depression years, most of the teachers were on hourly wages.[46] In 1932, Erskine announced pay reductions for instructors—by 10 percent for those earning more than $25 per hour and 5 percent for those earning below $25 per hour.[47] By mid-decade, he reduced his own annual salary to $10,000. At the same time, appeals reached Erskine and others with growing frequency about the plight of Jewish musical artists forced to leave Germany and other eastern European countries. New York financial mogul Felix Warburg often approached Erskine in an effort to place individuals such as German conductor Frieder Weissmann, Austrian composer Hans Gal, and violinist Klaus Liepmann. While the Juilliard trustees were reluctant to hire from abroad during reductions at home, Erskine did manage to contribute $5,000 from the Julliard Foundation to Warburg for the Musician's Emergency Fund.[48]

Although Erskine's own financial situation appeared on more solid footing than most in the Depression, his spending, borrowing, and investing resulted in constant monetary problems during and beyond those spare years. With his bon vivant lifestyle in full swing, he maintained his own apartment, as well as a Manhattan apartment and estate in Connecticut for his wife and children. In 1931, he complained to Laurance Chambers at Bobbs-Merrill: "My writing has brought in so little in the last year and a half that I am quite poor and want to make some money if that can be done without interfering with quality." He was working on a new novel, *Unfinished Business*, but worried that "if it does no better as a novel than *Uncle Sam* or *Sincerity*, there is not much point, financially speaking."[49] The situation improved only temporarily when movie rights to *Sincerity* sold to Universal Pictures, which brought it to film as *A Lady Surrenders*. In 1931, his novel *Unfinished Business* was published to lukewarm sales and reviews. Erskine was compelled to ask if Bobbs-Merrill anticipated enough sales to allow him to borrow $1,000, explaining: "My income tax next week will pretty well clean me out, and I hate to sell securities unless I have to."[50] His letters and notes to friend and publisher Laurance Chambers during the early Depression years were often impatient entreaties to sell additional foreign rights, push magazines to serialize, negotiate with motion picture companies, publicize more vigorously, and distribute more widely. Curbing his spending was not yet an option, even when his wife, Pauline, warned: "We have been living in a rich family's paradise on a poor family's income, and it just won't work." Although he rarely visited their Connecticut estate, he ignored Pauline's suggestion that it be sold.[51]

In response to his reduced income from book publishing, Erskine stepped up production of magazine articles. During the early 1930s, he managed to produce about a dozen a year, including essays and short stories in periodicals like *Woman's Home Companion*, *Collier's*, *Review of Reviews*, *Saturday Review of Literature*, and the *North*

American Review. He also received a retainer from the *Brooklyn Daily Eagle* to contribute regular columns. For his next book venture, he collected a number of stories written as imaginative sequels to well-know classics (e.g., *Cinderella, Beauty and the Beast, Sleeping Beauty*) into the volume *Cinderella's Daughter and Other Sequels and Consequences*. Sales were not encouraging, but Erskine pressed on. He suggested to Chambers that Bobbs-Merrill might consider bringing out a book of essays and speeches he had written "on education with special emphasis on the place of arts in education," but that venture never materialized.[52]

On the strength of good feedback from a story in *Collier's* about the mishaps of a college student named Felix, he decided to write a whole campus novel about student and faculty life at Columbia during the Depression. The result, *Bachelor—Of Arts*, was published in 1934.[53] Although one Bobbs-Merrill reader had warned that it was "adolescent" and "juvenilizing," Chambers convinced his acquisitions committee to take a chance on attracting a young audience.[54] Happily, excerpts of that book appeared in a number of Sunday newspaper magazines. Fox Film Corporation purchased the film rights, and the movie, filmed on the campus of Occidental College, appeared with popular actress Anita Louise in the starring role.

As the author of three books that had made their way to popular film in a half-dozen years, Erskine also enjoyed Hollywood connections, and he entertained William De Mille, Adolph Zukor, Douglas Fairbanks, Mary Pickford, and others when they came to New York. Erskine and Helen Worden also had made some good friends at whose summer homes they visited—including violinist Efrem Zimbalist and his soprano wife Alma Gluck, as well as the playwright Channing Pollock and his wife. Yet, the continuance of the Depression, the needs of his family, and his own spending guaranteed Erskine ongoing financial problems. He had moved to a large new duplex at 471 Park Avenue, which did not help his hefty living expenses. By 1934, he alerted Chambers that his travel might be curtailed: "Some outlying family members have been in trouble this year, and my brother and I have been glad to help, but the result is that we are down to the bare bone, and unless I sell some more manuscripts to magazines than at present seems likely, I expect to stay here pretty steadily."[55] His son Graham, working in Manhattan before going to architectural school in Italy, moved in with him for a while; while his daughter, Anna, began an acting career with a summer stock company in Westport,

Connecticut, and in small parts on Broadway. They cheered him greatly in difficult financial times and especially when, in 1934, his sister, Rhoda Erskine, died of cancer at age 41.

Helen Worden took an active part in encouraging sales of Erskine's writing, continually thinking of marketing ideas to present to Bobbs-Merrill. For example, she suggested that a group of columns Erskine wrote for the *Brooklyn Eagle* be "reprinted in a little folder or booklet...and distributed through the Woolworth stores." She also felt that press releases about upcoming Erskine books should go to city editors in towns where he had recently lectured or played piano, and Erskine proudly told Chambers, "She thinks publicity of this kind is worth quite as much as advertising."[56]

*　*　*

Erskine had numerous writing projects in various stages—as well as his work as president of a large music school, piano performer, and frequent lecturer—when composer George Antheil approached him about adapting *The Private Life of Helen of Troy* into opera form. Enthusiastic about American composers and intrigued by both the jazz and atonal modernist elements of Antheil's work, Erskine was interested in the idea. He considered Antheil a daring innovator—"a genius"—whose best-known work, the ear splitting and musically disappointing *Ballet Mecanique*, had debuted at Carnegie Hall in 1926 to the unanimous animosity of critics and most of the audience. However, he told Antheil that through negotiations about dramatic versions of his book, he had developed "a natural aversion...against reworking material which has already been put into a definite form." Nevertheless, he might be able to work on somewhat of a sequel to the story in his book, one that used a little-known story about Helen after the death of Menelaos, and turn it into a libretto for Antheil's music.[57]

The libretto for the opera *Helen Retires* was readied while Antheil completed the music. Finding a company to perform it was another matter. The Metropolitan Opera, with its European traditions, was out of the question. Leopold Stokowski was briefly interested, but then not. Albert Stoessel was unable to find a place for it at Chautauqua. The Philadelphia Opera was approached, but could not arrange to produce it. Finally, it was produced by the Juilliard School opera program in 1934 with Stoessel conducting. Erskine, who maintained that Antheil's music was "both beautiful and irritating," noted that the audience and critics "both damned and praised" the production. *New York Times* critic Olin Downes had positive comments about Erskine's libretto, but insisted that it was frequently overwhelmed by music "too much jazzed." He dismissed Antheil as a composer who "needs more technique, much more technique—technique of composition and technique of orchestration."[58] Antheil, grateful simply to have found a stage and orchestra for his work, wrote Erskine a long note of thanks for Erskine's "genius in writing the libretto" and "courage and faith" in producing the opera. He also expressed great pleasure in knowing that his collaborator "will not be swayed by these really ignorant critics who know absolutely nothing of either modern orchestral or stage tendencies in operatic music."[59] Erskine did manage to recoup some of his investment of time and energy when the *Golden Book* magazine published his libretto in two installments several months later.[60]

Erskine was determined that contemporary American opera would eventually win out over "European opera with its preposterous plots, its tiresome recitative, and its remoteness from American culture and American life."[61] He later wrote one more libretto, a version of his short story, "Cinderella's Daughter," retitled *Sleeping Beauty*, for Beryl Rubenstein at the Cleveland Institute of Music. However, his primary operatic involvement was in developing the Juilliard opera program. And, by extension, that meant dealing with the Metropolitan Opera, which had been vaguely mentioned for unspecified assistance in the Augustus Juilliard will. That assistance, initially discussed between the Juilliard Foundation trustees and Metropolitan Opera general manager Giulio Gatti-Cassazza, had been stalemated by disagreements concerning differences in aims and issues of control. Eventually, however, with several overlapping board members between Juilliard and the Met and with the Met's cushion of surplus funds annihilated during the early Depression years, discussions resumed. In 1933, Juilliard contributed $50,000 and in 1934, $40,000 toward whittling away at the Met's estimated $600,000 deficit. By 1935, a much fuller partnership was in the wings.[62]

The underlying problem for the Metropolitan Opera was rooted in its 1883 founding purposes as both a prestigious showcase for the best and most dramatic opera of the world and a highbrow gathering place for the social, and sometimes musical, upper crust. Fifty years later, the bulging of the American middle class suggested alternatives in musical entertainment for the masses, while the Depression suggested alternatives to excess for the elite. Erskine viewed the Metropolitan as too tied to the European system of showcasing big name stars in lavish productions of traditional European opera classics. He had often remarked about his and the general public's growing regard for Broadway musicals as a worthy alternative in talent and enjoyment, insisting: "All the elements that Americans enjoy are present in a good musical show. Dancing, the lyric quality in the songs, beauty of settings and of bodies, drama, comedy—they are all there in their elements in a show like 'Show Boat.' The opera used to have these elements, but they have dropped away. They are just concerts in costume now."[63]

In 1934, when some Met board members indicated they were ready to consider a Juilliard proposal for funding and policy control, Erskine made his move to renovate the opera and its management. His plan was for a leaner and more efficient operation that offered more American and contemporary fare and attracted—even "educated"—an audience that might include some of the middlebrow public. In a letter to Allen Wardwell, who was both a Metropolitan Opera board member and a Juilliard Foundation trustee, he offered $150,000 from the Juilliard Foundation in exchange for: Management personnel changes, a shorter main opera season, a six-month supplementary season "at popular prices" and featuring American singers, greater Juilliard representation on the board, a Metropolitan fundraising campaign, and a $100,000 underwriting commitment from the Metropolitan Opera Association. The boards of both entities accepted the plan and the funding. Erskine became a member of the Metropolitan Board of Directors and of the new Committee of Control he had proposed for overseeing his plan.[64]

Committed to the popularization of music and its comprehension among all classes of Americans, Erskine continued his quest to make the Juilliard School a central player in outreach to diverse populations and to communities throughout the country. While he realized that the Julliard mission to train expert performance and composition talent would always be foremost, he believed that such talent also could be urged to contribute outside the large urban areas in order to increase access to music in other places. Undoubtedly, some of his peers and even Juilliard students determined that his disdain for a strictly virtuoso system of music performance training was rooted in his own musical limitations as only a very competent amateur.

However, his leadership at Juilliard was more that of an institutional executive than a prominent musician—a new arrangement in the arena of music schools, but an appropriate concept when the Juilliard School was viewed as a music education entity within the Juilliard Musical Foundation. When Frank Damrosch retired from his leadership at the Institute of Musical Art in 1933, Erskine appointed Ernest Hutcheson as the new dean, adding to his position as dean of the Graduate School and creating more friendly ground for Erskine's ideas for the Juilliard School.

*   *   *

Shortly after assuming the presidency at Juilliard, Erskine had begun to receive communications from towns, schools, and colleges asking about the possibility of enhanced music education or performance at their own locations. A group in Atlanta, for example, asked about increasing interest in symphony and opera. A small contingent from Juilliard then traveled to Atlanta for a performance and to introduce the singer Helen Riley who would stay on to help Atlanta's musical cause. She eventually organized the Atlanta Symphony Guild, which enabled a sustained City Symphony. When New Mexico Agricultural and Mechanical University inquired about a violin instructor, the Juilliard sent talented Graduate School student Hine Brown and provided his initial teaching salary. That was supplemented by his additional conducting duties at the El Paso, Texas, Symphony. Later, Juilliard sent him to conduct the Louisville, Kentucky, Symphony. Jacques Jolas, a gifted young piano teacher, was first sent to Harrisburg, Pennsylvania, to help organize an orchestra. Eventually, he was sent to assist in the music program at Cornell College in Iowa, where Juilliard also sent Francis German to teach voice.

In essence, such appointments from the Juilliard Graduate School were in the nature of postdoctoral fellowships or internships. They bridged a gap between artistic excellence and practical career endeavors while they served Erskine's aim of musical outreach. Eventually, according to Erskine's estimate, there were 20 outreach endeavors called "Juilliard Centers," all under the supervision of Oscar Wagner, a gifted piano talent whom Ernest Hutcheson had brought to Juilliard as his assistant. Erskine and others visited them and gave lectures and performances while in town.[65]

Insisting that "the school that trains artists has some responsibility to prepare audiences for them," Erskine partnered with the

Carnegie Foundation in fielding requests from small communities for grants to increase musical education and performances in their towns.[66] He corresponded frequently with schools and colleges throughout the country, sharing ideas and advice widely. He later proposed direct Juilliard grants to music programs at small, struggling colleges in the South.[67] In 1932, he initiated a Juilliard summer school for music teachers from throughout the country. Five years later, summer attendance rose to nearly 1,000, and the effort expanded as a way for music students from outside large cities to test themselves with truly great teachers.

Erskine felt that even further educational outreach could occur to students and audiences of good music through radio. Yet, he was not enthusiastic about the idea of "educational broadcasting" that might need governmental support to sustain itself alongside commercial broadcasting. At Federal Communications Commission (FCC) hearings on the subject in 1934, he joined a group of well-known figures, including H. L. Mencken, who testified that commercial interests were doing a fine job of education. A staff commentator in the *New Republic* objected to their appearance before the FCC, citing Erskine and Mencken in particular and noting: "It would be interesting to know whether these and other celebrities appeared on their own initiative, and paid their own expenses, or were persuaded by the broadcasters to come forward and were given financial aid in doing so." Mencken, in his inimitable style, fumed to Erskine that the article was "a slimy insinuation typical of the kept men who run that great moral periodical." But Erskine simply responded to him: "I am accused of so many things that I have long ago developed a thick hide. It is a special pleasure to be insulted with you!"[68]

Erskine continued as a popular draw on the speaker circuit, rarely turning down an opportunity to appear before audiences in or outside New York. For example, during a speaking tour during May and June, 1935, he gave commencement addresses at Southwestern College (Memphis, Tennessee) and Boston University; Phi Beta Kappa addresses at University of Cincinnati and Swarthmore College; lectures at Illinois Wesleyan University and Temple University; and guest piano performances with the Chicago Symphony, the Minneapolis Symphony, and the Detroit Symphony. The following commencement season, he spoke at the University of Arizona, the University of Iowa, Oberlin College, Allegheny Institute, and the Westminster Choir School of Princeton University. During these years, he received honorary degrees at Rollins College, New York State Normal School,

Cornell College (Iowa), Illinois Wesleyan College, and Boston University. Closer to home, his speech to the National Institute of Arts and Letters in New York City, titled "The Human Grammar of Good Writing," drew a standing-room only, white-tie crowd.[69]

While Erskine's most frequent lecture topic was music education, he also still spoke on literature and his own books. His opinion was sought and reported on a wide range of issues, and he found himself quoted on the Nobel Prize award to Sinclair Lewis, on modern women, on school curriculum and pedagogy, on college student discipline, and on the potential of a music festival for the city of New Orleans. Wire services helped to trumpet his thoughts in newspapers throughout the country. Back in New York, Mayor LaGuardia appointed him to the Municipal Arts Commission. In 1935, he became vice president of the National Institute of Arts and Letters, soon to be renamed the National Academy of Arts and Letters, and he continued his service on the board of directors of the MacDowell Colony.

Somehow, the busy Juilliard president found time and optimism for continuing to produce book-length fiction. He may have reasoned that even though reviews and sales had slumped badly since his first three novels, net sales of the critically panned *Sincerity* had finally climbed over $42,000 (more than $500,000 in 2010), and *Bachelor—Of Arts*, dismissed by Bobbs-Merrill in-house reviewers, had made it to film.[70] During 1934, he tackled another light romance, this one about jealousy concerning lovers' pasts. Readers at Bobbs-Merrill had little good to say about the manuscript Erskine submitted, titled *Forget If You Can*, which would become his eleventh novel in 11 years. Editor Jessica Mannon summed up general office opinion concerning "exceedingly dull" dialogue and "unreal" characters, adding: "I cannot but believe we should be doing Dr. Erskine an ill favor to publish the manuscript as it now stands."[71] However, on the strength of a well-known author and a story that at least started strong and might improve some in copy-editing, Bobbs-Merrill brought out the book in early 1935. Literary criticism was mixed—one reviewer labeling the novel a "thoroughly trite story," but deciding it was still "fairly amusing reading." Sales were decidedly mediocre.[72]

Some of Erskine's Juilliard School colleagues and students dismissed his publishing and other outside endeavors as commercial, tasteless, and embarrassing to the school. Typically, they criticized his writing, from essays and fiction to opera librettos, as amateurish, and they viewed his outreach to mass, middle-class audiences as detracting from the elite-performance aims typical of fine music education. Nevertheless, within a half-dozen years at the helm of Juilliard, Erskine had added substantial value to the school as a leader with fresh and bold ideas and a national platform for widely broadcasting them, with appropriate social status and personal appeal to befriend large numbers of music lovers, with democratic ideals that could be widely admired as sincere and necessary, and with intellectual capacities that enabled him to interact with the top minds in education and music among his contemporaries. As its first president, Erskine was not the founder of the Juilliard School, but he was the craftsman who nudged together existing organizations, opportunities, and ideals in order to launch its enduring presence.

CHAPTER 10

SEGUES AND SECOND ACTS

Although his first half-dozen years as president of the Juilliard School of Music had produced numerous positive accomplishments, Erskine also encountered considerable frustrations. His leadership, especially in the case of amalgamating the two schools and in the issue of the Metropolitan Opera, was viewed by many music lovers as heavy handed. Intellectual and musical cynics saw his lectures and piano performances as commercial gimmicks. His novels and short stories struck some readers as too middlebrow to be truly literary. Detractors loved to recall his most commercial accomplishments rather than his academic achievements. An article about the Metropolitan Opera in *Time* magazine, for example, referred to him not as an academic leader, but as "John (*Helen of Troy*) Erskine."[1] Even Juilliard students did not hold him in the high esteem he had enjoyed among students at Columbia, although during his administration they had requested and acquired greater voice in decision making. However, that voice was dampened by Erskine's disdain for the more radical students—especially those who might be pacifists or communist sympathizers—and his opposition to some of their more political student organizations.[2]

Yet, in the midst of a continuing poor economic environment in the mid-1930s, Erskine could do little but plow ahead with plans and actions that might continue forward movement for Juilliard and for himself. Nearing 60 years old, he could not even begin to contemplate slowing the pace of his life, and he still needed to work frantically on his writing and his paid lecturing and performing to keep his complicated personal finances afloat. While supporting himself and his wife and children in separate households, he also aided his sisters, Helen and Anna, during the Depression years. He finally retreated to a tiny, much less expensive, apartment—two rooms plus kitchenette and bath—at 540 Park Avenue. He began to consider selling the property in Wilton. With renewed determination, he sought out opportunities to lecture, to give interviews, to perform, and to write.

Late in 1935, one of his lecture tours had him booked for an evening appearance in Lansing, Michigan, and a noon lecture in Detroit the next day. Friends were driving him to Detroit on the morning of his scheduled lecture when a Michigan State Highway pickup truck struck their car head on. All three in the car survived, but with serious injuries. Erskine suffered a skull fracture, a broken nose, and some broken finger bones. By his own estimate, he also lost over $7,000 in lecture engagements and writing payments over the next several months, in addition to medical costs. The state of Michigan eventually reimbursed him for his full medical costs and an additional $1,800 in lost earnings.[3]

The accident acted as the kind of near-death episode that serves as a warning about life—but only briefly. According to Erskine's memoir about his life in music, he did indeed take some of his recovery time to contemplate past mistakes and future directions. Yet, a month later, when he returned to New York upon his discharge from the Detroit hospital, he plunged back into his work at the Juilliard School and his writing, while practicing longer hours on the piano to "limber up the muscles of my right hand."[4] Within four months, he started another lecture tour with the engagement he missed in Detroit, and he then flew to Hollywood to broadcast on radio with Bing Crosby. Throughout 1936, his expanding radio work propelled him to guest appearances from New York on the ABC network to Oakland, California, on station KFSO. He was a regular judge on the Metropolitan Opera radio show "Radio Auditions" and a frequent interviewee about music, politics, and self-improvement on various stations.

*   *   *

Discouraged about the sales of his recent novels, *Forget If You Can* and *Solomon My Son*, Erskine eventually became reluctant to ask Laurance Chambers for further advances from Bobbs-Merrill based on future sales. "Has enough real cash come in," he finally ventured, "for me to make a raid on your treasury? I am in a jam over an income tax, and I am looking for about another $2,000."[5] He did manage somewhat improved sales with his controversial opinion book, *The Influence of Women and Its Cure*, a somewhat cynical rant against organized women in clubs and federations. Claiming that women were responsible for Prohibition, literary censorship, and the "unmitigated drudgery" of "enslaved" male wage earners, he advised women either to get busy with work that would leave them no time for group efforts or to go home and enjoy the leisure provided to them by men. Critics pointed to numerous and real flaws, such as Erskine's inability to propose any viable solutions to his perceived problems, but the controversial subject matter made for valuable publicity.[6]

Ever committed to leaving no stone unturned in digging his way out of financial predicaments, Erskine decided to turn his attention to a more steady source of writing income. He began crafting stories and essays for *Liberty* magazine, edited by his friend Fulton Oursler. Among his work in that publication was a series of stories about the fifteenth-century swashbuckling French poet, François Villon. After the accident in Michigan, he added detail and pulled together his stories into the book *The Brief Hour of François Villon*. A historical novel full of dangerous and humorous escapades, it was particularly well received for Erskine's own translations of approximately 20 Villon poems. One reviewer affirmed: "He has translated poetry as only a poet can translate." Another insisted: "It has been said of Erskine that he is a highbrow whom lowbrows like. It might be said of Villon that he was a lowbrow whom the highbrows like...Mr. Erskine has much of Mr. Villon's sex appeal. No matter what his age or his somewhat irregular features, he fascinates." Erskine was likely particularly pleased with the favorable *New York Times* review, given that paper's negative criticism of his recent books. This time the reviewer decided Erskine had brought his subject "vividly to life" in a tale full of "adventure" and "charm" that "grows naturally from Mr. Erskine's understanding and scholarship."[7]

Apparently, Erskine sensed no publishing momentum from the favorable reception of the François Villon stories and book, since sales barely reached 8,000; however, he was already working on another historical fiction novel about Walt Whitman.[8] Much to the chagrin of his friend Laurance Chambers, who had been made president of the Bobbs-Merrill Company in 1935, Erskine decided that his sales—especially foreign, film, and serialization rights—might improve with a new publisher. He wrote to Chambers that although he had "wrenchings of the heart" about leaving Bobbs-Merrill, he felt "something should be tried to remedy the fortune of my books." Chambers offered to come to New York and discuss the matter with him, but Erskine's mind was made up. He told Chambers that any further discussion "would be merely distressing to both of us" and pointed out that "each of the books seems to be a little less successful than the one before." Glumly, he had concluded that "I am not growing any younger, and if my books are getting worse I ought to prove it to myself and quit. On the other hand, if I can sell more copies, I need to do so."[9]

Chambers, disappointed and blindsided, reminded Erskine of their long history. Bobbs-Merrill had published 20 Erskine books and had brought out 6 others that had earlier been with other publishers. He responded to Erskine's explanations with: "I appreciate your paramount need of all the money you can make from your literary work. I wish you, with all my heart, success. I am sorry that we may no longer enjoy a close cooperation in the effort to achieve it. The best of luck! You have hit both my affection and my publishing pride, but the former remains constant."[10]

Erskine published his Whitman book, *Start of the Road*, and several others with Frederick A. Stokes Company. Although the volume followed Whitman's works and associations closely, it was a fiction of thoughts and conversations. Erskine was delighted when noted Whitman scholar Charles Nathan Elliot found it "fascinating" and inclusive of "authentic Whitman thoughts and utterances."[11] Perhaps not yet satisfied that he had a publisher who could maximize his earnings, he also later published with J. Messner, Inc., J. B. Lippincott, Macmillan, and Greenwood Press. Chambers was able to turn his attention to editing and marketing his many other authors, including the recently signed Irma Rombauer, whose *Joy of Cooking* was then on its way to becoming not only a best seller, but also a classic. Nine years later, Bobbs-Merrill would bring out a twentieth-anniversary edition of *The Private Life of Helen of Troy*.

* * *

Although Erskine lectured on the Columbia campus occasionally and kept in touch with several former colleagues and students, he had only passing contact with his alma mater after his indefinite leave of absence had been granted. He may have been more disappointed for students and some young faculty members than for himself when the course he initiated in Great Books was suspended a year after his departure. The official reason was to shift faculty teaching resources to a new core requirement for sophomores, Introduction to Contemporary Civilization. However, since Erskine's proposal had been only grudgingly approved and limited to upperclassmen in honors, it had never gained huge numbers of registrants, and, while younger faculty particularly enjoyed teaching the sections, many in the old guard still objected that classic works were being digested so quickly and without the interpretive aid of academic specialists.

In 1932, however, the defunct General Honors program was revived by Jacques Barzun, repositioned as a course offered to all undergraduates, and renamed "Colloquium on Important Books." With "only slight modifications," it followed "the selecting, grouping and staffing methods of the old Honors course without change."[12] Notably, this reintroduction of Great Books followed by two years their introduction at University of Chicago, where former Erskine student Mortimer Adler and University of Chicago president Robert Maynard Hutchins had introduced "General Honors Course 110" in 1930. That course served as the taproot for the many well-publicized ideas and initiatives that launched the University of Chicago's prominence in general education and solidified the mistaken impression that the notion of a "great books" curriculum started in Chicago. Barzun and Lionel Trilling co-taught Columbia's popular Colloquium on Important Books for a number of years, keeping alive the efficacy of undergraduate reading in great classics until the English faculty was ready to commit to an undergraduate core that required great books reading and discussion for all students.

By 1937, the Columbia faculty agreed to a bifurcated approach to students in the first two years and those in the upperclassmen years: two years of required courses in science, social science, and humanities sequences followed by two years of specialized and elective work. The first year of the humanities sequence—Literature Humanities—was recognized as "an offshoot of Professor Erskine's Honors Readings in Great Books."[13] As Erskine had originally and unsuccessfully proposed, the course was required for all freshmen. It now spanned only one year and met in small sections four times a week. Mark Van Doren, who taught the course for 15 years, maintained that "nothing I ever did with students was more fun...[The books] proved, as

Erskine had predicted, to be wise friends for freshmen...Important questions raised themselves again and again; and the freshmen were astonished by their own competence to deal with them."[14]

Also in 1937, the most enduring and successful Great Books program in higher education was initiated as a unified and required course of study at St. John's College, Annapolis, Maryland. Stringfellow Barr, a former history professor at University of Virginia, and Scott Buchanan, who had used Great Books in outreach endeavors of the People's Institute of Cooper Union, convinced the St. John's trustees to try one last experiment to save the college from financial free fall. The results proved spectacular and lasting.[15]

While Erskine was pleased with the revival of the reading program that he had developed and nurtured into being, he also remained somewhat cynical about its termination and resuscitation. He reminded Clifton Fadiman:

> As soon as I left Columbia the course was abandoned. I felt that a good arrow had been shot into the air, and that was that. But, afterwards the Columbia alumni protested the abandoning of the course, and the authorities observed—I believe to their astonishment—that [University of] Chicago and St. John's [College] thought well of what they had failed to appreciate, so the reading course went back, stronger than ever.[16]

* * *

Early in 1937, John Erskine suffered a stroke that left him partially paralyzed on his right side, mostly in bed for several months, and deeply depressed. Although he slowly recovered most of his energy and his agility over a six-month period, he knew he would never be able to seriously perform at the piano again. His right hand, injured in the earlier auto accident and barely brought back with therapy, could never regain full strength after the initial paralysis from the stroke. He announced to the Juilliard board of directors that he would retire from the presidency on July 1, 1937, and he proposed that Ernest Hutcheson be appointed to succeed him. His health and his dream of "finding time to write, to study and to think" prompted him to give up his position of ten years with little hesitation or regret.[17]

A number of his friends and former Columbia colleagues thought the timing was right for him to return to Columbia and perhaps manage the new Literature Humanities course sections. His sister, Helen, for example, had urged him to announce his intent to resign from Juilliard as soon as possible so that President Butler might feel free to encourage him to end his indefinite leave of absence and return to teaching. "The members of the English Department who wish to have you return would be strengthened in their demands if it were known that you will be free," she wrote to him. She worried that "as far as Butler and these others know you may be so pleased with the work at the Juilliard that you have given up all thoughts of returning to teaching anywhere."[18]

Erskine's closest friend among former colleagues, Raymond Weaver, launched a campaign in the English Department to get him back. He reported to Erskine: "I spoke to [Department Chair Harrison R.] Steeves suggesting this as an eminently appropriate occasion for inviting you to help put 'Humanities' in effect. Steeves was frigidly evasive." Exasperated, Weaver decided that Steeves would "frustrate any attempt to resuscitate his lifeless department," so he took his suggestion to get Erskine back directly to Dean Herbert Hawkes. He was surprised when Hawkes insisted, "But Erskine is no longer on leave; he's off the books."[19]

In fact, Erskine had indeed been quietly removed from the books. It is likely that word of his Juilliard resignation had reached those Columbia administrators who didn't welcome the idea that he might end his indefinite leave and reappear on campus. Worried that he could insist on his right to return to a position from which he never resigned, they would have then maneuvered to prevent that possibility. Although Erskine had no idea it was in the works, a letter arrived from President Butler informing him that the trustees had voted to turn his leave into a retirement, effective July 1, 1937. In doing so, they designated him Professor Emeritus, an infrequent award and great honor, but nevertheless a retirement. In his letter, Butler put a positive, but unconvincing, spin on the move by reminding Erskine that the emeritus designation "ensures that your name will be carried on the university rolls and that you will continue as a member of the University family."[20]

*   *   *

Although Erskine was no longer president of Juilliard or an active faculty member at Columbia, he had not retired. He remained chairman of the board of directors of the Metropolitan Opera, a member of the board of directors of the Juilliard School of Music, and a trustee of the Juilliard Foundation. He was also a member of the board of directors of the Episcopalian schools, Trinity and St. Agatha, and of the MacDowell Colony, as well as a member of the Trinity vestry. Shortly after his resignation from Juilliard, he put finishing touches on the libretto he wrote for *The Sleeping Beauty*, a new opera composed by Cleveland Institute of Music director Beryl Rubinstein. It premiered at the Juilliard School early in 1938 and then moved to Ohio with the Cleveland Symphony Orchestra. Later that year, Erskine dove back into teaching. He commuted weekly to Pittsburgh to join conductor Fritz Reiner of the Pittsburgh Symphony in instructing a course in music appreciation offered by five local colleges at Carnegie Institute of Technology.

Even without the addition of piano solos at the conclusion of his addresses, Erskine's lecture touring schedule continued at a whirlwind pace. After finishing his teaching commitments in Pittsburgh, he made a swing through the South where he renewed his earlier acquaintance with DuBose and Dorothy Heyward in Charleston, South Carolina. He then spent a week lecturing at the University of Miami's Winter Institute, which he repeated annually for several more years. From there, he moved on to lecture in several Texas locations. Back in New York, he gave a lecture series on the evolution of music for Cooper Union.[21]

In mid-1939, he spent six weeks in Hollywood recording for West Coast radio programs and interviewing celebrities for his series of articles for *Liberty*. The latter endeavor, a more likely assignment for a rookie journalist than an educator of Erskine's stature, may have testified to either his extreme need of funds or his hearty enthrallment with Hollywood glitterati—or perhaps both. Among the articles he produced were: "Clark Gable's Secret Wish," "Mickey Mouse—Supported by Stokowski," and "Can Hollywood Stars Afford to be Good Actors?"[22] He made another trip to Hollywood the following year and reported "having a very delightful time" socializing with the three Marx brothers; meeting Walt Disney, Sinclair Lewis, and Robert Nathan; and working some at MGM on dialogue for a movie from the play *Kismet*. "The possibilities of life are so numerous in Hollywood," he exclaimed.[23]

Erskine's already substantial platform for speaking about music and literature was further enlarged in 1940 with his election to the post of chairman of the National Committee for Musical Appreciation, a fairly well-endowed private effort at musical understanding for everyone through accessible performances and recordings. His lecturing advanced under a new agent, Margaret Miller, who billed him as ready to deliver something for nearly everyone—whether on or off the course of his recognized expertise—through talks titled: "My America," "Abraham Lincoln," "Patrick Henry," "The Moral Obligation to Be Intelligent," "A Better Education," "The Fine Arts in Education," "The Art of Self-Education," "Walt Whitman and the Fine Arts," "Motion Pictures as an Art Form," "Transcendentalism and the Fine Arts," "The Influence of Women and Its Cure," and "The Adventure of Novel Writing."[24]

Eager to reiterate friendly international allegiances just prior to US involvement in World War II, the US State Department invited Erskine to join a small group of artists and writers who would tour South America to lecture, meet their counterparts, and generally spread neighborly cheer. The three-month goodwill junket, May through July, 1941, started with a three-week ocean voyage and included stops in Brazil, Uruguay, and Argentina. Erskine immediately delighted in a rhythm of daytime writing and evening socializing. Among the many artistic and business hotshots on board, those Erskine spent time with included: acclaimed operatic bass Salvatore Baccaloni, violinist Yehudi Menuhin, and Price Waterhouse partner Percival Brundage. Erskine's schedule at each stop was organized by US Embassy personnel and generally included frequent lectures, sometimes in French; lunches and dinners with South American writers, critics, academics, dramatists, and musicians; attendance at plays, film screenings, and cocktail parties; and interviews with local newspapers and magazines.

The only low point in Erskine's enjoyment of the countries he visited was a brief stop in Barbados. There, he became insular: "If England tries to give us the West Indies, we ought to throw them back. These little colonies are out of date and utter failures, and the colored people are now a headache for England and would be worse for us."[25] However, he was delighted with Rio de Janeiro, where the Rio Branca reminded him of a more sun-drenched version of boulevards in Paris and some of the downtown appeared a little like the oldest sections of New Orleans. Of Montevideo, he claimed "I lost my heart to the place at once." And in Buenos Aires, he thought again of Paris when he found "the same newspaper kiosks, the same cafes, the same old women selling papers or flowers, and the same damp coffee smell, particularly at night, when the mist is easy to see."[26]

During the trip, Erskine managed to write some nearly every-day and finish another book, *Song Without Words: The Story of Felix Mendelssohn*, published in 1941. When he returned, his writing continued from the spacious new apartment he had moved into at his 540 Park Avenue building, and he published articles in *Liberty*, *Collier's*, *Reader's Digest*, *Saturday Review of Literature*, the *North American Review*, the *New York Times Magazine*, and others.

Radio proved an ever-enlarging medium for Erskine as it expanded from music and talk to quiz shows, book readings, and celebrity interviews. He became a frequent guest on the quiz show "Information Please," where his former student Clifton Fadiman was master of ceremonies, and on discussion forum shows, like "The Mary Margaret McBride Program," "American's Town Meeting of the Air," and "Sunday Evening at Fannie Hurst's." He was typically introduced as "John Erskine, the administrator, author, editor, teacher, poet, novelist, dramatist, and musician."[27] Just prior to the US entrance into World War II, he often attached his promotion of music and literature to love of country and democracy. "Amateur music making should characterize a democracy and in favorable circumstances set an example for the practice of the arts," he told listeners to the NBC radio show "Get Ready for Tomorrow" in 1939, insisting that "the proper use of the arts is to articulate our ideals." Determined that censorship was particularly undemocratic, he maintained: "I regret the emotional condition of those fellow writers who refuse to have their books published in Germany. Should the Germans be deprived of democratic books just because Hitler attacks democracy? Or are we afraid that our books are not really representative of democracy?"[28]

* * *

By the decade of the 1940s, Erskine longed for his marital situation to be settled in a formal separation agreement, preferably a divorce. His son Graham had earned a doctorate in architecture from the University of Rome in 1937 and was thriving in the profession. His daughter Anna had attended acting school and was enjoying both some writing and some stage parts in New York. There was little reason for any charade of marital attachment. In 1941, pleading financial problems occasioned by medical bills, he suggested to Pauline that they "straighten out personal affairs" with a divorce.[29] She did not agree, but they did list their Wilton, Connecticut, property for sale. When it sold, Pauline, charged with the packing and moving chores, wrote a final letter from Wilton to her husband: "The Wilton chapter of my life is almost over. Looking back I find no romance, but much satisfaction—in the two splendid children I have raised, in this place (every room, shrub, flower and blade of grass bears witness to my care), and in my relations to the community...When you bought this place, I little thought this Herculean task of sorting and packing would fall to me to do alone."[30] Erskine was careful to let family members know that the sale of the Wilton property was leaving Pauline with "a quite considerable sum."[31]

In 1944, after at least 15 years of living almost completely separately, Pauline signed a separation agreement. Erskine committed to monthly alimony checks. Writing of the separation and impending divorce to his son, then an army engineer in Italy, he noted that he need not worry about his mother's financial well-being: "With whatever your mother inherits from [her mother] Grandma Ives and with her investment of the Wilton money, plus whatever else she had, she now will be pretty well off." A disciplined saver and conservative spender, unlike her husband, Pauline informed him and their son and daughter that she was saving money so that they could inherit. "She must do what she thinks is right, of course," a peevish Erskine told his son. "While you were children not able to take care of yourselves, I felt a special obligation toward you. Your mother apparently feels one still. I confess I am a bit disgusted to hand over money for investment purposes when I have no money to invest on my own account."[32] The divorce settlement gave Pauline one-fourth of Erskine's net income, after taxes, up to $2,400 a year.[33]

Pauline was as hurt as John Erskine was ecstatic about ending their marriage, and she was particularly protective about her relationship with her two adult children. When she got news that she was mentioned in his discussions with them, she wrote: "I have never interfered by word or deed in the children's relationship with you and think you might accord me a like courtesy. You are a strange man John Erskine. You used to say I did not understand you. The trouble was I understood you only too well and you knew and resented it."[34]

Erskine spent time in Reno, Nevada, during the spring and summer of 1945 and compiled the required six weeks of residency to qualify for the lenient divorces notable in that state. At 65 years old, his love for Helen Worden was stronger than ever, and he wrote her constantly while eagerly waiting for the divorce and his chance to marry her. He was elated to realize that their "unbelievable happiness together" was so near. He wrote of missing her and of planning for their life together, signing his letters, "Yours always, only yours."[35] They were married in Albuquerque, New Mexico, on July 3, 1945, just days after Erskine's 35-year marriage to Pauline ended in divorce. Earlier that week, his daughter Anna had married in New York City the playwright and producer Russel Crouse.[36]

*   *   *

Erskine's writing life came almost full circle back to his youthful start as an essayist. Perhaps sensing that his fiction had run its course, he turned to nonfiction historical treatments and essays for his book-length projects. Announcing his competence as a historical researcher and analyst, he authored *The Philharmonic Symphony Society of New York: Its First Hundred Years*, published in 1943 as both a chronological narrative and a reference volume—including the reproduction of many years of concert programs.[37] Next came *The Complete Life*, a book of essays on attaining cultured self-actualization in areas ranging from religion and politics to conversation and manners. Appropriately, he started the book with topics in which he could claim recognizable expertise: Reading and writing, followed by music. Only near the end of the volume did he tackle chapters on love, marriage, and parenting. His general thesis was that the active life is the good life. He promoted learning as essential to fulfillment and experience as essential to learning, apparently still viewing his own life as the struggle to balance intelligence and action that he first contemplated when he encountered George Edward Woodberry. Or perhaps he sought to justify choices he made that might seem untoward to others. His somewhat obscure codicil to his call to action warned: "Experience is of little value until sublimated by the mind and the spirit...possible only through the training and use of intelligence. But if this is the end of wisdom, the beginning is a willingness to keep our feet on the ground, to deal with experience as destiny flings it at us, and to be aware of all that is around us."[38] Peppered with examples from his own experiences from boyhood to adulthood, as well as with ample references to history and literature, the book won from reviewers adjectives like "fascinating," "fresh," and "stimulating."[39]

Barely two years later, Erskine attempted to explain Jesus in *The Human Life of Jesus*. Using passages from various versions of the Bible, as well as ancient and modern literature, he constructed a birth to resurrection biography. As if to warn off anyone seeking religious scholarship, he wrapped the narrative in his own brand of plain speak and meta-discourse: "We shall never know the whole truth about the innkeeper. His profession obscures his character." And, "If we had a full record of his boyhood, I think we should find him brooding even then on the puzzle of his life and, like other boys, the puzzle of himself."[40]

Undoubtedly, these books helped maintain Erskine's popular recognition and prompt the continuing invitations he received to lecture throughout the country and to write in mass-market magazines. His name was still widely recognized, and, as one Kansas City journalist reminded, "His distinction is sealed and certified by thirteen academic and honorary degrees."[41] Consumer advice articles added to his usual essay and opinion pieces with titles like: "Your Letters Speak for You" (in *Senior Scholastic)* and "The Happy Art of Conversation" and "Build Your Own Library" (in *Coronet*).[42]

* * *

During the World War II years and heated postwar period, it was inevitable that Erskine would be pressed for his opinions on political and social controversies. He gave them freely, but not with any particular unity of direction. For example, when he congratulated Amherst professor George Whicher (also a former Erskine student) on his public stand against college fraternities, Erskine noted that he too felt "Negroes, Jews, and other minority groups" should "be treated on an equality with the traditionally respectable and dumb" members of Greek organizations. He concluded to Whicher: "I'm glad you said a fair word for the Communists. If Karl Marx and the Russian Socialists after him hadn't believed that an attack on religion was essential to progress in economic and social justice, every intelligent Christian would have been a Communist long ago."[43] Yet, he soon decided to quit the National Institute of Arts and Letters because he viewed it as a "Communist-governed group."[44]

When the National Institute of Arts and Letters, in defense of the Screen Writers' Guild, decided to send a letter to the US House of

Representatives protesting the processes of the House Un-American Activities Committee (HUAAC), Erskine was one of a small minority of members who would not sign on. Explaining that he was "unwilling to approve or back or come to the rescue of the Communistic writers in Hollywood," he especially objected to individuals who refused to answer HUAAC questions about Communist organization membership. "I see no reason why they should ask or expect to have any privilege of secrecy which would enable them to continue to advance subversive purposes," he fumed.[45]

It is possible that Erskine was becoming more cranky than conservative. Although he had voted twice for Roosevelt and considered himself a liberal, by 1944 he decided that "if he insists on being president again, the disaster to the ideals he has stood for will be great."[46] And he emphatically felt the Columbia trustees, in their embrace of glamor and notoriety, had made a grievous mistake in selecting General Dwight Eisenhower as the university's president in 1948. If asked about where he leaned politically or socially, Erskine himself would probably have countered that he simply looked at every issue on its merits, without concern about inconsistent liberal versus conservative labels. Thus, the issue of censorship of the book *Forever Amber*, brought to his attention by Macmillan Company chairman, George P. Brett, Jr., put him in a real quandary. He despised censorship of all kinds, but he also disdained *Forever Amber* on literary grounds. When Brett asked him to put in writing an opinion that would help defend against Commonwealth of Massachusetts action to declare the book obscene and indecent, he owned up to both his views:

> I haven't read *Forever Amber*. From the reviews and from the remarks of those who had read it, I gathered that it would add nothing to my knowledge of life and manners during the Restoration... Its appeal to many people would lie in the frankness which for the same kind of reader would constitute the merit, let us say, of the Diary of Samuel Pepys. I cannot believe that you or the house of Macmillan would offer the public a book which seemed to you objectionable, and I believe your judgment is pretty sound. As for the sensors of Massachusetts, they have demonstrated so often their capacity for misjudging an excellent book that *Forever Amber* may be a far more important work of art than I supposed. If this statement would be helpful, you are welcome to use it.[47]

As the war years morphed into the boom years, Erskine's financial situation improved a bit. In 1948, the Juilliard trustees elected him president of the Juilliard Foundation and paid him well in the position. He and Helen were comfortable in their large apartment on Park Avenue, and they had a secretary and a cook. Although he regretted that he "hadn't yet piled up any reserves," he told his brother Bob that he was simply grateful "to scrape together a comfortable living from year to year."[48]

In a manner, Erskine also continued to teach as he neared his seventieth year. For several autumns, each week for ten weeks, a group of friends and acquaintances gathered in his living room to hear him lecture on, and then discuss, both current reading and ancient classical works. This time, Erskine was following in the footsteps of one of his students. Mortimer Adler had begun leading informal adult Great Books groups in Highland Park, Illinois, in 1930, shortly after he arrived at the University of Chicago. He later expanded with a downtown Chicago businessmen's group that he led with the University of Chicago president Robert Maynard Hutchins. When they formalized the endeavor by creating the Great Books Foundation, one of the first to lead an adult Great Books group under those auspices was another of Erskine's early General Honors students, Paul L. Myers, an Elkhart, Indiana, attorney.[49]

Erskine's involvement with Great Books also included his service on the editorial advisory board of the Encyclopedia Britannica publishing venture, *The Great Books of the Western World*, with Robert Maynard Hutchins as editor. Hutchins assured Erskine that he was his first selection for board membership, "since you are the father of this kind of study in the United States."[50] Others on the board comprised a veritable reunion of Erskine cronies in advocating for the humanities, including Mark Van Doren, Alexander Meiklejohn, Mortimer Adler, Scott Buchanan, and Stringfellow Barr. The meetings to select a list of books, as well as letters exchanged between meetings, were steeped in criticism, passion, and bartering, as books were proposed and choices were horse-traded. Hutchins sent out an initial list of 82 authors that contained most of Erskine's favorites, although he did suggest it "should be stronger in modern mathematics and works in natural science."[51] Demonstrating his enduring commitment to flexibility and revision in book listing, he stuck up for the inclusion of Mark Twain and Charles Dickens, although neither of them was on the original Columbia General Honors list. Likewise, neither made the final *Britannica* 54-volume list. He struggled against the tide to get Molière included, and he was a minority of one against Melville. He lost both those battles. Promoting Balzac, he complained to

Hutchins, "Your committee seem on the whole not much given to the study of French literature."[52]

Erskine's defeat in many of the book-choosing skirmishes was muted by his sense of little personal investment in the outcome. Later, he noted that he had readily recognized and somewhat enjoyed "very much the same kind of discussion which delayed the original selection of the great books for the Columbia course." He was pleased to find himself "amazed that my simple suggestion for studying great books by the most natural of all methods should have led us so far."[53]

As Erskine scanned back over the horizon of his life, he determined that a summing up was due. True to the expansive manner and multitudinous interests that had marked his journey from public intellectual to prominent celebrity, he planned not a single memoir, but a four-volume series. The first would summarize his life broadly, while the other three would hone in on his teaching, his music, and his writing. All would skip briefly over his personal life and concentrate on his professional accomplishments and friendships. *The Memory of Certain Persons*, first in the planned quartet, was labeled "an autobiography" and proceeded chronologically through Erskine's early years and on to his professional pursuits. His personal life was somewhat skewed toward his experiences with his son Graham and his early years with his siblings and parents. Tellingly, nearly 20 percent of the book was dedicated to fewer than two years of his life: his time in France during World War I—the glory days that introduced him to the heady sense of action and company of active people who would attract him ever after. Only a scant five pages described his experience in initiating and teaching Great Books. True to its title, the book emphasized Erskine's friends and associates through the years—from Mortimer Adler and George Antheil to Carl Zigrosser and Hans Zinsser. Appropriately enough, his memories side stepped romantic interests, such as Anaïs Nin or Adeline Atwater, although he did briefly own up to a first wife. His former friend and publisher Laurance Chambers was not included in the more than 700 personalities who marched through the pages. Nevertheless, the volume added some valuable life and detail to the turn-of-the-century history of Columbia University, the establishment of the AEF University in France, and the early machinations at the Juilliard School. Erskine was not particularly disappointed to realize that the volume "made no great commotion." Instead, he was exceedingly pleased that it spurred numerous letters to him from former colleagues and students.[54]

The next two Erskine memoirs closed out the planned set of four as a trilogy: *My Life as a Teacher* and *My Life in Music*, published in 1948 and 1950 respectively. Episodic narratives, they explained and justified some elements of Erskine's professional life, such as his use of Juilliard funds to take control of the Institute of Musical Art and the Metropolitan Opera. They also described his philosophies of education in literature and music. Apparently, fiction writing was still as much a reflex as an art for Erskine. He found a way, among his memoir writing, to reach into his grab bag of genres past and create another novel based on ancient Greek mythology relocated to contemporary society. In *Venus, the Lonely Goddess*, he again launched ancient gods and mortals into bemused modern dialogue about love and life, adding thoughts about war and its role in defining the differences between men and women.[55]

The third memoir, *My Life in Music*, marked the end of Erskine's professional activities. Late in 1948, he fought off a work hiatus of several months occasioned by high blood pressure and then optimistically began planning for ventures that included more articles, lectures, a motion picture script, and travel. However, the next year he suffered a cerebral hemorrhage. After six months, he had recovered his speech but only some slight walking ability. While he could not make public appearances, friends and colleagues stopped by the apartment frequently, and his adoring Helen stayed at his side 24 hours a day. When he was unable to attend a thirtieth anniversary celebration of the Columbia General Honors Course that had been arranged by Jacques Barzun, he penned a greeting to be read to the group with the pithy and cogent statement: "You of my original Great Books course are living proof that Columbia did not sink to the complacent scholastic level of universities where the most adventurous theories are heard without the flutter of a whisker since everybody knows nothing will be done about it."[56]

Erskine recovered just enough energy to determine he must make one last trip to France to see his beloved Beaune. The seven-month trip with Helen, a nurse, a wheelchair, many pieces of luggage, a pet parrot, and medicines did nothing for his health and seemed to include more small embolisms, one that caused aphasia. He was disappointed in Beaune; by then it had attracted far too many tourists for his taste. Most of the stay in Europe was spent consulting doctors in Paris and London. Helen thought of taking him to a nursing home in France, but the doctors advised that he return to the United States. Back in

New York in May, 1951, he was a complete invalid dependent on a day and a night nurse. He could do little but enjoy the homey comfort of his surroundings, especially the wall in his apartment devoted to France and displaying his certificate of honorary Beaune citizenship and his diplomas of honorary degrees from the Universities of Bordeaux and Burgundy. Columbia Journalism School student Jules Witcover was hired to come read to him on weekends.[57]

John Erskine died at home on June 2, 1951. His funeral, at Columbia University's St. Paul's Chapel, was attended by 300 friends and family members. Fittingly for one whose very finest work was as an educator, it included a eulogy by his former student Clifton Fadiman, hymns sung by the Columbia student choir, and a casket draped with the blue and white Columbia University flag adorned with its emblematic crown.[58] Erskine had determined that a life ended was not as disturbing to him as a life forgotten. Perhaps explaining his lifelong impulse to implement ideas, influence students, acquire renown, and leave behind ample material evidence in more than 30 published volumes, he had admitted: "I have little fear of death, yet I cannot contemplate with equanimity the fact that on this earth I shall some day be altogether forgotten, and my place shall know me no more."[59]

CODA

The most tempting, and perhaps least complicated, interpretation of John Erskine's life narrative is the rise and fall story: the tale of a brilliant and multi-talented educator who sold out to commercial inclinations and undisciplined impulses. A wider angle perspective, however, could elevate Erskine to the pedestal of benevolent caretaker over middlebrow masses, chipping away at the barricades of cultural elitism and enabling average citizens access to emblems of good taste and able intellect. Still another explanation might focus on his pioneering expedition into celebrity professor territory, a journey that broke trail for a long line of media-savvy academics to follow—exemplified post-Erskine by Bergen Evans, Carl Sagan, and Pepper Schwartz on the small screen; by Lionel Trilling, Saul Bellow, James Dickey, and Henry Louis Gates in print; and by Cornel West everywhere.

None of these interpretive possibilities are inaccurate or unrealistic. Each easily clarifies Erskine's contributions and limitations, and each alleviates the complexity of multidimensional achievement that has confounded his lasting recognition as an important educator. Even taken together, however, these summary analyses fail to account for larger contexts undergirding Erskine's life and work. His public fame was launched by his fiction writing and cemented by his appearances with great symphony orchestras, in lecture halls and on radio. His academic prominence was rooted in his poetry and essays, supported by lectures on campuses throughout the country. But his most significant achievements were in other areas. His design of a Great Books reading and discussion program gave impetus to scores of outreach efforts and curricular designs aimed at resuscitating liberal education and modeling a common core. His development of the unique American Expeditionary Forces (AEF) University in France demonstrated conceptual and administrative possibilities for higher learning beyond the confines of traditional academic structures and models. And his leadership in setting the Juilliard School on a path to continuing national prominence established Erskine as an exceptional educational executive.

Upon his death, Erskine was most frequently viewed as a well-known personality, a popular author, and—most pleasing to himself—a superb teacher and mentor whose hundreds of grateful students were forging their own paths of cultural and creative influence. A reassessment with the dual advantages of longitudinal perspective and decades of historical reconstructions further illuminates his life and contributions.

*   *   *

As Erskine enlarged his role as a traditional professor and scholar to embrace action and creativity, he proved particularly adept at combining his high regard for the comforts of an upscale Victorian upbringing with his enjoyment of the more spirited imperatives of a new generation. Rather than choosing either, he managed to adopt both of what George Santayana identified as "two mentalities, one a survival of the beliefs and standards of the fathers, the other an expression of the instincts, practice, and discoveries of the younger generations."[1] Santayana, however, was primarily concerned with how the opposing elements of romantic complacency and assertive action shaped American cultural and intellectual life. While the philosopher referred to a collective genteel American mind and enterprising American will, Erskine demonstrated the possibility that the same duality could inhabit a single individual.[2]

Both sides of Santayana's bifurcated representation served Erskine well. His self-discipline at writing, practicing piano, and remaining uninvolved in academic quarrels echoed the moral obligations of his privileged and Protestant youth. His romantic attraction to poetry, music, and the sound of ancient languages, as well as his lifelong fascination with the idea of beauty, signaled the lingering presence of that earlier life. These were the elements loudly scorned by the disaffected Randolph Bourne, but Bourne's analysis proved only partial, truncated by his early death. By piling on multiple talents and activities, Erskine managed to deftly sidestep many negative outcomes of gentility, identified by Van Wyck Brooks as "the spiritual inadequacy of American life...provincialism, colonialism, naiveté, and romantic self-complacency."[3] While he admired and even enjoyed some particulars wrought by Victorian highbrows, Erskine was on guard against the disengagement from reality and risk that defined their world. His AEF University undertaking in France convinced him that he could confront difficulties and initiate action, even amid the messiness of unforeseen challenges and unknowable consequences. He then began to favor bold strokes in his writing and his music and, most notably, in launching the Great Books curriculum and the Juilliard School of Music. His ensuing high-wire act became a precarious and lifelong balancing trick between the sweet comfort of gentility and the heady opportunity of action. A misstep too far in one direction would mean a slip into irrelevance, while a move too far in the other would mark a slide into crude commercialism or personal smallness.

Just as Erskine embodied the two sides of Santayana's split personality nation, his life chronology straddled what Robert Wiebe viewed as an American march away from anchorless dislocation and toward orderly continuity. At the time of Erskine's birth, according to Wiebe, Americans were in a state of post-Reconstruction chaos and indecision that pervaded economic, commercial, and political life. "Americans in a basic sense no longer knew who or what they were. The setting had altered beyond their power to understand it."[4] An emerging middle class in the early twentieth century finally tackled the job of sense making by embracing bureaucracy, professionalism, standardization, and rationality—crucial tools of the progressive impulse. The academic world that Erskine entered was a microcosm of Gilded Age ways and values, with its keen sensibilities about identity and propriety and its germination of isolated groups and individuals untouched by larger forces. But by 1920, the changes incubated in the middle class search for order, as well as the success of the military bureaucracy, signaled for Erskine a new and welcome world indeed. His support for widespread educational access and for common coursework, combined with his enthusiasm for professional groups of writers, intellectuals, and musicians, began here.

The shifts observed by Wiebe played out in Erskine's career and creative endeavors. It was not surprising that he opted to exchange his professorial position for the life of the academic executive, a place where outcomes were clear and isolation was unlikely. It was also possible for Erskine to find continuity of outlook—an ordering—in his other varied endeavors, particularly the intersection of his fiction and popular nonfiction writing, his musical performance, and his presence in radio and print media. He convinced himself that his teaching (especially of the Great Books), his writing (especially its treatment of characters from ancient history and mythology), and his musical performances (especially those with small-town civic orchestras) had a unifying theme of bringing social and intellectual evidence of good breeding and good taste to wider audiences. However, that interpretation may have been as much rationalization as rationale—a comforting notion that fit well with the national dash toward middlebrow culture but failed to fully explain human motivations. By his own admission, Erskine thoroughly enjoyed action, applause, popular renown, and the bon vivant life; while his spending habits required commercial success. The confluence of timing, national mood, and personal preference was ideal for enabling the multi-talented Erskine both to widely and significantly contribute and to individually and significantly benefit.

Only in more localized ways—especially concerning his first wife—did Erskine fall short of the success he sought. By the time they divorced, he had spent more years committed to other women than to Pauline. Although he grumbled about her behavior during the final breakup, he knew he had handled the marital disintegration badly. His children grew into successful adults, but he observed their sadness with his general absence occasioned by a second life on his own. His friendships and professional associations were many, but as he became more politically conservative, some inevitably fizzled. He puzzled about academic advancement, never reaching department chair, much less president, at Columbia. When he might have returned to campus after his Juilliard resignation, the leave-of-absence rug was pulled out from under him. Yet, there is no evidence that these circumstances left Erskine with great regrets or any sense that he had paid too high a price for his commitment to experience, enjoyment, and recognition.

* * *

While Erskine's notoriety was rooted in his popular novels and subsequent radio engagements, scriptwriting gigs, lectures, concerts, and articles, his lasting legacy clearly was shaped by his initiation of a Great Books curriculum and his presidency of the Juilliard School of Music. And that is as it should be, for in launching these entities he led a charge for survival of the arts and humanities against a tidal wave of academic specialization and professional training. Convinced that the "average citizen" could benefit from learning music, reading great literature, and numerous other areas of liberal learning, he insisted that "a truly liberal education would offer instruction in all subjects...and in every subject we should aim at knowledge rather than at information or opinion."[5]

Judged by its spread and endurance, the idea of the Great Books as college curriculum was a spectacular success. Mortimer Adler was the first to nurture an offshoot when he convinced Scott Buchanan that the idea was a perfect fit for the "People's Institute," an outreach project of Cooper Union. Buchanan and others (mostly former Columbia "General Honors" students) then taught the Great Books in public libraries throughout New York City. Buchanan eventually landed at University of Virginia, where he teamed with Stringfellow Barr in initiating a Great Books honors program. Shortly after Robert Maynard Hutchins was appointed president of the University of Chicago in 1929, he had dinner with Adler. They had become friends during Hutchins's years as dean of the Yale Law School, and Hutchins confessed that he had not given much thought to education beyond legal learning. Adler could only tell him "what had been the most important factor in my own education—the Erskine General Honors course at Columbia [which] had done more for my mind than all the rest of the academic pursuits in which I had been so far engaged."[6] Adler soon joined the faculty at the University of Chicago, brought Buchanan and Barr to the campus for a year of consultation, and nurtured the presence of the Great Books at Chicago and elsewhere. Buchanan and Barr then took the idea to St. John's College, Annapolis, Maryland, launching the enduring flagship among colleges wholly built on the curricular foundation of reading in Great Books.[7] Great Books reading programs at community colleges, summer schools, adult education ventures, and local reading groups were soon to follow, often aided by the Great Books Foundation and various publishing programs that continue to promote Great Books access.[8]

Measured by its influence on scores of Erskine students—many of whom later influenced their own students, readers, audiences, and institutions—the Great Books idea gathered intergenerational steam. Adler, Trilling, Fadiman, Barzun, and dozens of others fanned out to craft new curriculums, teach, lead reading groups, and extol the virtues of Great Books. The idea became one of three major streams that developed to keep liberal education alive in the twentieth century, according to Stanley N. Katz. The first was the "distribution system" of selection from a wide variety of arts and humanities courses, as pioneered at Princeton in the late nineteenth century. The idea of a common core came next, initiated by both

Erskine's reading curriculum and the Contemporary Civilization survey course at Columbia after World War I and later taken up at the University of Chicago and Harvard. The third and final stream was a process-oriented approach emphasizing reflective thought and individual cognitive development, rather than content, favored by John Dewey and his band of progressive educators. These streams remain foundational to various current approaches to liberal education, observed Katz: "The challenge has seemed to be modifying the historical principles of general education in order to bring them up to date."[9]

Erskine's move to Juilliard, just when his General Honors course was winning over some skeptical colleagues and growing in student numbers, was somewhat of a mystery. The Juilliard Foundation trustees were indecisive about direction; its Graduate School was a loose group of isolated teaching projects; and squabbles among those involved were well publicized. Yet, Erskine jumped into the fray. Perhaps he determined that any ladder climbing at Columbia was stymied by his commercial success in popular fiction. His colleagues were undoubtedly somewhat envious and more than a little irked that his major work had no relationship to the studious, if plodding, scholarship that was the academic coin of the realm. Additionally, by the time he agreed to assume the presidency of the Juilliard School of Music, he was a public figure with an estate in Connecticut, an apartment in Manhattan, speaking tours, admirers, a mistress, and a heady social life. He was well primed for an enthusiastic leap into the unknown.

Erskine was a compromise choice between those who wanted the Juilliard presidency but polarized the trustees and those who solidified trustee agreement but didn't want the job. But he turned out to be exactly what the school needed—someone with new ideas about the place of music education in the arts and humanities, a democratic commitment to access and outreach, enthusiasm for contemporary and American musical arts, and national name recognition that could draw attention to the school. He was able to connect Juilliard to not only music lovers, but also to interested individuals in a wide range of endeavors, whether highbrow or middlebrow. His leadership, couched in intuitive behavior and personal characteristics, rather than goals and strategies, set the Juilliard School of Music on its path to eminence—now as The Juilliard School (including Divisions of Dance and Drama) located at Lincoln Center and responsible for the careers of hundreds of great contributors to the fine arts throughout the world.

Inevitably, Erskine's ideas for increased access to great literature and fine music would quickly attract what Jacques Barzun observed as "the fatal stain" of "popularity"—especially since Erskine's approach also included popularizing revered ancient stories in contemporary novels and modern musical librettos.[10] Yet Barzun also comprehended far more about the nature of culture and knowledge than the stain painters and may have recalled his teacher John Erskine when he concluded: "The highbrow guardians failed to understand how the things they cherished depend on stirrings down below. A chance encounter with a novel, a symphony, a painting, will impel a young mind to go on—and up...Knowledge lives by being known, not stored. Like religion, like culture, it is a possession held in common as widely as possible."[11]

* * *

In addition to the rise of the Great Books and of the Juilliard School, Erskine's legacy as a writer continued for some time after his death through a small flurry of reprints and new editions. In 1966, Kennikat Press republished his 1920 *The Kinds of Poetry: And Other Essays,* and Books for Libraries Press brought out his 1910 *Leading American Novelists.* Appearing since then have been editions of *The Moral Obligation to Be Intelligent* (1969, Books for Libraries Press); *The Literary Discipline* (1970, Scholarly Press); *The Complete Life* (1971, Books for Libraries Press); *My Life in Music* (1973, Greenwood Press); and *The Delight of Great Books* (1974, Scholarly Press). However, Erskine would have been most delighted to see that even with reprints and new editions of his work, his popularity in print eventually would be eclipsed by his grandson, Timothy Crouse, whose 1973 best seller, *The Boys on the Bus,* remains in print in its second paperback edition.

Erskine also would have been pleased at the publishing success of many of his students and young friends, perhaps particularly Anaïs Nin. In 1928, after Nin read to him some of her diary entries about himself, he decided she was a particularly perceptive writer. He asked her to hold onto her insights and write about them in a biography after his death.[12] Possibly sensing too little distance—in time and emotion—for an appropriate treatment of his life, she ignored the request. Her response was appropriate for a subject of inordinate capacity driven by enigmatic motivations. Lloyd Morris, the successful former student so taken by Erskine's first reading of his first novel, attempted an explanation: "For Erskine, the challenge of opportunity was always to be irresistible, and perhaps because it was, it was likewise incessant. His versatility astonished any average mind. Mere ambition seemed an inadequate explanation. One had to look deeper to find the secret spring."[13] In fact, Morris oversimplified. For Erskine, that spring was a complex network of swirling and sometimes counter-directional tributaries that defined his talents and interests. Pooled together, those disparate energies surfaced as enduring achievements, earning Erskine's legacy as the leading activist for the academic survival and popular expansion of fine arts and humanities.

Abbreviations

ACASC	Amherst College Archives and Special Collections
COCSC	College of Charleston Special Collections (Addlestone Library, Charleston, SC)
CUAC	Columbia University Archives
CUOHR	Columbia University Oral History Research Office
CURBM	Columbia University Rare Book and Manuscript Library (Butler Library, New York, NY)
IUMD	Indiana University Manuscripts Department (Lilly Library, Bloomington, IN)
JCA	Juilliard College Archives
LOCMD	Library of Congress Manuscript Division
LOCRS	Library of Congress Recorded Sound Reference Center
NLALAP	Newberry Library Adeline Lobdell Atwater Papers (Chicago, IL)
UPRBML	University of Pennsylvania Annenberg Rare Book and Manuscript Library

NOTES

INTRODUCTION

1. Lloyd Morris, *A Threshold in the Sun* (New York: Harper and Brothers, 1943), 89–90. Also see Jerry E. Patterson, *Fifth Avenue: The Best Address.* (New York: Rizzoli International, 1998); and Francis Steegmuller, "Oldest Hotels," *The New Yorker*, September 22, 1934, 18.
2. Quoted in Oscar James Campbell, "The Department of English and Comparative Literature," in *The Faculty of Philosophy*, ed. D. C. Miner (New York: Columbia University Press, 1957), 79.
3. Morris, *A Threshold in the Sun* and John Erskine, *The Memory of Certain Persons* (Philadelphia, PA: J.P. Lippincott, 1947), 356.
4. Quoted in Helen Huntington Smith, "Professor's Progress," *The New Yorker*, December 27, 1927, 28.
5. Morris, *A Threshold in the Sun*, 90.
6. Ibid.
7. John Carter, "The Wit and Wisdom of Helen of Troy," *New York Times*, November 9, 1925, 15.
8. D. Laurance Chambers. Typescript memo to files, January 4, 1926. The Bobbs-Merrill Manuscript Collection (hereafter referred to as Bobbs-Merrill MSS), Box 48, IUMD.
9. John Erskine to D. Laurance Chambers, April 20, 1926. John Erskine to D. Laurance Chambers, February 4, 1927. D. Laurance Chambers to John Erskine, February 23, 1927. Bobbs-Merrill MSS, Box 48, IUMD.
10. John Erskine to D. Laurance Chambers, December 29, 1925. D. Laurance Chambers to John Erskine, February 23, 1927. Bobbs-Merrill MSS, Box 48, IUMD.
11. Earlier popular academics and public intellectuals (e.g., Webster, Emerson, James) relied on lecture touring and writing to achieve widespread acclaim. Technological advances in printing and entertainment uses of radio, however, marked a new age for mass appeal among marketable personalities.
12. Lionel Trilling, "Some Notes for an Autobiographical Lecture," in *The Last Decade: Essays and Reviews, 1965–1975*, ed. D. Trilling

(New York: Harcourt Brace, 1979), 234. Although Erskine first suggested a course in great books for all undergraduates in 1915, his colleagues turned it down. They reconsidered during the post–World War I impulse for Western foundations, but limited the audience to honors students. The reading list, modified regularly, was laden with Greek and Roman philosophers, as well as Western European authors such as Dante, Montaigne, Shakespeare, Voltaire, and Rousseau.

13. Untitled typescript, course list, 1895. Erskine Papers, Uncatalogued, Box 7, CURBM (hereafter referred to as Erskine Papers).

14. Joan Shelley Rubin, *The Making of Middlebrow Culture* (Chapel Hill: The University of North Carolina Press, 1992), 151.

15. John Erskine, *The Memory of Certain Persons* (Philadelphia: J.B. Lippincott, 1947), 94.

16. Ibid., 74.

17. David J. Leese, "The Pragmatic Vision: Columbia College and the Progressive Reorganization of the Liberal Core—the Formative Years, 1880–1941" (PhD diss., Columbia University, 1987), 119. See also Robert A. McCaughey, *Stand, Columbia: A History of Columbia University in the City of New York, 1754–2004* (New York: Columbia University Press, 2003).

18. Frank Bowles, "Annual Report of the Director of University Admissions," 1951, Central Records, Bowles folders, CUAC.

19. J. David Hoeveler, *The New Humanism: A Critique of Modern America, 1900–1940* (Charlottesville: University Press of Virginia, 1977), 3.

20. Jacques Barzun, *From Dawn to Decadence: 500 Years of Western Cultural Life* (New York: Harper Collins, 2000), 606–607.

21. Ibid., 5.

22. Gerald Graff, *Professing Literature: An Institutional History* (Chicago: The University of Chicago Press, 1987), 55.

23. Ibid., 94.

24. Quoted in Randolph Bourne, "The Professor" in *The History of a Literary Radical and Other Essays*, ed. Van Wyck Brooks (New York: B.W. Heubsch, 1920), 94.

25. See John Erskine, *The Moral Obligation to be Intelligent* (New York: Duffield and Company, 1915).

26. Alan Willard Brown, "The Columbia College Colloquium on Important Books," *Journal of General Education* (July 1, 1948): 278–286.

27. Robert H. Wiebe, *The Search for Order: 1877–1920* (New York: Hill and Wang, 1967), 287.

28. John Erskine to Rhoda Erskine, January 14, 1919. Erskine Papers, Correspondence Files, Box 6, CURBM.

29. Barzun, *From Dawn to Decadence*, 714, 717.
30. See, for example, David Riesman, Nathan Glazer, and Reuel Denney, *The Lonely Crowd: A Study of the Changing American Character* (New Haven: Yale University Press, 1950); Rubin, *The Making of Middlebrow Culture*; and Warren I. Susman, *Culture as History* (New York: Pantheon, 1984).
31. Erskine, *The Memory*, 343.
32. Well received among Erskine's published volumes by 1925 were: *Actaeon and Other Poems* (New York: J. Lane Co., 1907); *Great American Writers* (with W. P. Trent) (New York: Henry Holt, 1912); *The Moral Obligation to be Intelligent* (New York: Duffield and Company, 1915); *The Kinds of Poetry and Other Essays* (Port Washington, NY: Kennikat Press, 1920); *Democracy and Ideals: A Definition* (New York: George H. Doran, 1920); and *The Literary Discipline* (New York: Duffield and Company, 1923). He also coauthored with his sister, Helen Erskine, an English text book: *Written English: A Guide to the Rules of Composition* (New York: The Century Co., 1914). For reference to "presidencies," see Erskine, *The Memory*, 341, and Anna Erskine Crouse, interview with the author, March 26, 2008.
33. Erskine, *The Memory*, 357.
34. See Dwight Macdonald, "Masscult and Midcult: I," *Partisan Review* 27 (Spring 1960): 203–233 and "Masscult and Midcult: II," *Partisan Review* 27 (Fall 1960): 589–631. Macdonald noted "midcult" as the more dangerous of the two, especially in terms of tendencies he viewed in its vulgarization of the arts.
35. Janice Radway, "The Scandal of the Middlebrow: The Book-of-the-Month Club, Class Fracture, and Cultural Authority," *South Atlantic Quarterly* 89 (Fall 1990): 714.
36. Richard Hofstadter, *Anti-Intellectualism in American Life* (New York: Alfred Knopf, 1963).
37. David O. Levine, *The American Culture and the Culture of Aspiration, 1915–1940* (Ithaca, NY: Cornell University Press, 1986), 102.
38. Helen Lefkowitz Horowitz, *Campus Life: Undergraduate Cultures from the End of the Eighteenth Century to the Present* (New York: Alfred A. Knopf, 1987).
39. Rubin, *The Making of Middlebrow Culture*, 16.
40. Ibid., 18.
41. John Erskine, "Afterthoughts of Lady Godiva," *Cosmopolitan* (March 1929), 10–35, 192. "The Candor of Don Juan," *Cosmopolitan* (November 1931), 58–61, 122–126.
42. See Erskine, *The Memory* and Erskine, *My Life in Music* (Westport, CT: Greenwood Press, 1950).

43. Reviewer letter, N.A., n.d. Bobbs-Merrill MSS, Box 49, "Bachelor of Arts" Folder, IUMD. Jessica Mannon, internal memo, n.d. Bobbs-Merrill MSS, Box 49, "Forget if You Can" Folder, IUMD. Laurance Chambers to John Erskine, January 31, 1938. Bobbs-Merrill MSS, Box 48, IUMD.

44. See Katherine R. Chaddock, "A Canon of Democratic Intent: Reinterpreting the Roots of the Great Books Movement," *The History of Higher Education Annual* 22 (2003); and Hugh S. Moorhead, "The Great Books Movement" (PhD diss., University of Chicago, 1964).

45. Helen H. Smith, "Professor's Progress," *The New Yorker*, December 19, 1927, 27.

46. Edna Levey, "John Erskine Discourses Lightly on Art, Music Morals, and Female Intelligence," unpublished typescript, January 22, 1931, 2. Bobbs-Merrill MSS, Box 48.

47. William S. Knickerbocker, "John Erskine: Enough of His Mind to Explain His Art," *Sewanee Review* 35 (April 1927): 155.

48. Morris, *A Threshold in the Sun*, 85–86.

1 Gifted Boy of the Gilded Age

1. John Erskine, *The Memory of Certain Persons* (Philadelphia, PA: J. P. Lippincott, 1947), 20.

2. For family background and boyhood information, see the memoirs: Erskine, *The Memory*, 9–49; and John Erskine, *My Life in Music* (Westport, CT: Greenwood Press, 1950), 1–10.

3. George Santayana, "The Genteel Tradition in American Philosophy (1911)," in *Nine Essays by George Santayana*, ed. Douglas L. Wilson (Cambridge: Harvard University Press, 1967), 39–41.

4. John Erskine to Laurance Chambers, October 28, 1929. Bobbs-Merrill MSS, Box 48, IUMD.

5. John Erskine, *The Kinds of Poetry* (New York: Duffield and Company, 1920), 44.

6. John Erskine to "*Santa Claus*," n.d., 1888. Erskine Biographical File, Box 4, CURBM.

7. John Erskine, *The Complete Life* (New York: Jullian Messner, 1943), 125–128.

8. Erskine, *The Memory*, 23.

9. Erskine, *The Complete Life*, 78. Also see Erskine, *My Life in Music*, 2.

10. Erskine, *My Life in Music*, 8.

11. Ibid., 9.

12. Horace Coon, *Columbia: Colossus on the Hudson* (New York: E.P. Dutton, 1947), 146–149.

13. Erskine, *The Memory*, 62.

14. Melville Cane, *All and Sundry: An Oblique Autobiography* (New York: Harcourt, Brace & World, 1968), 169.
15. John Erskine, handwritten notes. Erskine Papers, Uncatalogued, "Columbia" Folder, Box 7, CURBM.
16. Erskine, *The Memory*, 63.
17. Cane, *All and Sundry*, 170.
18. Erskine, *The Memory*, 66.
19. Cane, *All and Sundry*, 169.
20. Erskine, *The Memory*, 67.

2   THE COLUMBIA STAMP

1. Virginia Gildersleeve, *Many a Good Crusade* (New York: Macmillan, 1954), 42.
2. Ludwig Lewisohn, *Upstream: An American Chronicle* (New York: Boni and Liveright, 1922), 104.
3. Frederick P. Keppel, *Columbia* (New York: Oxford University Press, 1914), 80–81.
4. Melville Cane, "Reminiscences," typescript, 1956, 11, CUOHR.
5. Gildersleeve, *Many a Good Crusade*, 42.
6. Keppel, *Columbia*, 275–276.
7. Melville Cane, *All and Sundry: An Oblique Autobiography* (New York: Harcourt, Brace & World, 1968), 103.
8. John Erskine, *The Memory of Certain Persons* (Philadelphia, PA: J. P. Lippincott, 1947), 96.
9. Erskine described Harrison as a "kindly humorist" who sat near him in classes due to alphabetical ordering; he referred to Alsberg as a "strangely gifted…poet and cello player" (*The Memory*, 81). See Henry S. Harrison, *Queed* (Boston: Houghton Mifflin, 1911). For information on Alsberg's experiences as a radical among Russian anarchists and his work with the Federal Writers' Project, see Jerre Mangione, *The Dream and the Deal: The Federal Writers' Project, 1935–1943* (Syracuse, NY: Syracuse University Press, 1996).
10. N.A., "The New Columbia Professor," *Harper's Weekly*, April 1882, 268–269.
11. Erskine, *The Memory*, 86.
12. Ferris Greenslet, *Under the Bridge: An Autobiography* (Boston: Houghton Mifflin, 1943), 49.
13. Upton Sinclair, *The Goose-Step* (Pasadena, CA: Published by the Author, 1922), 12.
14. Sinclair, *The Goose-Step*, 15.
15. George Edward Woodberry, *Heart of Man, and Other Papers* (New York: Harcourt, Brace and Howe, 1920).

16. Hans Zinsser, *As I Remember Him: The Biography of R.S.* (Boston: Little, Brown, and Co., 1940), 46.

17. Joel Spingarn, "George Edward Woodberry," in *Dictionary of American Biography, Volume X*, ed. M. Dumas (New York: Charles Scribner's Sons, 1937), 479.

18. Lionel Trilling, "The Van Amringe and Keppel Eras," in *A History of Columbia College on Morningside*, ed. Irwin Edman (New York: Columbia University Press, 1954), 125. For discussions of Woodberry's close philosophical kinship with Matthew Arnold and influence from Charles Eliot Norton, see David J. Leese, "The Pragmatic Vision: Columbia College and the Progressive Reorganization of the Liberal Core—The Formative Years, 1880–1941" (PhD diss., Columbia University, 1987); and Joan Shelley Rubin, *The Making of Middlebrow Culture* (Chapel Hill: The University of North Carolina Press, 1992).

19. Spingarn, "George Edward Woodberry," 481.

20. Brander Matthews, "Literary Men and Public Affairs," *North American Review*, April 1909, 533.

21. Brander Matthews, *The Historical Novel and Other Essays* (New York: Charles Scribner's Sons, 1901). See also, Oscar James Campbell, "The Department of English and Comparative Literature," in *A History of the Faculty of Philosophy*, ed. Jacques Barzun (New York: Columbia University Press, 1957), 58–101.

22. George Edward Woodberry, *The Appreciation of Literature* (New York: Baker & Taylor, 1907), 176.

23. William James to Mrs. Henry Whitman, June 7, 1899, *The Letters of William James*, ed. Henry James, Vol. 2 (Boston: The Atlantic Monthly Press, 1920), 89.

24. N.A., "Trouble at Columbia," *New York Times*, April 28, 1902, 2.

25. Erskine, *The Memory*, 87.

26. Woodberry to Low, September 9, 1898, quoted in Trilling, *A History of Columbia College*, 73.

27. Matthews to Low, November 9, 1899, quoted in Trilling, *A History of Columbia College*, 73.

28. Greenslet, *Under the Bridge*, 54.

29. Erskine, *The Memory*, 93.

30. Ibid., 93–94.

31. Edward MacDowell to Seth Low, April 27, 1896 and Seth Low to Edward MacDowell, June 4, 1896. Low Papers, Box 11, CUAC.

32. Erskine, *The Memory*, 74. See also, Douglas Moore, "The Department of Music," in *A History of the Faculty of Philosophy*, ed. Jacques Barzun (New York: Columbia University Press, 1957), 269–288.

33. John Erskine, "MacDowell at Columbia: Some Recollections," *The Musical Quarterly* 28, no. 2 (October 1942): 397–398.

34. Erskine, *The Memory*, 78.

35. The Marching Song words: "When you're marching for Columbia, you better march like men; and every mile you march with her you'll wish were eight or ten. When you're marching for Columbia, your four years won't be long; and then you'll wish you back again to sing her marching song." Typescript in Erskine Papers, Uncatalogued, Box 7, CURBM.

36. Melville Cane, "Reminiscences," 1956, CUOHR. Also see Von W. Boardman, "After Class," in *A History of Columbia College on Morningside*, ed. Irwin Edman (New York: Columbia University Press, 1954), 163–198. For a detailed description of the Columbia University commencement exercises, see "Class Day at Columbia," *The New York Times*, June 12, 1900, 5.

37. Erskine was appointed "Proudfit Fellow in Letters" at $555 annually during his first two years in graduate school. Erskine Papers, Uncatalogued, "Columbia" Folder, Handwritten Notes, Box 7.

38. Seth Low (1850–1916) lost his bid for reelection as mayor in 1903. He served as president of the National Civic Federation and, from 1907 to 1916, as chairman of the Board of Trustees of Tuskegee Institute. Nicholas Murray Butler (1862–1947) ran unsuccessfully for vice president with Howard Taft in 1912, and he failed at two efforts to secure the Republican presidential nomination—1920 and 1928. He shared the 1931 Nobel Peace Prize with Jane Addams for his work in founding and managing the Carnegie Endowment for International Peace and other global peace efforts.

39. Erskine, *The Memory*, 105.

40. Lewisohn, *Upstream*, 107–108. See also, Ralph Melnick, *The Life and Work of Ludwig Lewisohn* (Detroit: Wayne State University Press, 1998). Lewisohn's remarks about his experiences at Columbia may be at least somewhat shaded by a number of disappointments: his difficulties in convincing the English faculty to agree to his proposed dissertation topic; his inability to find a faculty mentor who could replace his College of Charleston undergraduate champion, Professor Lancelot Minor Harris; his failure to secure the fellowship he sorely needed to ease his grim financial situation; and his sense that, as a Jew, many cards were stacked against him. He left Columbia in 1904 without completing his doctorate. His first novel, *The Broken Snare*, was published in 1908, and in 1948, he became a founding faculty member of Brandeis University.

41. Sinclair, *The Goose-Step*, 10.

42. Sinclair, *The Goose-Step*, 13.

43. The editors to John Erskine, June 13, 1899. Erskine Biography File, Box 4, CURBM.

44. *The Century Magazine*, published from 1881 to 1930, was the successor to *Scribner's Monthly Magazine*. "Actaeon" was published in its January 1901 edition.

45. Abraham Flexner, *The American College: A Criticism* (New York: The Century Co., 1908), 29–30.

46. Erskine, *The Memory*, 111. See also, Oscar J. Campbell, "The Department of English and Comparative Literature," in *A History of the Faculty of Columbia University*, ed. Jacques Barzun (New York: Columbia University Press, 1957), 58–101.

47. N.A., "Elizabethan Songs: John Erskine's Study of Their Poetry and Music," *New York Times Book Review*, October 24, 1903, 5.

48. Alexander Meiklejohn, "College Education and the Moral Ideal," *Education* XXVIII, 1908, 558.

49. Laurence R. Veysey, *The Emergence of the American University* (Chicago: The University of Chicago Press, 1965), 209.

50. Erskine, *The Memory*, 115.

3   The Gown Is the Town

1. Richard Hofstatder, *Anti-Intellectualism in American Life* (New York: Alfred Knopf, 1963), 408.

2. Laurence R. Veysey, *The Emergence of the American University* (Chicago: The University of Chicago Press, 1965), 233–234.

3. George Harris, speech at Boston alumni dinner, February 5, 1906. Quoted in N.A., "Dr. Harris on Football," *Boston Evening Transcript*, February 6, 1906, 2. For a history of the early years at Amherst College, see Thomas Le Duc, *Piety and Intellect at Amherst College* (New York: Columbia University Press, 1946).

4. Van Wyck Brooks, *America's Coming of Age* (New York: E.P. Dutton, 1915), 13.

5. Hofstatder, *Anti-Intellectualism*, 404.

6. John Erskine, *My Life as a Teacher* (Philadelphia: J.B Lippincott, 1948), 20.

7. Ibid., 16.

8. See John Erskine, *The Memory of Certain Persons* (Philadelphia: J.B Lippincott, 1947), 119–170. Also see, Claude M. Cuess, *Amherst: The Story of a New England College* (Boston: Little, Brown, & Co., 1935).

9. Erskine, *My Life as a Teacher*, 34.

10. John Erskine to Alexander Meiklejohn, January 9, 1917. Meiklejohn Papers, Box II, Folder 9, ACASC.

11. John Erskine to Alexander Meiklejohn, April 25, 1915. Meiklejohn Papers, Box II, Folder 9, ACASC. See also, Erskine, *The Memory*, 144–146. George Bosworth Churchill had been a high school teacher and an assistant editor at *Cosmopolitan* magazine when he was appointed to the Amherst faculty in 1898. While on the faculty, he also served in the Massachusetts legislature. He was elected to the US House of Representatives in 1925 but served only three months before his death.

12. William T. Bigelow to John Erskine, February 20, Erskine Papers, Box 1, Folder 3, ACASC. See also, Erskine, *The Memory*, 166–167.

13. Erskine, *The Memory*, 135.

14. John Erskine to Curtis H. Page, October 4, 1945. Erskine Papers, Box 1, Folder 2, ACASC.

15. Jerome Liebling, Christopher Benfey, Polly Longworth, and Barton Levi St. Armand, *The Dickinsons of Amherst* (Hanover, NH: University Press of New England, 2001). Martha Dickinson Bianchi, *The Life and Letters of Emily Dickinson* (Boston: Houghton Mifflin, 1924).

16. Martha Dickinson Bianchi to John Erskine, n.d. Alfred Haufman to John Erskine, August 29, 1947. Erskine Papers, Box 1, Folder 2, ACASC. Erskine sent Martha Dickinson copies of almost all his books as soon as they were published.

17. John Erskine to Jan Crowell, October 11, 1945. Erskine Papers, Box 1, Folder 2, ACASC. See also, George F. Whicher, *This Was a Poet: A Critical Biography of Emily Dickinson* (New York: Scribner's Sons, 1938).

18. Erskine, *My Life as a Teacher*, 21.

19. Ibid., 20.

20. John Erskine, "The Teaching of Literature in College," *The Nation*, September 3, 1908.

21. The *Boston Evening Transcript*, February 6, 1906, quoted George Harris speaking at an alumni dinner: "The educated man is the all-round man, the symmetrical man. The one-sided man is not liberally educated. The aim of a college is not to make scholars. The aim is to make broad, cultivated men, physically sound, intellectually awake, socially refined and gentlemanly."

22. Le Duc, *Piety and Intellect*, 139–140.

23. Erskine, *The Memory*, 164.

24. Ibid., 164.

25. Ibid., 166.

26. George F. Whicher, *Mornings at 8:50: Brief Evocations of the Past for a College Audience* (Northampton, MA: The Hampshire Bookshop, 1950), 115.

27. See *Selections from Spencer's The Faerie Queene*, ed. John Erskine (New York: Longmans, Green and Co., 1905).

28. See John Erskine, *Actaeon and Other Poems* (New York: John Lane, 1907). William A. Bradley, "Two Young Poets of Idealism," *New York Times Review of Books*, March 2, 1907, 132.

29. Erskine, *The Memory*, 182–183.

30. John Erskine, *Leading American Novelists* (New York: Henry Holt, 1910). Erskine's book was part of a series, "*Biographies of Leading Americans*," edited by his Columbia professor William P. Trent.

31. John Erskine to Pauline Ives, July 10, 1907. Erskine Papers, Uncatalogued, Box 15: Scrapbooks, CURBM.

32. Frederick P. Keppel to John Erskine, March 7, 1906. Erskine Biographical Files, Box 7, Columbia Folder, CURBM.

33. Erskine, *The Memory*, 162.

34. Nicholas M. Butler, *Across the Busy Years: Recollections and Reflections* (New York: Scribner's Sons, 1939), 148–149.

35. McCaughey, *Stand, Columbia: A History of Columbia University in the City of New York, 1754–2004* (New York: Columbia University Press, 2003), 211.

36. N.A., "Trouble at Columbia," *New York Times*, April 28, 1902, 2.

37. Michael Rosenthal, *Nicholas Miraculous: The Amazing Career of the Redoubtable Dr. Nicholas Murray Butler* (New York: Farrar, Straus and Giroux, 2006), 150–153. See also, Editorial, *Columbia Spectator*, April 29, 1902.

38. N.A., "Criticises Butler and Quits Columbia: Professor MacDowell Follows Professor Woodberry in Resigning," *New York Times*, February 4, 1904, 12. See also, Rosenthal, *Nicholas Miraculous*, 153–155.

39. Ibid.

40. Erskine, *The Memory*, 148.

41. The Department of English, amidst unprecedented growth of the student population, requested two new faculty members, John Erskine and George P. Krapp, to replace Professor Carpenter. President Butler approved both. Ashley Thorndike to Nicholas Murray Butler, April 26, 1909. Central Files, Box 331, Folder 4, CUAC.

42. Erskine, *The Memory*, 189–190.

43. Plimpton to Erskine, May 3, 1909. Erskine Papers, Box 1, Folder 36, ACASC.

4 GROWING PAINS AT A NEW COLUMBIA

1. Randolph Bourne to Simon Barr, December 14, 1913, *The Letters of Randolph Bourne*, ed. Eric J. Sandeen (Troy, NY: Whitston, 1981),

188. Randolph Bourne to Sarah Bourne, September 12, 1913, *The Letters of Randolph Bourne*, 136. See also, Bruce Clayton, *Forgotten Prophet: The Life of Randolph Bourne* (Baton Rouge: Louisiana State University Press, 1984).

2. George Santayana, credited with coining the phrase "genteel tradition," noted in a lecture delivered at the University of California, Berkeley in 1911 that America was of two minds: an "American spirit" marked by "industry and invention" and an "American intellect" found "floating gently in the back-water." See George Santayana, "The Genteel Tradition in American Philosophy," *University of California Chronicle* XII, no. 4 (October 1911): 358.

3. Randolph Bourne to Elsie Clews Parsons, May 9, 1917, Eric J. Sandeen, "Bourne Again: The Correspondence between Randolph Bourne and Elsie Clews Parsons," *American Literary History* 1 (1989): 502.

4. Nicholas Murray Butler, *Scholarship and Service* (New York: Scribner's and Sons, 1921).

5. Randolph Bourne, "The Two Generations," in *Youth and Life* (Boston: Houghton Mifflin, 1913), 31. Originally in *Atlantic Monthly*, CVII (May 1911), 591–598.

6. Irwin Edman, "The College: A Memoir of Forty Years," in *A History of Columbia College on Morningside Heights*, ed. Dwight C. Miner (New York: Columbia University Press, 1954), 8.

7. John Erskine, *The Memory of Certain Persons* (Philadelphia, PA: J. P. Lippincott, 1947), 195.

8. Randolph Bourne, "From Olympus," *Columbia Monthly* VIII (December 1910), 71.

9. Randolph Bourne, "The Professor," *The New Republic*, July 10, 1915, 257–258.

10. Joyce Kilmer, "The College Student Has Changed Greatly," *The New York Times Sunday Magazine*, February 21, 1915, 21.

11. Clayton, *Forgotten Prophet*, 133.

12. Erskine, *The Memory*, 195.

13. John Erskine to Carl Zigrosser, August 9, 1911. Manuscript Collections, Correspondence with Carl Zigrosser, University of Pennsylvania Libraries, Annenberg Rare Book and Manuscript Library (UPARML). Frederick P. Keppel, *Columbia* (New York: Oxford University Press, 1914), 275–277. Zigrosser had a notable career as an expert in print art and museum curator.

14. Michael Rosenthal, *Nicholas Miraculous: The Amazing Career of the Redoubtable Dr. Nicholas Murray Butler* (New York: Farrar, Straus and Giroux, 2006), 37.

15. Lionel Trilling, "The Van Amringe and Keppel Eras," in *A History of Columbia College on Morningside*, ed. Irwin Edman (New York: Columbia University Press, 1954).

16. Erskine, *The Memory*, 69. Erskine claimed that in his graduate student years he once found Peck in his office with his arm around the waist of a pretty student.

17. Harry Thurston Peck to the Trustees of Columbia College, September 21, 1910. Peck File, Box 1, CURBM.

18. John Erskine, *My Life as a Teacher* (Philadelphia: J.B Lippincott, 1948), 108–109. For an analysis of Butler's handling of the Peck case and other controversial faculty members, see Laurence R. Vesey, *The Emergence of the American University* (Chicago: The University of Chicago Press, 1965), 426–428.

19. Joel E. Spingarn, quoted in Rosenthal, *Nicholas Miraculous*, 209–210.

20. Erskine, *My Life as a Teacher*, 109.

21. Rosenthal, *Nicholas Miraculous*, 211.

22. Erskine, *My Life as a Teacher*, 110. Spingarn, who had independent means, established a career as an influential and successful activist for racial equality, eventually as president of the NAACP.

23. Joel E. Spingarn, "Harry Thurston Peck," *The International* VIII, no. 4 (April 1914), 107.

24. John Erskine to Nicholas M. Butler, January 11, 1913 and February 14, 1913; Nicholas M. Butler to John Erskine, May 6, 1915. Central Files, 1890–1971, John Erskine File, CUAC.

25. Alexander Meiklejohn to John Erskine, July 6, 1915; Stuart Sherman to John Erskine, August 1, 1915. Erskine Papers, Box 1, Folders 14 and 23, ACASC.

26. Talcott Williams to Alexander Meiklejohn, March 10, 1913. Meiklejohn Papers, Box 2, Folder 9, ACASC.

27. John Erskine to Herbert Lord, July 11, 1917. Erskine Papers, Uncatalogued, Box 13 (Pol-S), CURBM. Helen W. Erskine, "Reminiscence," 1961, CUOHR.

28. Nicholas Murray Butler to Ashley H. Thorndike, December 4, 1913. Central Files: Thorndike, 1890–1971, Box 340, Folder 6, CUAC.

29. John Erskine, *Leading American Novelists* (New York: Henry Holt, 1910). The book was part of the series *Leading Americans: A New Set of Biographies*, ed. W. P. Trent.

30. See Lawrence J. Oliver, *Brander Matthews, Theodore Roosevelt, and the Politics of American Literature, 1880–1920* (Knoxville: University of Tennessee Press, 1992).

31. Trilling, "The Van Amringe and Keppel Eras," 24.

32. Anna Erskine Crouse (telephone interview, August 6, 2007) noted that Matthews was a "very big influence" on her father during his Columbia faculty years.

33. See William Peterfield Trent, John Erskine, Stuart P. Sherman, and Carl Van Doren, eds., *The Cambridge History of American Literature* (New York: George Putnam's Sons, 1917). See also, Kermit Vanderbilt, *American Literature and the Academy* (Philadelphia: University of Pennsylvania Press, 1986); and Oliver, *Brander Matthews, Theodore Roosevelt, and the Politics of American Literature.* Although Oliver noted that Putnam, who was friendly with Matthews, initially proposed a Matthews and Trent coeditor arrangement, Vanderbilt did not mention this in his exhaustive study of the beginnings of the *Cambridge History.*
34. John Erskine, *My Life in Music* (Westport, CT: Greenwood Press, 1950), 26–27.
35. John Erskine, *The Shadowed Hour* (New York: Lyric, 1917).
36. John Erskine, *The Moral Obligation to Be Intelligent* (New York: Duffield and Co., 1915), 23.
37. N.A., "Reviews," *Boston Evening Transcript*, December 24, 1915, 6. N.A., "Recent Essays," *Springfield Republican*, December 26, 1915, 27.
38. Wendell T. Bush, "Reviews and Abstracts of Literature," *The Journal of Philosophy, Psychology and Scientific Methods* 13, no. 25 (December 7, 1916), 696. Alex Mackendrick, "Intelligence as a Moral Obligation," *The Dial* (February 3, 1916), 118.
39. Erskine, *The Memory*, 229.
40. Lionel Trilling, "Notes for an Autobiographical Lecture" in *The Last Decade: 1965–75*, ed. Diana Trilling (New York: Harcourt Brace Jovanovich, 1978), 122.
41. John Erskine, "Notes," in *More One-Act Plays*, ed. Helen Louise Cohen (New York: Harcourt, Brace and Company, 1927), 77.
42. Lloyd Morris, *Threshold in the Sun* (New York: Harper and Brothers, 1943), 86–87.
43. Frank Ernest Hill, "Reminiscences," 1961, CUOHR.
44. Horace Coon, *Columbia: Colossus on the Hudson* (New York: E.P. Dutton, 1947), 181–182.
45. Oscar James Campbell, "The Department of English and Comparative Literature," in *A History of the Faculty of Philosophy, Columbia University*, ed. Jacques Barzun (New York: Columbia University Press, 1957), 84–85.
46. Irwin Edman, *Philosopher's Holiday* (New York: Penguin, 1938), 144.
47. Morris, *Threshold in the Sun*, 86–87.
48. Quoted in Clifton Fadiman, "Some Recollections of Great Teachers" in *University on the Heights*, ed. Wesley First (New York: Doubleday, 1969), 66.

49. Corey Ford, "The Jester and the Times" in *University on the Heights*, ed. Wesley First (New York: Doubleday, 1969), 83.

50. Erskine, *The Memory*, 241.

51. Erskine, *The Memory*, 342. See also, John Erskine to Scott Buchanan, December 27, 1938. Erskine Papers, Alphabetical Files, Box 10 (G-K), CURBM.

52. Ashley Thorndike to Nicholas Murray Butler, November 2, 1917. Central Files: Thorndike, 1890–1971, Box 340, Folder 6, CUAC.

5 WORLD WAR I AND THE FRENCH SEDUCTION

1. John Dewey had managed to support both peace and preparedness, but became fully antipacifist by 1918. See Gary Bullert, *The Politics of John Dewey* (Buffalo, NY: Prometheus Books, 1983), 35–43.

2. Gerald Graff, *Professing Literature: An Institutional History* (Chicago: The University of Chicago Press, 1987), 128.

3. William James, "The Moral Equivalent of War," *McClure's Magazine* (August 1910), 464. The essay was based on an address by James at Stanford University in 1906.

4. Francis Bangs to Nicholas Murray Butler, February 14, 1918. Francis S. Bangs Papers, CUAC.

5. Charles Beard to Columbia University Trustees, October 8 1917. Quoted in Robert A. McCaughey, *Stand, Columbia: A History of Columbia University in the City of New York, 1754–2004* (New York: Columbia University Press, 2003), 251 and in Horace Coon, *Columbia: Colossus on the Hudson* (New York: E.P. Dutton, 1947), 148.

6. See McCaughey, *Stand, Columbia*, 245–255; and Joseph Freeman, *An American Testament: A Narrative of Rebels and Romantics* (London: Victor Gollancz Ltd., 1938), 101–108.

7. John Erskine, *The Memory of Certain Persons* (Philadelphia: J.B Lippincott, 1947), 243. See also, Freeman, *American Testament*, 100.

8. John Erskine to Henry W. L. Dana, September 17, 1917. Erskine Papers, Uncatalogued, Box 7, CURBM. John Erskine to Alexander Meiklejohn, October 9, 1917. Meiklejohn Papers, Box 2, Folder 9, ACASC.

9. Freeman, *American Testament*, 112. John Erskine to Henry W. L. Dana, August 19, 1937. Erskine Biography File, Box 7, CURBM.

10. Erskine, *The Memory*, 252–253.

11. Freeman, *American Testament*, 105.

12. Joan Shelley Rubin, *The Making of Middlebrow Culture* (Chapel Hill: The University of North Carolina Press, 1992), 161.

13. John Erskine to Nicholas Murray Butler, December 17, 1917. Central Files 1890–1971, Box 665, CUAC.

14. John Erskine to Eliza Hollingsworth Erskine, March 1918. Erskine Biographical File, Box 1, CURBM.

15. John Erskine, "Report of Progress to July 1, 1918," in *Educational Plans for the American Army Abroad*, ed. A. P. Stokes (New York: Association Press, 1918), 53–66.

16. John Erskine to Nicholas Murray Butler, May 18, 1918. Central Files 1890–1971, John Erskine File, CUAC.

17. John Erskine, "Educational Opportunities for Our Army Abroad," *The Columbia University Quarterly* (October 1918): 358.

18. Anson Phelps Stokes, "Educational Memorandum No. II: Report Giving Approved Plan for Work During Demobilization," February 16, 1918, in *Educational Plans for the American Army Abroad*, ed. A. P. Stokes, (New York: Association Press, 1918), 31–40. Colonel [James A.] Logan to Mr. [Edward Clark] Carter, telegram, February 28, 1918, *Educational Plans for the American Army Abroad*, ed. A. P. Stokes, (New York: Association Press, 1918), 12. George S. Hellman, "The A.E.F. Schools of Art," *New York Times*, July 17, 1919, 70.

19. Erskine, "Report of Progress to July 1, 1918," 53–66.

20. "Agreement for Temporary Duty in the U.S. Army," April 16, 1919. Erskine Papers, Uncatalogued, Typescript in Box 6 (A-B), CURBM.

21. Erskine, "Report of Progress to July 1, 1918," 59–61.

22. For details on the initiation of the AEF University during demobilization, see Alfred Emile Cornebise, *Soldier-Scholars: Higher Education in the AEF, 1917–1919* (Philadelphia: American Philosophical Society, 1997); Erskine, *The Memory*, 295–337; and Rae W. Rohfeld, "Preparing World War I Soldiers for Peacetime: The Army's University in France," *Adult Education Quarterly* 39 (1989): 187–198.

23. John Erskine to Scott Buchanan, December 27, 1938. Erskine Alphabetical Files, Box 10 (G-K), CURBM.

24. John J. Pershing, quoted in Erskine, *The Memory*, 303.

25. John Erskine, *My Life as a Teacher*, (Philadelphia: J.B Lippincott, 1948), 131. General Order Number 6 is reprinted in *My Life as a Teacher*, 132–134.

26. John Erskine, "Train Conscripts for War—and for Peace," *Reader's Digest* (October 1940), 57; and John Erskine, "American Expeditionary Forces," n.d. Erskine Papers, Uncatalogued, Typescript in Box 6 (A-B), CURBM.

27. John Erskine to Corporal Henry, March 14, 1919; and John Erskine to Francis Call Woodman, March 11, 1919. Both in Negroes Folder,

Entry 409, National Archives, Washington, DC, quoted in Rohfeld, "Preparing World War I Soldiers for Peacetime," 191.

28. Erskine, *The Memory*, 315.
29. Ibid., 329.
30. Ibid.

6   A Canon for the Rest of Us

1. Mark Van Doren, *The Autobiography of Mark Van Doren* (New York: Harcourt, Brace & Co., 1939), 131; Jacques Barzun, "The Great Books," *The Atlantic Monthly* (December 1952), 79–84. Van Doren characterized Erskine's wartime canon as a reading list he developed for himself and his friends while waiting to come home. Barzun described it as a reading program for the students at Beaune. Later, Gerald Graff continued the mistaken myth of Beaune roots for Great Books in Gerald Graff, *Professing Literature: An Institutional History* (University of Chicago Press, 1987), 133.

2. John Erskine to Scott Buchanan, December 27, 1938. Erskine Papers, Alphabetical Files, Box 6 (A-B), CURBM.

3. The address, "University Leadership," delivered on September 24, 1919, at Columbia, became a chapter in John Erskine, *Democracy and Ideals* (New York: George H. Doran Co., 1920), 134–135, 136. The Butler Medal was awarded "to that graduate of Columbia University, in any of its parts, who has during the year preceding shown the most competence in philosophy, or in educational theory, practice or administration, or who has during this time made the most important contribution to any of these." See Frederick Woodbridge to Nicholas M. Butler, April 11, 1919. Central Files 1890–1971, Frederick Woodbridge File, CUAC.

4. John Erskine, *The Memory of Certain Persons* (Philadelphia: J.B. Lippincott and Co., 1947), 111.

5. David O. Levine, *The American College and the Culture of Aspiration, 1915–1940* (Ithaca, NY: Cornell University Press, 1986), 39. Levine used enrollment figures from the biennial surveys of the US Bureau of Education.

6. Ibid., 139.

7. N.A., "The American College," *The New Republic*, October 25, 1922, 208.

8. Noah Porter, *Books and Reading: Or What Books Shall I Read and How Shall I Read Them* (New York: Charles Scribner, 1881); John Lubbock, *The Hundred Best Books* (London: Keegan Paul, 1897); Charles Eliot Norton, ed., *The Heart of Oaks Books* (Boston: D.C. Heath and Co., 1902); Charles W. Eliot, ed., *The Harvard Classics,*

50 vols. (New York: P.F. Collier, 1909–10). For a thorough discussion of early book lists and advice, as well as its influence on Erskine and others, see Hugh S. Moorhead, *The Great Books Movement* (PhD diss., University of Chicago, 1964). Moorhead traces the use of the adjective "great" to several nineteenth-century advice books, including *The Choice of Books* by Charles F. Richardson (1881) and *Choice of Books* by Frederic Harrison (New York: Macmillan, 1893).

9. Benjamin P. Kurtz, *Charles Mills Gayley*, (Berkeley: University of California Press, 1943).
10. Brander Matthews, "The Study of Fiction," in *Counsel Upon the Reading of Books*, ed. Henry Van Dyke (Boston: Houghton, Mifflin and Company, 1901), 175–212. George E. Woodberry, "Introduction," in *One Hundred Books Famous in English Literature* (New York: The Grolier Club of the City of New York, 1902), xiii.
11. George E. Woodberry, *The Appreciation of Literature* (New York: Baker & Taylor Col, 1907), 172.
12. Ibid., 191–192.
13. John Erskine, "The Teaching of Literature in College," *The Nation*, September 3, 1908, 203.
14. Justus Buchler, "Reconstruction in the Liberal Arts," in *A History of Columbia College on Morningside* (New York: Columbia University Press, 1954), 68.
15. Committee on Instruction on the Establishment of a System of Honors and Sequential Courses, January 21, 1910. Pamphlet in John Erskine File, Central Files 1890–1971, University Archives, CUAC.
16. John Erskine, "General Honors at Columbia," *The New Republic*, October 25, 1922, 13.
17. John Erskine to Carol Zigrosser, August 9, 1911. Correspondence with Carl Zigrosser, Ms. Collection 6, Rare Book and Manuscript Library, UPRBML.
18. "Preliminary Report," *Columbia College Gazette*, December 1916. Columbiana Collection, CUAC.
19. John Erskine to Robert E. Spiller, March 5, 1942. Erskine Papers, Alphabetical Files, CURBM.
20. John Erskine, *My Life as a Teacher* (Philadelphia: J.B. Lippincott Co., 1948), 166.
21. Joan Shelley Rubin, *The Making of Middlebrow Culture* (Chapel Hill: The University of North Carolina Press, 1992), 167. Jacques Barzun, "Reminiscences of the Columbia History Department, 1923–75," in *Living Legacies at Columbia*, ed. Theodore deBary (New York: Columbia University Publications, 2006), 370.
22. Buchler, "Reconstruction," 114.

23. Quoted in Erskine, *My Life as a Teacher*, 167–168. Erskine kept the author of the letter to Keppel anonymous.
24. Ibid., 166.
25. Erskine, *The Memory*, 343.
26. Moses Hadas, "The Department of Greek and Latin," in *A History of the Faculty of Philosophy, Columbia University*, ed. Dwight Miner (New York: Columbia University Press, 1957), 177.
27. Mortimer J. Adler, *Philosopher at Large: An Intellectual Autobiography* (New York: Macmillan Publishing Co., 1977), 56.
28. The rationale, proposal, and revised proposal were published in the faculty newsletter, *Columbia College Gazette*, December 1916 and May 1917. For a thorough treatment of the events and lists, see Moorhead, *The Great Books Movement*, 71–80. See also, David Joseph Leese, *The Pragmatic Vision: Columbia College and the Progressive Reorganization of the Liberal Core—The Formative Years, 1880–1941* (PhD diss., Columbia University, 1987), 390–423.
29. Diana Trilling, ed., *The Last Decade: Essays and Reviews, 1965–1975/ Lionel Trilling* (New York: Harcourt Brace Jovanovich, 1979), 234.
30. Moorhead (see note above) included three full Columbia lists and the Lubbock list in his appendix. See also, Amy Apfel Kass, *Radical Conservatives for a Liberal Education* (PhD diss., The Johns Hopkins University, 1973), 20–23.
31. *Columbia College Gazette*, May, 1917. Columbiana Collection, CUAC.
32. Quoted in Leese, *The Pragmatic Vision*, 414.
33. Herbert Lord to John Erskine, March 17, 1918. Erskine Papers, Alphabetical Files, Box 6, CURBM.
34. Rubin, *The Making of Middlebrow Culture*, 176–177.
35. Dean Frederick Keppel left Columbia to join the War Department in Washington, DC, in 1917 as an assistant secretary. He was appointed president of the Carnegie Corporation in 1924.
36. Jacques Barzun to F. Champion Ward, March 15, 2006. Instruction: Core Curriculum Files, CUAC.
37. For thorough treatments of the Columbia core curriculum, especially Introduction to Contemporary Civilization, see Timothy P. Cross, *An Oasis of Order: The Core Curriculum at Columbia College* (New York: Office of Columbia University Publications, 1995) and Committee on Plans, *A College Program in Action: A Review of Working Principles at Columbia College* (New York: Columbia University Press, 1946).
38. Jacques Barzun to F. Champion Ward, March 15, 2006. Instruction: Core Curriculum Files, CUAC. For a discussion of the separate and distinguishing emphases on literature in General Honors

versus sociology and history in Contemporary Civilization, see Graff, *Professing Literature*, 133–137.

39. Adler, *Philosopher*, 30.
40. Erskine, *My Life as a Teacher*, 168.
41. Erskine, *The Memory*, 342.
42. Erskine, "General Honors at Columbia," 13.
43. "Outline of Readings in Important Books," 1926 typescript. Erskine Papers, Alphabetical Files, Box 10 (G-K), Rare Book and Manuscript Library, Columbia University, New York. On the original list were: Homer, Herodotus, Thucydides, Aeschylus, Sophocles, Euripides, Aristophanes, Plato, Aristotle, Lucretius, Vergil, Horace, Gardner, Plutarch, Aurelius, St. Augustine, St. Thomas Aquinas, Dante, Galileo, Grotius, Montaigne, Shakespeare, Cervantes, Bacon, Descartes, Hobbes, Milton, Molière, Locke, Montesquieu, Voltaire, Rousseau, Gibbon, Smith, Kant, Goethe, American State Papers, Hugo, Hegel, Lyell, Balzac, Malthus, Bentham, Mill, Darwin, Pasteur, Marx, Tolstoy, Dostoevsky, Nietzsche, and James.
44. For example, although Santayana was not on the original 1919 list, Erskine later recalled to student Clifton Fadiman the "excitement among us when we were reading Santayana's 'Unknowable' in the slender offprint." John Erskine to Clifton Fadiman, September 22, 1941. Erskine Biographical Files, Box 7 (Columbia Students), Rare Book and Manuscript Library, Columbia University, New York.
45. Leese, *The Pragmatic Vision*, 420.
46. Adler, *Philosopher*, 60.
47. See Erskine, "The Teaching of Literature," 202, and Woodberry, "Introduction," xiii.
48. Erskine, *My Life as a Teacher*, 168–169.
49. Stringfellow Barr, quoted in Harris Wofford, Jr., ed., *Embers of the World* (Santa Barbara, California: Center for the Studies of Democratic Institutions, 1969), 182.
50. Adler, *Philosopher*, 30. Clifton Fadiman, *Reading I've Liked* (New York: Simon and Schuster, 1941), 29. Erskine to Fadiman, September 22, 1941. Erskine also used the phrase "so-called Honors Course" in his introduction to Alan Willard Brown, ed., *Classics of the Western World, Third Edition* (Chicago: American Library Association, 1943), 13. See also, Erskine, *My Life as a Teacher*, 155–175.
51. Robert A. McCaughey, *Stand, Columbia: A History of Columbia University in the City of New York, 1754–2004* (New York: Columbia University Press, 2003), 292.
52. The registration figures are quoted in Moorehead, *The Great Books Movement*, as produced in official records of the Columbia University Registrar's Office.

53. Van Doren, *The Autobiography*, 131–132.
54. Jacques Barzun, *From Dawn to Decadence: 500 Years of Western Cultural Life* (New York: HarperCollins, 2000), 746.
55. Jacques Barzun to F. Champion Ward, March 15, 2006, 3. Instruction: Core Curriculum Files, CUAC
56. Adler, *Philosopher*, 57.
57. See Van Doren, *The Autobiography*, 132.
58. Leon Keyserling to William Keyserling, November 8, 1926. Keyserling Family Papers, Box 4, Special Collections, College of Charleston, Charleston, South Carolina (hereafter cited as Keyserling Family Papers).
59. Fadiman, *Reading*, xxix–xxx.
60. N.A., *Outline of Readings in Important Books* (New York: Columbia University Press, 1924), v, 5, 9, 97.
61. Adler, *Philosopher*, 61. Adler recalled the 76 works that constituted the modified Erskine list as the reading list that he and Robert Maynard Hutchins later used, with minimal changes, in teaching Great Books at the University of Chicago.
62. Leon Keyserling to William Keyserling, March 23, 1927. Keyserling Family Papers, Box 4.
63. See Katherine Chaddock Reynolds, "A Canon of Democratic Intent: Reinterpreting the Roots of the Great Books Movement," *History of Higher Education Annual*, 22 (2002), 5–32. While Adler later took the idea to the University of Chicago, Buchanan and his colleague Stringfellow Barr took it to St. John's College where they initiated the Great Books curriculum in 1937.
64. Trilling, *The Last Decade*, 234.
65. "John Erskine: Author of Private Life of Helen of Troy." Typescript in Bobbs-Merrill MSS. IUMD, Box 48.
66. Erskine, *The Memory*, 341–342.
67. Henry Morton Robinson, "John Erskine—A Modern Actaeon," *The Bookman* 67 (August 1927), 617–618.
68. N.A., "Courses at Columbia 'Razzed' by Students," *New York World*, April 28, 1927, 4.
69. Alan Willard Brown, "The Columbia College Colloquium on Important Books," *Journal of General Education* (July 1948), 279.
70. Adler, *Philosopher*, 30–31.

7   CELEBRITY ATTRACTION

1. John Erskine, *My Life in Music* (Westport, CT: Greenwood Press, 1950), 33–35.
2. John Erskine, *The Memory of Certain Persons* (Philadelphia: J.B. Lippincott and Co., 1947), 346.

3. Jacques Barzun, *From Dawn to Decadence: 500 Years of Western Cultural Life* (New York: HarperCollins Publishers, 2000), 734–735.

4. Barzun, *From Dawn*, 737.

5. For more comprehensive information on the early history of radio see Lloyd Morris, *Not So Long Ago* (New York: Random House, 1949) and Anthony Rudel, *Hello, Everybody: The Dawn of American Radio* (Orlando, Florida: Harcourt, 2008).

6. John Erskine, "University Leadership," in *Democracy and Ideals*, ed. Erskine (New York: George H. Doran Company, 1920), 150.

7. N.A., "Dr. Erskine on Democracy," *New York Evening Post*, September 4, 1920, 6.

8. See John Erskine, *The Kinds of Poetry* (New York: Duffield and Company, 1920).

9. See John Erskine, *Collected Poems: 1907–1922* (New York: Duffield and Company, 1922). Lloyd Morris, "Review" in *International Book Review*, December 1922, 32.

10. John Erskine, *The Literary Discipline* (New York: Duffield and Company, 1923), ix.

11. Lloyd Morris, "Professor Erskine Drops the Literary Sounding-Line," *New York Times Book Review*, May 6, 1923, 9.

12. Joseph Wood Krutch, "Pseudo-Classic," *The Nation*, August 15, 1923, 168.

13. See John Erskine, *The Enchanted Garden* (Cedar Rapids, IA: The Torch Press, 1925). Copy number seven, inscribed to Lloyd Morris, is now in the possession of the University of Wyoming Library, Laramie.

14. John Erskine, "Sonata," 1–12 and "The Poetic Bus Driver," 34–44, in *Sonata and Other Poems* (New York: Duffield, 1925). See also, Percy A. Hutchison, "Poetry with a Cosmic Urge and a Bus Driver's Dream of Beauty," *New York Times Book Review*, May 31, 1925, 11.

15. Erskine, "The Poetic Bus Driver," 37.

16. John Erskine, "Mass Education," *The Bookman* LX, no. 1 (September 1924), 1–2.

17. Erskine, "Mass Education," 3.

18. Quoted in Mrs. Anna Erskine Crouse. Interview with the author. New York, March 26, 2008.

19. John Erskine, "The Liberal College," *The New Republic*, April 15, 1925, 203.

20. David O. Levine, *The American College and the Culture of Aspiration, 1915–1940* (Ithaca: Cornell University Press, 1987), 18–19.

21. John Erskine, "Teaching Literature: Chapter Two," *The Bookman* 56, no. 1 (September, 1922), 4.

22. Ibid., 6.

23. John Erskine, "Spotlight or Fame?" *The Bookman* 55, no. 5 (July 1922), 450.

24. John Erskine, "Present Tendencies in American Literature," *New York Times Book Review*, December 23, 1923, 3.

25. Henry Morton Robinson, "John Erskine as i Knew Him," *Columbia Alumni News*, March 1957, 9.

26. John Erskine, *My Life in Music*, 36.

27. John Erskine, Typescript of "Valentine for the First Year of Wilton." Erskine Papers, Uncatalogued, Box 15 (Scrapbooks), Rare Book and Manuscript Library, Columbia University, New York.

28. Erskine, *The Memory*, 347. See also, Erskine, *My Life in Music*, 36–50.

29. Erskine, *The Memory*, 347.

30. John Erskine to Walter Mohr, October 7, 1949. Erskine Papers, Uncatalogued, Box 7 (Columbia), Rare Book and Manuscript Library, Columbia University, New York. See also, Henry Morton Robinson, "John Erskine—A Modern Actaeon," *The Bookman* 65, No. 6 (August 1927), 613–618.

31. J. M. Thomas to John Erskine, February 21, 1925; John Erskine to J. M. Thomas, February 27, 1925. John Erskine Papers, Box 1, Archives and Special Collections, Amherst College Library, Amherst, Massachusetts.

32. Anaïs Nin, *The Early Diary of Anaïs Nin: Volume Two, 1920–1923* (New York: Harcourt Brace Jovanovich, 1978), 300.

33. Nin, *The Early Diary, Two*, 393.

34. Anaïs Nin, *The Early Diary of Anaïs Nin: Volume Three, 1923–1927* (New York: Harcourt Brace Jovanovich, 1983), 28, 37, 73–74.

35. Erskine, *The Memory*, 354–355.

36. John Erskine, *The Literary Discipline* (New York: Duffield and Company, 1923).

37. D. Laurance Chambers to John Erskine, June 17, 1925. Bobbs-Merrill MSS, Box 48, IUMD.

38. John Erskine to H. H. Howland, June 24, 1925. Bobbs-Merrill MSS, Box 48, IUMD.

39. Bliss Perry to D. Laurance Chambers, November 5, 1925; Henry van Dyke to D. Laurance Chambers, October 20, 1925. Bobbs-Merrill MSS, Box 48, IUMD.

40. Laurance Chambers to John Erskine, August 3, 1925; John Erskine to Laurance Chambers, August 5, 1925. Bobbs-Merrill MSS, Box 48, IUMD.

41. Erskine, *The Memory*, 357.

42. John Erskine, *The Private Life of Helen of Troy* (Indianapolis, IN: The Bobbs-Merrill Company, 1925), 54, 273, 64.

43. John Erskine, "John Erskine Reviews John Erskine's Books," *Delineator* 116 (May 1930), 84.
44. John Erskine to Laurance Chambers, December 18, 1925. Bobbs-Merrill MSS, Box 48, IUMD.
45. John Carter, "Wit and Wisdom of Helen of Troy," *New York Times*, November 8, 1925, X15.
46. Ernest Boyd, "Readers and Writers," *The Independent*, December 12, 1925, 683.
47. N.A. Internal Memo, Bobbs-Merrill to Laurance Chambers, January 4, 1926. Bobbs-Merrill MSS, Box 48, IUMD.
48. Nin, *The Early Diary, Three,* 169.
49. Ibid., 174–175.
50. Ibid., 174.
51. Laurance Chambers to John Erskine, February 3, 1926. Bobbs-Merrill MSS, Box 48, IUMD.

8 FAME AND LOATHING ON MORNINGSIDE HEIGHTS

1. N.A., "John Erskine Returns to Find Himself a Wit," *New York World*, January 24, 1926, 2.
2. Debois K. Wiggins, "Made Helen a Real Person," *Sunday Brooklyn Eagle Magazine* (October 31, 1926), 5. See *Delineator*, volumes 109 and 110 (1926 and 1927) and *Century*, volumes 114 and 115 (1927 and 1928).
3. Oscar Campbell, "The Department of English and Comparative Literature," in *A History of The Faculty of Philosophy, Columbia University*, ed. Dwight Miner (New York: Columbia University Press, 1957), 93.
4. John Erskine to Laurance Chambers, February 8, 1926. Bobbs-Merrill MSS, Box 48, IUMD.
5. John Erskine to Laurance Chambers, April 20, 1926 and August 31, 1926. Bobbs-Merrill MSS, Box 48, IUMD.
6. John Erskine to Laurance Chambers, August 31, 1926 and October 1, 1926. Bobbs-Merrill MSS, Box 48, IUMD. Although turned down by Bobbs-Merrill, Dabbs eventually became a well-known author and early civil rights leader.
7. Calculated using Consumer Price Index adjustments. See www.measuringworth.com (accessed June 4, 2011).
8. Emma Fanton, quoted in Norman F. Boas, *Nod Hill, Wilton, Connecticut Reminiscences* (Mystic, CT: Privately published, 1997), 27–28.

9. John Erskine to Laurance Chambers, December 18, 1925. Chambers to Erskine, July 13, 1926. Bobbs-Merrill MSS, Box 48, IUMD.

10. John Erskine, "John Erskine Reviews John Erskine's Books," *Delineator* 116 (May 1930), 84.

11. Isabel Paterson, "Reviews," *New York Herald Tribune*, November 14, 1926, 5; N.A., "Culling the Sweet and Bitter Fruits of Six Months' Fiction," *New York Times*, December 5, 1926, Book Review 5; Elmer Davis, "Guinevere Runs Off with Mr. Erskine's 'Galahad'," *New York Times*, November 14, 1926, Book Review 2.

12. Maxwell Aley to Laurance Chambers, October 23, 1926. Bobbs-Merrill MSS, Box 48, IUMD.

13. John Erskine to Laurance Chambers, December 28, 1926. Bobbs-Merrill MSS, Box 48, IUMD.

14. Laurance Chambers to John Erskine, April 26, 1927. Bobbs-Merrill MSS, Box 48, IUMD.

15. Quoted in Marion A. Knight, Mertice James, Matilda Berg, eds., *Book Review Digest* (New York: H.W. Wilson Co., 1927), 237.

16. Margaret Miller to Laurance Chambers, January 2, 1929. Bobbs-Merrill MSS, Box 48, IUMD. In 1927, $71,000 was comparable to approximately $879,000 in 2011 (calculated using Consumer Price Index adjustments). See www.measuringworth.com/ppowerus/ (accessed May 30, 2011).

17. Quoted in N.A., "Helen and Galahad Under Fire," *The Literary Digest* 92 (January 8, 1927) 26–27 and N.A., "Dr. Wise Denounces Erskine's Novels," *New York Times*, December 13, 1926, 24.

18. "John Erskine's Radio Speech," September 18, 1927. Typescript in Bobbs-Merrill MSS, Box 48, IUMD.

19. Helen Gahagan to John Erskine, December 31, 1926. Telegram in Erskine Clipping Files Juilliard School Library and Archives.

20. George Gershwin, "Critic Artist, Artist Critic in This Review of Concert," *New York World*, January 22, 1927, 10.

21. John Erskine, *The Memory of Certain Persons* (Philadelphia, PA: J.P. Lippincott, 1947), 362.

22. John Erskine, *My Life in Music*, (Westport, CT: Greenwood Press, 1950), 238.

23. Committee for the Suppression of Irresponsible Censorship statement quoted in "Authors Organize Censorship Fight," *New York Times*, May 1, 1927, 7.

24. John Erskine, "The Irony of Censorship," *National Board of Review Magazine* (March 1927), 4–5. Reprinted from a speech delivered at the twelfth annual luncheon of the National Board of Review.

25. Quoted in N.A., "Erskine Sees Drys and Bible at Odds," *New York Evening Sun*, December 9, 1927, 3.

26. The major New York newspapers covering Erskine were: *The New York World, The New York Telegram, The New York Post, The New York Times,* and *The New York Herald Tribune.* See N.A., "Professor Erskine in Hospital," *The New York World,* March 18, 1927, 3.

27. John Erskine as Told to Elinore Elgin, "I Blame Wives' Physical Decline For Husbands' Seeking New Loves," *New York Evening Graphic,* August 28, 1926, Magazine Section 1–2.

28. Anaïs Nin, *The Early Diary of Anaïs Nin: Volume Four, 1927–1931* (New York: Harcourt Brace Jovanovich, 1985), 123.

29. Adeline Lobdell Atwater, *Autobiography of an Extravert,* typescript, n.d., 245. Adeline Lobdell Atwater Papers, Box 1, The Newberry Library, Roger and Julie Baskes Department of Special Collections.

30. John Erskine to Olga Samaroff, December 18, 1930. Olga Samaroff to John Erskine, May 29, 1931. Archives, Juilliard School of Music, Office of the President, General Administration Records, 1914–1951, Box 4/5.

31. Atwater, *Autobiography.* Also see, Adeline Atwater: Group I, Woman's Party Collection, US Library of Congress, Washington, DC.

32. Ibid., 246.

33. Adeline Atwater Pynchon to Fulton Oursler, August 21, 1951. Erskine Biographical File, Box 4, Rare Book and Manuscript Library, Columbia University, New York. Atwater's 1951 letter to Oursler indicated she had saved 400 letters, all addressed to "Lilith," sent by Erskine from 1926 to 1931; however, none of these have been found for use in this biography.

34. Anaïs Nin, *Early Diary, Four,* 127.

35. John Erskine, "John Erskine Reviews John Erskine's Books," *Delineator* 116 (May, 1930), 84.

36. John Erskine, *My Life as a Teacher* (Philadelphia: J.B. Lippincott Co., 1948), 208–210.

37. Ibid., 208.

38. "Lecture Engagements for John Erskine." Typescript in Bobbs-Merrill MSS, Box 48, IUMD.

39. Nin, *Early Diary, Four,* 122.

40. Ibid., 131–132, 144.

41. Pauline Erskine to Laurance Chambers, December 30, 1928, Bobbs-Merrill MSS, Box 48, IUMD.

42. Deidre Bair, *Anaïs Nin: A Biography* (New York: G.P. Putnam's Sons, 1995), 89.

43. Nin, *Early Diary, Four,* 189–190.

44. John Ferrone to Graham Erskine, March 22, 1982, quoted in Bair, *Anaïs Nin,* 539.

45. Nin, *Early Diary, Four,* 227.

46. Ibid., 229.
47. John Erskine, *The Delight of Great Books* (Indianapolis: The Bobbs-Merrill Co, 1928), 28–29.
48. F. L. Robbins, "Book Review: Sincerity," *The Outlook* 153 (November 13, 1929), 428; R. G. E., "Sincerity," *The New Republic* 61 (January 8, 1930), 204.
49. John Erskine to Anne Johnston, November 20, 1929, Bobbs-Merrill MSS, Box 48, IUMD.
50. N.A., "Net Sales," typescript, April 30, 1930. Bobbs-Merrill MSS, Box 48, IUMD.
51. Laurance Chambers to John Erskine, January 11, 1929. Bobbs-Merrill MSS, Box 48, IUMD.
52. William L. Chenery to John Erskine, May 14, 1929. John Erskine to William L. Chenery, May 22, 1929. Bobbs-Merrill MSS, Box 48, IUMD.

9   RAISING JUILLIARD

1. John Erskine, *My Life in Music* (Westport, CT: Greenwood Press, 1950), 83.
2. Ibid., 81.
3. F. W. Strehlau, "Baltimore Symphony Orchestra Pleases Record Audience in First Appearance of Season," *Baltimore Evening Sun*, November 19, 1928, 3.
4. The trustees named in the Juilliard will were: Frederic Juilliard, nephew of Augustus Juilliard; Charles Hl Sabin, president of the Guarantee Trust Company; and James N. Wallace, president of Central Trust Company (who soon died and was replaced by his banking successor, George W. Davison).
5. N.A., "A Magnificent Gift," *The Etude* (October 1919), 9.
6. The major source of information on the planning and founding of The Juilliard School of Music is Andrea Olmstead, *Juilliard, A History* (Urbana: University of Illinois Press, 1999).
7. James Loeb to Frank Damrosch, November 8, 1923. Quoted in Olmstead, *Juilliard*, 72.
8. Erskine, *My Life in Music*, 52.
9. The "graduate school" designation meant nothing, since students were required only to have high school graduation equivalency. There was no formal curriculum, but means for each student to take private lessons in a single instrument, voice, or composition. Selectivity was guaranteed by the funding of full fellowships for all students. The first group of 81 students comprised a majority of females, including two African Americans. See Olmstead, *Juilliard*.

NOTES 217

10. See George Martin, *The Damrosch Dynasty* (Boston: Houghton Mifflin Company, 1963), 296–303.
11. Erskine, *My Life in Music*, 71.
12. Ibid.
13. James Loeb to John Erskine, March 20, 1928. Quoted in Erskine, *My Life in Music*, 72.
14. Quoted in N.A., "Dr. Erskine Heads Juilliard School," *New York Times*, February 23, 1928, 17.
15. Quoted in Marguerite Barzun to Katherine Chaddock, February 27, 2008.
16. John Erskine, quoted in Olmstead, *Juilliard*, 103.
17. Quoted in N.A., "More Music Study Is Urged by Erskine," *New York Times*, June 5, 1928, 28.
18. Quoted in Cobina Wright, Universal Service, "John Erskine Turns from Novels to Discuss Musical Education, *West Palm Beach Post*, July 7, 1928, 3.
19. Quoted in N.A., "Wants Fewer Virtuosos," *New York Times*, July 20, 1928, 23.
20. John Erskine, "De-Centralizing Our Music," *Music Supervisors Journal* 16 (1930), 23.
21. John Erskine to Ezra Pound, May 10, 1928. Box 3/2, Office of the President, General Administration Records: 1914–1951, JCA.
22. John Erskine to Ezra Pound, May 10, 1928. Box 3/2, Office of the President, General Administration Records: 1914–1951, JCA.
23. Quoted in Helen Worden Erskine, unpublished typescript dated January 2, 1958, 3. Box 5, John Erskine Biographical Files, Rare Book and Manuscript Library, Columbia University.
24. Quoted in Edna Levey, "John Erskine Discourses Lightly on Art, Music, Morals, and Female Intelligence," unpublished typescript, January 22, 1931, 1–2. Bobbs-Merrill MSS, Box 48, IUMD.
25. George Martin, *The Damrosch Dynasty: America's First Family of Music* (Boston: Houghton Mifflin, 1983), 302.
26. Erskine, *My Life in Music*, 74.
27. Ibid., 116
28. John Erskine to Ernest Hutcheson, June 6, 1927. Office of the President, General Administration Records: 1914–1951, Box 2/5, JCA. In 1966, the Metropolitan Opera House opened its new facility at Lincoln Center. The Juilliard School of Music moved to the Lincoln Center Complex in 1969.
29. Quoted in Erskine, *My Life in Music*, 118.
30. See Olmstead, *Juilliard* and Erskine, *My Life in Music*.
31. N.A., "Sharp Increase Marks Broadcast of Second Radio Lesson," *New York Times*, April 1, 1931, 4.

32. Erskine, *My Life in Music*, 141.

33. John Erskine to Hugh Guiler, December 9, 1930. John Erskine Biographical Files, Box 10, CURBM.

34. Hugh Guiler to John Erskine, August 1, 1931. John Erskine Biographical Files, CURBM.

35. Anaïs Nin, *The Early Diary of Anaïs Nin: Volume Four, 1927–1931* (New York: Harcourt Brace Jovanovich, 1985), 378. John Erskine to Alfred Knopf, March 4, 1931; to Frank Crowninshield, September 10, 1931; to Samuel Chotzinoff, October 7, 1931. John Erskine Biographical Files, Box 10, CURBM.

36. Ibid., 396.

37. Ibid., 378.

38. Noel Riley Fitch, *Anaïs: The Erotic Life of Anaïs Nin* (Boston: Little Brown and Co., 1993), 119–120. See also, John Erskine to Hugh Guiler, March 4, 1931. Box 10, Erskine Biography Files, CURBM.

39. Laurance Chambers to John Erskine, July 11, 1930. Box 48, Bobbs-Merrill MSS, Lilly, IU.

40. John Erskine to Laurance Chambers, March 18, 1931. Box 48, Bobbs-Merrill MSS, Lilly, IU. See Adeline Atwater, *The Marriage of Don Quixote* (Indianapolis: Bobbs-Merrill, 1931). Also see, John Erskine to Bill Maloney, March 10, 1931. Erskine Biographical Files, Box 4, CURBM.

41. The passenger list from the SS Paris and Aquitania crossings were saved by Helen Worden and found in Erskine Biographical Files, Box 8, CURBM. See also, Erskine, *My Life in Music*, 112–114.

42. Helen Worden wrote the "About People" column for the *Herald Tribune* and the "That's Life" column for the *Hall Syndicate*. From 1959–1964, she wrote the Dorothy Dix advice column for the *Bell Syndicate*.

43. Quoted in Nin, *Early Diary, Four*, 475.

44. See Helen Worden, *The Real New York* (Indianapolis: Bobbs-Merrill, 1932) and *Round Manhattan's Rim* (Indianapolis: Bobbs-Merrill, 1933).

45. Anna Erskine to John Erskine, August 26, 1930. Erskine Biographical Files, Box 8, CURBM.

46. Using Consumer Price Index calculation basis, $15,000 in 1932 is equivalent to $239,000 in 2010.

47. John Erskine to "The Faculty," September 26, 1932. Office of the President, General Administration Records, 1914–1951, JCA.

48. John Erskine to Felix Warburg, June 21, 1933 and August 23, 1933. Office of the President, General Administration Records, 1914–1951, Box 3, JCA.

49. John Erskine to Laurance Chambers, March 18, 1931. Bobbs-Merrill MSS, Box 48, IUMD.
50. John Erskine to Laurance Chambers, March 10, 1932. Bobbs-Merrill MSS, Box 48, IUMD.
51. Pauline Erskine to John Erskine, December 5, 1934. Erskine Biographical Files, Box 7, CURBM.
52. John Erskine to Laurance Chambers, November 13, 1933. Box 48, Bobbs-Merrill MSS, Lilly, IUMD.
53. See John Erskine, "Fair College Day," *Collier's* 92 (December 1933); and John Erskine, *Bachelor—Of Arts* (Indianapolis: Bobbs-Merrill Co., 1934).
54. N.A., n.d. Typescript memo in Bobbs-Merrill MSS, Box 48, IUMD.
55. John Erskine to Laurance Chambers, January 24, 1934. Bobbs-Merrill MSS, Box 48, IUMD.
56. John Erskine to Laurance Chambers, December 5, 1932 and March 27, 1933. Bobbs-Merrill MSS, Box 48, IUMD.
57. Erskine, *My Life in Music*, 126. John Erskine to George Antheil, June 7, 1929. George Antheil Collection, Box 5, Library of Congress, Washington, DC.
58. Olin Downes, "Helen Retires Has Premiere at the Julliard School," *New York Times*, March 1, 1934, 22.
59. George Anthiel to John Erskine, March 3, 1934. Office of the President, General Administration Records: 1914–1951, Box 3, JCA.
60. John Erskine, "Helen Retires," *The Golden Book*, May 1934, 537–548.
61. Quoted in *The Nation*, October 1, 1930.
62. John Erskine, "What Kind of Opera Production?" *New York Times*, June 12, 1932, X4–6. N.A., "Juilliard's Bargain," *Time Magazine*, March 18, 1935.
63. Ruth Seinfel, "Erskine Sees Broadway Shows Guiding Our Future Opera," *New York Evening Post*, September 25, 1930, 3.
64. John Erskine to Allen Wardwell, n.d., quoted in Erskine, *My Life in Music*, 196–197. Also see, N.A., "Juilliard's Bargain," *Time Magazine*, March 18, 1935.
65. For detail on Erskine's early work at Juilliard, see Erskine, *My Life in Music*, 93–96 and Olmstead, *Juilliard*, 102–103.
66. John Erskine, *The Memory of Certain Persons* (Philadelphia, PA: J.P. Lippincott, 1947), 374.
67. Report to the Directors, February 10, 1941. Office of the President, General Administration Records: 1914–1951, Box 3, JCA. Erskine's proposal was to set up music centers at: Fisk College

(TN), Converse College (SC), University of Chatanooga (TN), and Hendrix College (AR).

68. N.A., "Around Town," *The New Republic*, November 28, 1934, 17. H. L. Mencken to John Erskine, December 12, 1934. John Erskine to H. L. Mencken, December 14, 1934. Office of the President, General Administration Records: 1914–1951, Box 2, JCA.

69. N.A., "Itinerary," n.d. Typescript in Box 48, Bobbs-Merrill MSS, Lilly, IU. N.A., "John Erskine, Resume," 1937. Typescript in Erskine Biography File, Box 1, CURBM.

70. N.A., "Net Sales," typescript, April 30, 1930. Box 48, Bobbs-Merrill MSS, Lilly, IU.

71. Jessica Mannon, n.d., internal memo. Typescript in Bobbs-Merrill MSS, Box 48, IUMD.

72. N.A., "A Study of Jealousy," *New York Times*, February 17, 1935, 15. See John Erskine, *Forget If You Can* (Indianapolis: Bobbs-Merrill Company, 1935).

10 Segues and Second Acts

1. N.A., "Music: Juilliard's Bargain," *Time Magazine*, March 18, 1935, 58.

2. See Andrea Olmstead, *Juilliard, A History* (Urbana: University of Illinois Press, 1999), 114–115. Erskine was particularly unsympathetic with activist students in a chapter of the National Student League and in the Juilliard chapter affiliated with the American League against War and Fascism.

3. J. M. Kane to Frank D. Eaman, July 22, 1936. Erskine Biographical File, Box 1, CURBM.

4. John Erskine, *My Life in Music* (Westport, CT: Greenwood Press, 1950), 165.

5. John Erskine to Laurance Chambers, July 31, 1935. Bobbs-Merrill MSS, Box 48, IUMD.

6. John Erskine, *The Influence of Women and Its Cure* (Indianapolis: Bobbs-Merrill Company, 1936). See also, John Chamberlain, "Books of the Times," *New York Times*, January 31, 1936, 13.

7. Merab Eberle, "Erskine Writes Biography of François Villon," *Dayton Journal* (August 1, 1937), Editorial Section, 3. J. S., "For Angus," n.d. Typescript in Bobbs-Merrill MSS, Box 48, IUMD. K. W., "John Erskine's Vivid Portrait of Villon," *New York Times*, August 8, 1937, 85. See John Erskine, *The Brief Hour of François Villon* (Indianapolis: Bobbs-Merrill Company, 1937).

8. Helen Worden Erskine to Lucy Kroll, September 21, 1966. Box 734, Lucy Kroll Collection, Library of Congress, Washington, DC.

In the years after Erskine's death in 1951, Helen Worden Erskine approached several film producers and directors about buying the film rights to *The Brief Hour of François Villon* and other Erskine books, but to no avail.

9. John Erskine to Laurance Chambers, January 21, 1938 and January 26, 1938. Bobbs-Merrill MSS, Box 48, IUMD.
10. Laurance Chambers to John Erskine, January 31, 1938. Bobbs-Merrill MSS, Box 48, IUMD.
11. Charles N. Elliot to John Erskine, February 4, 1942, Charles N. Elliot Collection, Box 1, LOCMD.
12. Committee on Plans, *A College Program in Action: A Review of Working Principles at Columbia College* (New York: Columbia University Press, 1946), 165.
13. Ibid., 22.
14. Mark Van Doren, *The Autobiography of Mark Van Doren* (New York: Harcourt, Brace and Company, 1958), 211.
15. For information on the route taken by Barr and Buchanan toward the founding of the program at St. John's see Katherine Chaddock Reynolds, "A Canon of Democratic Intent: Reinterpreting the Roots of the Great Books Movement," *History of Higher Education Annual* 22 (2002), 5–32.
16. John Erskine to Clifton Fadiman, September 22, 1941. Erskine Biographical File, Box 1, CURBM.
17. Erskine, *My Life in Music*, 180.
18. Helen Erskine to John Erskine, n.d., 1937. Erskine Biographical File, Box 1, CURBM.
19. Raymond Weaver to John Erskine, December 3, 1937. Erskine Biographical File, Box 7, CURBM.
20. Quoted in Erskine, *My Life in Music*, 174.
21. See Erskine, *My Life in Music*, 181–209.
22. John Erskine, "Mickey Mouse—Supported by Stokowski," *Liberty*, October 28, 1939, 10–12; "Can Hollywood Stars Afford to Be Good Actors?" *Liberty*, December 2, 1939, 14–16; "Clark Gable's Secret Wish," *Liberty*, January 27, 1940, 14–16.
23. John Erskine to Mary Margaret McBride, November 4, 1941. Interview recording RWC 7039 A3, LOCRS. See also, Erskine, *My Life in Music*, 199.
24. N.A., n.d. Erskine Alphabetical File, Box 11, CURBM.
25. John Erskine, "Diary, So. America," 4. Typescript. Erskine Biographical File, Box 7, CURBM.
26. Ibid., 9–11.
27. William J. Shimer on NBC Radio, "Get Ready for Tomorrow," 1939. Recording RWA 4990 B2, LOCRS.

28. John Erskine on NBC Radio, "Get Ready for Tomorrow," 1939. Recording RWA 4990 B2, LOCRS.

29. John Erskine to Pauline Erskine, April 10, 1941. Erskine Biographical File, Box 7, CURBM.

30. Pauline Erskine to John Erskine, October 23, 1941. Erskine Biographical File, Box 7, CURBM.

31. John Erskine to Helen ("Sister") Erskine, October 15, 1941. Erskine Biographical File, Box 7, CURBM.

32. John Erskine to Graham Erskine, August 7, 1944. Erskine Biographical File, Box 2, CURBM.

33. Melville Cane to John Erskine, June 16, 1944. Erskine Biographical File, Box 2, CURBM. Using CPI calculations, $2,400 in 1944 is equivalent to approximately $30,000 in 2011.

34. Pauline Erskine to John Erskine, August 2, 1944. Erskine Biographical File, Box 2, CURBM.

35. John Erskine to Helen Worden, n.d., 1945. Erskine Biographical File, Box 7, CURBM.

36. John Erskine to Edward Lunsford, September 6, 1945. Erskine Biographical File, Box 8, CURBM. N.A., "Erskines Divorced After 35 Years," *New York Times*, July 1, 1945, 19; and N.A., "Erskine Weds in the West," *New York Times*, July 4, 1945, 22.

37. John Erskine, *The Philharmonic Symphony Society of New York: Its First Hundred Years* (New York: The Macmillan Co., 1943).

38. John Erskine, *The Complete Life* (New York: Julian Messner, Inc., 1943) 4.

39. Thomas Sugrue, "A Civilized Man's Guide to Culture," *New York Times Book Review*, April 25, 1943, 9.

40. John Erskine, *The Human Life of Jesus* (New York: William Morrow Co., 1945), 4, 12.

41. L. M., "Several Careers in the Arts Are Combined in Work of John Erskine," *Kansas City Star*, March 25, 1946, 3. At that writing, Erskine held three degrees from Columbia University, as well as honorary degrees from Norwich College, Amherst College, Hobart College, University of Bordeaux, Columbia University, Rollins College, New York State Normal College, Cornell College, Illinois Wesleyan University, and Boston University.

42. John Erskine, "Your Letters Speak for You," *Senior Scholastic* 50 (March 1947), 13, 19; "The Happy Art of Conversation," *Coronet* 25, no. 5 (March 1949), 37–40; "Build Your Own Library," *Coronet* 26, no. 1 (May 1949), 108–110.

43. John Erskine to George Whicher, July 19, 1944. Erskine Biographical File, Box 4, CURBM.

44. John Erskine to Austin Strong, January 26, 1948. Erskine Correspondence, Box 6, CURBM.

45. John Erskine to Douglas Moore, January 21, 1948. Erskine Alphabetical File, Box 6, CURBM. Among the more than 100 National Institute of Arts and Letters members who signed the protest against HUAAC were: Conrad Aiken, Van Wyck Brooks, Henry Canby, Aaron Copland, W. E. B. DuBois, Edna Ferber, Joseph Wood Krutch, Sinclair Lewis, Archibald MacLeish, Walter Lippmann, Lewis Mumford, Eurgene O'Neill, Katherine Anne Porter, William Saroyan, Upton Sinclair, Carl Van Doren, Mark Van Doren, and Thornton Wilder. Erskine was among 30 who registered their objections to protest.

46. John Erskine to Jo Davidson, January 19, 1944. Erskine Biographical File, Box 10, CURBM.

47. John Erskine to George Brett, Jr., September 19, 1946. Erskine Biographical File. Box 14, CURBM.

48. John Erskine to Robert Erskine, May 4, 1948. Erskine Biography Files, Box 1, CURBM.

49. Paul L. Myers to John Erskine, November 15, 1947. Erskine Alphabetical Files, Box 11, CURBM. Myers' Elkhart group of nearly 40 participants represented graduates of 15 different universities, as well as some high school dropouts. Adler and Hutchins established the Great Books Foundation in 1947 to encourage liberal education through reading and discussion of Great Books among readers of all socioeconomic and educational backgrounds.

50. Robert Maynard Hutchins to John Erskine, October 13, 1943. Quoted in Hugh S. Moorhead, *The Great Books Movement* (PhD diss., University of Chicago, 1964), 422.

51. John Erskine to Robert Maynard Hutchins, November 5, 1945. Quoted in Moorhead, *Great Books Movement*, 427.

52. Discussions of committee deliberations can be found in Alex Beam, *a Great Idea at the Time: The Rise, Fall, and Curious Afterlife of the Great Books* (New York: Public Affairs, 2008) and Moorhead, *Great Books Movement*. John Erskine to Robert Maynard Hutchins, January 3, 1944. Quoted in Moorhead, *Great Books Movement*, 430.

53. John Erskine, *My Life as a Teacher* (Philadelphia: J. B Lippincott, 1948), 174. A 1990 revised edition did finally add works by Twain, Dickens, Balzac, and Molière. See Robert M. Hutchins, ed., *Great Books of the Western World* (Chicago: Encyclopedia Britannica, 1955) and Mortimer Adler, ed., *Great Books of the Western World* (Chicago: Encyclopedia Britannica, 1990).

224   NOTES

54. John Erskine to Robert Erskine, May 4, 1948. Erskine Biographical Files, Box 1, CURBM.
55. John Erskine, *Venus, the Lonely Goddess* (New York: William Morrow and Co., 1948).
56. John Erskine to Jacques Barzun, March 1950. Erskine Biographical Files, Box 2, CURBM.
57. Helen Worden Erskine to Gene Fowler, May 7, 1951. Erskine Biographical Files, Box 9, CURBM.
58. N.A., "Rites at Columbia for John Erskine," *New York Times*, June 5, 1951, 31.
59. Erskine, *The Complete Life*, 231.

CODA

1. George Santayana, "Genteel Tradition in American Philosophy," in *Gentile Tradition: Nine Essays*, ed. Douglas Wilson (Cambridge: Harvard University Press, 1967), 39.
2. Malcolm Cowley first explored Santayana's concept in one individual, Andrew Carnegie, in an essay, "The Revolt against Gentility," in *After the Genteel Tradition American Writers Since 1910*, ed. Malcolm Cowley (New York: W.W. Norton, 1937).
3. Van Wyck Brooks, "Introduction," in *The History of a Literary Radical*, ed. Randolph Bourne (Van Wyck Brooks) (New York: B.W. Huebsch, 1920), xix.
4. Robert Wiebe, *The Search for Order, 1877–1920* (New York: Hill and Wang, 1967), 42.
5. "Teaching of Facts Is Held Outmoded," *New York Times*, October 14, 1931, 9.
6. Mortimer J. Adler, *Philosopher at Large: An Intellectual Autobiography* (New York: Macmillan Publishing Co., 1977), 129.
7. St. John's College later opened a second campus in Santa Fe, NM. Other colleges presently based on a Great Books curriculum include: Gutenberg College (Eugene, OR), Shimer College (Chicago, IL), Thomas Aquinas College (Santa Paula, CA), and C.S. Lewis College (Northfield, MA).
8. Nearly 100 years after he first proposed the reading program in classics at Columbia, Erskine continued to regularly capture founding honors, most recently in: Louis Menand, *The Marketplace of Ideas* (New York: W.W. Norton & Co., 2010) and Alex Beam, *A Great Idea at the Time: The Rise, Fall, and Curious Afterlife of the Great Books* (New York: Public Affairs, 2008).
9. Stanley N. Katz, "Liberal Education on the Ropes," *Chronicle of Higher Education* 51, no. 30 (April 1, 2005), B6–9.

10. Jacques Barzun, "The Tenth Muse," *Harper's Magazine* 303 (September, 2001), 77.
11. Ibid., 80.
12. Anaïs Nin, *The Early Diary of Anaïs Nin: Volume Four, 1927–1931* (New York: Harcourt Brace Jovanovich, 1985), 144.
13. Lloyd Morris, *A Threshold in the Sun* (New York: Harper and Brothers, 1943), 89.

BIBLIOGRAPHY

MANUSCRIPT COLLECTIONS

Amherst College Library, Archives and Special Collections. Amherst, MA.
  Erskine, John. Papers.
  Meiklejohn, Alexander. Papers.
College of Charleston, Addlestone Library, Special Collections. Charleston, SC.
  Keyserling Family Papers.
Columbia University, Low Library, University Archives, Central Files. New York, NY.
  Butler, Nicholas Murray. File.
  Columbia College Files.
  Committee on Education Files.
  Erskine, John. File.
  Keppel, Frederick. File.
  Matthews, Brander. File.
  Spingarn, Joel. File.
  Thorndike, Ashley. File.
Columbia University, Butler Library, Oral History Research Office. New York, NY.
  Reminiscences of Jacques Barzun.
  Reminiscences of Melville Henry Cane.
  Reminiscences of Helen Worden Erskine.
  Reminiscences of Virginia C. Gildersleeve.
  Reminiscences of Oscar Hammerstein.
Columbia University, Butler Library, Rare Book and Manuscript Library. New York, NY.
  Erskine, John. Alphabetical Files.
  ———. Biographical Files.
  ———. Correspondence Files.
  ———. Uncatalogued Papers.
Harvard University, Houghton Library, Manuscript Collection. Cambridge, MA.
  Buchanan, Scott M. Papers.
  Woodberry, George Edward. Correspondence.

Indiana University, Lilly Library, Manuscripts Department. Bloomington, IN.
 Bobbs-Merrill Manuscripts Collection.
The Juilliard School Library, Archives. New York, NY.
 Juilliard Archival Scrapbook Collection.
 Office of the Dean, General Administrative Records, 1917–1945.
 ———, General Administrative Records, 1919–1948.
 Office of the President, General Administrative Records, 1904–1938.
 ———, General Administrative Records, 1914–1951.
Library of Congress, Manuscript Division. Washington, DC.
 Antheil, George. Collection.
 Elliot, Charles N. Collection.
 Kroll, Lucy. Collection.
 National Woman's Party Collection.
Library of Congress, Prints and Photographs Collection. Washington, DC.
Library of Congress, Recorded Sound Reference Center. Washington, DC.
 Radio Broadcast Collection.
 Special Collections.
Newberry Library. Chicago, IL.
 Atwater, Adeline Lobdell. Papers.
St. John's College, Greenfield Library, Archival Collections. Annapolis, MD.
 Barr-Buchanan Collection.
 Barr, Stringfellow. Personal Papers.
University of Chicago Library (Regenstein), Special Collections Research
 Center, Chicago, IL.
 Adler, Mortimer J. Papers.
 McKeon, Richard P. Papers.
University of Pennsylvania, Annenberg Rare Book and Manuscript Library.
 Philadelphia, PA.
 Zigrosser, Carl. Correspondence.

INTERVIEWS WITH THE AUTHOR

Barzun, Jacques and Marguerite. February 27, 2008.
Crouse, Anna Erskine. August 6, 2007; March 26, 2008.

BY JOHN ERSKINE: BOOKS
(ENGLISH EDITIONS ONLY)

Actaeon and Other Poems. New York: John Lane, 1907.
Leading American Novelists. New York: Henry Holt & Co., 1910.
Great American Writers. New York: Henry Holt & Co., 1912.
Great Writers of America. London: Williams and Norgate, 1912.

Written English: A Guide to the Rules of Composition. New York: Century, 1913.

Contemporary War Poems. New York: American Association for International Conciliation, 1914.

The Moral Obligation to Be Intelligent and Other Essays. New York: Duffield, 1915.

The Shadowed Hour. New York: Lyric, 1917.

Democracy and Ideals: A Definition. New York: George H. Doran, 1920.

Hearts Enduring: A Play in One Scene. New York: Duffield, 1920.

The Kinds of Poetry: And Other Essays. New York: Duffield, 1920.

Collected Poems. New York: Duffield, 1922.

The Literary Discipline. New York: Duffield & Co., 1923.

The Literary Discipline. New York: Duffield, 1924.

The Enchanted Garden. Chicago: Bookfellows, 1925.

The Private Life of Helen of Troy. Indianapolis: Bobbs-Merrill, 1925.

Sonata and Other Poems. New York: Duffield, 1925.

Galahad: Enough of His Life to Explain His Reputation. Indianapolis: Bobbs-Merrill, 1926.

Adam and Eve: Though He Knew Better. Indianapolis: Bobbs-Merrill, 1927.

American Character and Other Essays. Chautauqua, NY: Chautauqua Press, 1927.

The Cambridge History of American Literature, edited by William Peterfield Trent, John Erskine, Stuart P. Sherman, and Carl Van Doren. New York: G. P. Putnam's Sons, 1927.

The Cambridge History of American Literature, edited by William Peterfield Trent, John Erskine, Stuart P. Sherman, and Carl Van Doren. Cambridge: University Press, 1927.

Prohibition and Christianity; and Other Paradoxes of the American Spirit. Indianapolis: Bobbs-Merrill, 1927.

The Delight of Great Books. Indianapolis: Bobbs-Merrill, 1928.

Penelope's Man: The Homing Instinct. Indianapolis: Bobbs-Merrill, 1928.

Sincerity, A Story of Our Time. Indianapolis: Bobbs-Merrill, 1929.

Cinderella's Daughter and Other Sequels and Consequences. Indianapolis: Bobbs-Merrill, 1930.

Uncle Sam: In the Eyes of His Family. Indianapolis: Bobbs-Merrill, 1930.

Cinderella's Daughter and Other Sequels and Consequences. London: Putnam, 1931.

Jack and the Beanstalk, a Fairy Opera for the Childlike. Indianapolis: Bobbs-Merrill, 1931.

Unfinished Business. Indianapolis: Bobbs-Merrill, 1931.

Tristan and Isolde Restoring Palamede. Indianapolis: Bobbs-Merrill, 1932.

Bachelor—of Arts, 1st ed. Indianapolis: Bobbs-Merrill, 1934.

Helen Retires; an Opera in Three Acts. Indianapolis: Bobbs-Merrill, 1934.

Forget If You Can, A Novel. Indianapolis: Bobbs-Merrill, 1935.

A Musical Companion: A Guide to the Understanding and Enjoyment of Music. New York: A. A. Knopf, 1935.

Solomon, My Son. Indianapolis: Bobbs-Merrill, 1935.

Sonata and Other Poems. Indianapolis: Bobbs-Merrill, 1935.

With Franklin D. Roosevelt, Rupert Hughes, Samuel Hopkins Adams, Anthony Abbot, Rita Weiman, and S. S. Van Dine. *The President's Mystery Story.* New York: Farrar & Rinehart, 1935: 177–202.

The Influence of Women and Its Cure. Indianapolis and New York: Bobs-Merrill, 1936.

Young Love; Variations on a Theme. Indianapolis and New York: Bobbs-Merrill, 1936.

The Brief Hour of Francois Villon. Indianapolis and New York: Bobbs-Merrill, 1937.

The Start of the Road. New York: Frederick A. Stokes, 1938.

Give Me Liberty: The Story of an Innocent Bystander. New York: Frederick A. Stokes, 1940.

Casanova's Women, Eleven Moments of a Year. New York: Frederick A. Stokes, 1941.

Mrs. Doratt. New York: Frederick A. Stokes Co., 1941.

Song without Words, the Story of Felix Mendelssohn. New York: Julian Messner, 1941.

The Complete Life. New York: Julian Messner, 1943.

The Philharmonic-Symphony Society of New York, Its First Hundred Years. New York: Macmillan, 1943.

The Voyage of Captain Bart. Philadelphia: J. B. Lippincott, 1943.

What Is Music? Philadelphia: J. B. Lippincott, 1944.

The Complete Life, a Guide to the Active Enjoyment of the Arts and of Living. London: A. Melrose, 1945.

The Human Life of Jesus. New York: William Morrow & Co., 1945.

The Memory of Certain Persons. Philadelphia: J. B. Lippincott, 1947.

My Life As a Teacher. Philadelphia: J. B. Lippincott, 1948.

Venus, the Lonely Goddess. New York: William Morrow & Co., 1949.

My Life in Music. New York: William Morrow & Co., 1950.

BY JOHN ERSKINE: ARTICLES, ESSAYS, STORIES AND CHAPTERS

"Actaeon." *Century Magazine* 63, no. 3 (January 1902): 379–382.

"The Teaching of Literature in College." *The Nation* 87, no. 2253 (September 3, 1908): 202–204.

"The Kinds of Poetry." *The Journal of Philosophy, Psychology and Scientific Methods* 9 (November 7, 1912): 617–627.

"The Moral Obligation to be Intelligent." *The Hibbert Journal* 12 (October 1913): 174–185.

"Virtue of Friendship in the Faerie Queene." *PMLA* 30, n.s. 23 (December 1915): 831–850.

"Ode to Dr. Abraham Flexner." *Independent and the Weekly Review* 86 (May 1916): 349.

"Immortal Things." *The Columbia University Quarterly* 19 (March 1917): 97–105.

"The Sons of Metanaira." *The Lyric* 1, no. 2 (June 1917): 1–13.

"Theme of Death in Paradise Lost." *PMLA* 32, n.s. 25 (December 1917): 573–582.

"Educational Opportunities for Our Army Abroad." *The Columbia University Quarterly* 20 (October 1918): 353–364.

"Report of Progress to July 1, 1918." In *Educational Plans for the American Army Abroad*, edited by A. P. Stokes, 53–66. New York: Association Press, 1918.

"American Character." *Fortnightly Review* 111 (May 1919): 706–722.

"Society as a University." *Educational Review* (Garden City, NY) 58 (September 1919): 91–108.

"Universal Training for National Service." *Review of Reviews* (New York, NY: 1890) 60 (October 1919): 416.

"Poetry and Work." *The Nation* 111 (October 1920): 473–475.

"Spotlight or Fame?" *Bookman* 55 (July 1922): 449–451.

"Teaching Literature." *Bookman* 56 (September 1922): 1–7.

"General Honors at Columbia." *The New Republic* 32 (October 1922): 13.

"Literary Discipline." *The North American Review* 216 (November 1922): 577–591.

"Present Tendencies in American Literature." *New York Times Book Review*, December 23, 1923, BR3.

"New Poetry." *The Outlook* (1893) 136 (February 1924): 317–318.

"Mass Education." *Bookman* 60 (September 1924): 1–4.

"Sleeping Beauty." *Forum* (New York: 1886) 72 (September 1924): 396–397.

"Valentine to One's Wife." *Harper Magazine* 150 (February 1925): 170.

"Outlines." *Bookman* 61 (March 1925): 29–32.

"Do Americans Speak English?" *The Nation* 120 (April 1925): 410–411.

"The Liberal College." *The New Republic* 42 (April 1925): 203–205.

"George Edward Woodberry." *Saturday Review of Literature* 1 (May 1925): 761.

"Explaining Helen." *Delineator* 109 (October 1926): 9.

"Chivalry, Ever Old, Ever New." *Delineator* 109 (November 1926): 9.

"Are These Your Favorite Fiction Characters?" *American Magazine* 102 (December 1926): 7–9.

"There's Fun in Famous Books." *Delineator* 109 (December 1926): 14–15.

"Notes." In *More One-Act Plays*, edited by Helen Louise Cohen, 77. New York: Harcourt Brace & Co., 1927.

"Paradise Lost." *Delineator* 110 (January 1927): 30.

"The Professorial Life." *Columbia Alumni News*, January 7, 1927, 259–260.

"Huckleberry Finn." *Delineator* 110 (February 1927): 10.

"The Irony of Censorship." *National Board of Review Magazine* (March 1927): 4–5.

"Novel All Parents Should Read: The Ordeal of Richard Feverel." *Delineator* 110 (April 1927): 19.

"Further Gossip about King Arthur's Court." *Delineator* 110 (May 1927): 44.

"Behavior of Words." *Century* 114 (June 1927): 245–250.

"Great Teller of Lively Stories." *Delineator* 111 (July 1927): 38.

"Liberty to Live By." *Century* 114 (July 1927): 312–317.

"Nausicaa Receives." *Collier's* 80 (July 1927): 5.

"Changing the Past." *Century* 114 (August 1927): 499–504.

"Adam and Eve." *Collier's* 80 (September 1927): 5–7, 38, 40–43.

"Flight." *Century Magazine* 114 (September 1927): 5–7.

"Secret of Sane Living." *Delineator* 111 (October 1927): 8.

"Modesty." *Century* 115 (November 1927): 115–120.

"Tact, It Is a Warrant of Our Own Integrity." *Century* 115 (December 1927): 195–200.

"The Last Voyage of Odysseus." *Cosmopolitan* (December 1927): 32–35, 182–186.

"Romantic Autobiography." *Delineator* 112 (January 1928): 49.

"Taste." *Century* 115 (January 1928): 296–301.

"Humor, a Sense of It, Is a Thing to Cultivate and Achieve." *Century* 115 (February 1928): 421–426.

"Integrity." *Century* 115 (March 1928): 587–592.

"Self-reliance." *Century* 115 (March 1928): 587–592.

"Taking Up Music in Later Life." *Etude* 46 (March 1928): 187–188.

"Culture." *Century* 116 (May 1928): 83–88.

"Most Public School Pupils Should Receive Piano Instruction." *Musician* 33 (May 1928): 11.

"Urgent Need for Better Music Teaching." *Musician* 33 (August 1928): 9.

"What Education Means to Me." *American Magazine* 106 (October 1928): 12–13.

"Peter Kills the Bear." *Collier's* 82 (December 1928): 5.

"The Afterthoughts of Lady Godiva." *Cosmopolitan* (March 1929): 30–35, 192.

"Beauty and the Beast." *Cosmopolitan* (May 1929): 42–45, 106, 108, 110.

"Is There a Career in Music?" *World's Work* 58 (June 1929): 36–39.

"Whale of a Story." *Delineator* 115 (October 1929): 15.

"Amateur Music and Recreation Leadership." *Playground and Recreation* 23 (December 1929): 569–574.

"Uncle Sam." *Collier's* 85 (January 1930): 7–9.

"We Have with Us." *Collier's* 85 (January 1930): 22.

"Clothes Didn't Make the Greeks." *Mentor-World Traveler* 18 (February 1930): 34–37.

"College Here and Abroad." *World's Work* 59 (February 1930): 81–83.

"John Erskine Reviews John Erskine's Books." *Delineator* 116 (May 1930): 21, 84–86.

"Our Particularly Happy Opportunity." *The Survey* (1909) 64 (May 1930): 151.

"Drawbacks of an Isolated Music Training." *Musician* 3 (August 1930): 9.

"After Sophistication, What?" *Review of Reviews* 82 (August 1930): 87–88.

"Vergil, the Modern Poet." *Harper's Magazine* 161 (August 1930): 280–286.

"Amateur Music-Maker." *Woman's Home Companion* 57 (September 1930): 25–26.

"Pity the Music Critic." *Musician* 35 (October 1930): 12.

"Love." *Literary Digest* 107 (November 1930): 24.

"Adult Education in Music." *School and Society* 32 (November 1930): 647–653.

"De-Centralizing Our Music." *Music Supervisors Journal* 16 (May 1930): 21–33.

"The Cannibal King." In *The Second Mercury Story Book*, edited by J. C. Squire, 312–324. New York: Longmans, Green & Co., 1931.

"At the Front." *Literary Digest* 108 (January 1931): 38.

"Adult Education in Music." *School Music* 31, no. 153 (January/February 1931): 3–6.

"Give Music a Larger Place in Education." *Music Educators Journal* 17, no. 4 (March 1931): 17–18, 29.

"The Private Life of the Wife of That Hard-Riding Revolutionary Hero: But What about Mrs. Paul Revere?" *Cosmopolitan* 90 (April 1931): 46–49, 146, 148, 150–151.

"American Business in the American Novel." *Bookman* 73 (July 1931): 449–457.

"Teaching of Facts Is Held Outmoded." *New York Times*, October 14, 1931.

"Teaching Piano by Radio." *Woman's Home Companion* 58 (October 1931): 34.

"The Candor of Don Juan: A Thitherto Hidden Episode from the Private Life of the World's Greatest Lover." *Cosmopolitan* 91 (November 1931): 58–61, 122, 124, 126.

"What Kind of Opera Production?" *The New York Times Magazine,* 10 (June 12, 1932): 4–6.

"Our College Degree Tag." *Review of Reviews* 86 (July 1932): 45–46.

"New Education." *Saturday Review of Literature* 8 (July 1932): 813–814.

"Undercover Man." *Collier's* 90 (December 1932): 7.

"New Council Aids Adult Education." *New York Times,* February 3, 1933, 3.

"Erginette." *Collier's* 91 (March 1933): 10.

"Music Takes Off Its High Hat." *American Magazine* 115 (April 1933): 24–25.

"Human Spirit." *Saturday Review of Literature* 10 (August 1933): 25–26.

"Marriage in Moderation." *Collier's* 92 (November 1933): 19.

"Fair College Day." *Collier's* 92 (December 1933): 18.

"Guest Editor Takes a Bow." *Golden Book Magazine* 19 (March 1934): 24a–25a.

"Helen Retires." *Golden Book Magazine* 19 (May 1934): 537–548.

"Radio and Education." *Vital Speeches of the Day* 1 (November 1934): 86–89.

"The Future of Radio as a Cultural Medium." *The Annals of the American Academy of Political and Social Science* 177 (January 1935): 214–219.

"Newsreels Should Be Seen and Not Heard." *American Mercury* 35 (June 1935): 219–222.

"You're Not Too Old to Play the Piano." *Rotarian* 47 (December 1935): 16–18.

"Are Women a Menace?" *Delineator* 128 (April 1936): 12.

"Have You a Little Prodigy?" *Rotarian* 49 (August 1936): 6–9.

"What Is Contemporary Poetry?" *The North American Review* 242 (September 1936): 171–180.

"Invent Your Own Career." *Reader's Digest* 31 (September 1937): 59–62.

"More Music in Small Towns." *Magazine of Art* 31 (May 1938): 264–265.

"Listen and Learn." *Listener's Digest* 1, no. 2 (March 1939).

"Mickey Mouse—Supported by Stokowski." *Liberty,* October 28, 1939, 10–12.

"Can Hollywood Stars Afford to Be Good Actors?" *Liberty,* December 2, 1939, 14–16.

"Clark Gable's Secret Wish." *Liberty,* January 27, 1940, 14–16.

"Trojan Horse: Symbol for Our Time." *The New York Times Magazine* (May 1940): 5.

"Do You Call It Isolation?" *The American Scholar* 9, no. 4 (October 1940): 387–388.

"Train Conscripts for War, and for Peace." *Reader's Digest* 37 (October 1940): 57–61.

"Do Writers Borrow?" *Saturday Review of Literature* 23 (November 1940): 11.

"When Will the Poets Speak?" *The American Scholar* 10, no. 1 (January 1941): 59–66.

"A Draft for Peace." *American Magazine* 131 (February 1941): 52–54.

"West of the Hudson." *Rotarian* 58 (May 1941): 16–19, 67–68.

"Little at a Time." *Reader's Digest* 38 (June 1941): 10–11.

"Music is Good Society." *House Beautiful* 83 (October 1941): 71–73, 99.

"Be Fair to France." *Collier's* 108 (December 1941): 18.

"England and the English-Speaking People." *The American Scholar* 11, no. 1 (January 1942): 45–58.

"Women Don't Believe in Books." *The Saturday Evening Post* 215 (August 1942): 28.

"Helen of Troy and Helen of Gotham." *The New York Times Magazine* (September 1942): 40.

"MacDowell at Columbia: Some Recollections." *The Musical Quarterly* 28 (October 1942): 395–405.

"Neglected Art of Cursing." *American Mercury* 55 (November 1942): 564–569.

"My Son Has Gone to War." *Collier's* 110 (December 1942): 106.

"Introduction." In *Classics of the Western World, Third Edition*, edited by Alan Willard Brown, 13. Chicago: American Library Association, 1943.

"The World Will Belong to the Women." *The New York Times Magazine* (March 14, 1943): 15.

"Humanities in the Americas." *The American Scholar* 13, no. 1 (January 1944): 58–69.

"Our Hardy Annual Crop of Ph.D.'s." *The New York Times Magazine* (June 1945): 17–43.

"Dickinson Saga." *The Yale Review* 35, no. 1 (September 1945): 74–83.

"You're Not Too Old to Play the Piano." *Rotarian* 57 (December 1945): 16–18.

"Lawrence Johnston Burpee." *Canadian Geographical Journal* 33 (November 1946): 240.

"The Reading Course in Great Books." *The Humanities Review* (January 1947): 1–4.

"Your Letters Speak for You." *Scholastic* 50 (March 1947): 13–19.

"Ultimate Courage." *Reader's Digest* 53 (September 1948): 7.

"The Happy Art of Conversation." *Coronet* 25 (March 1949): 37–40.

"Build Your Own Library." *Coronet* 26 (May 1949): 108–110.

SECONDARY SOURCES

Adler, Mortimer J., ed. *Great Books of the Western World*. Chicago: Encyclopedia Britannica, 1990.

Adler, Mortimer J. *Philosopher at Large: An Intellectual Autobiography*. New York: Macmillan Publishing Co., 1977.

"The American College." *The New Republic*, October 25, 1922, 208–209.

"American Composers Offered $40,000 in Prizes." *New York Times*, March 3, 1929.

Antheil, George. *Helen Retires*. Indianapolis and New York: Bobbs-Merrill, 1934.

"Around Town." *The New Republic*, November 28, 1934, 17.

Atwater, Adeline. *The Marriage of Don Quixote*. Indianapolis: Bobbs-Merrill, 1931.

"Authors Organize Censorship Fight." *New York Times*, May 1, 1927, 7.

"Author Tells Hidden Meaning in Old Books." Reno, *Nevada State Journal*, June 9, 1945.

Babbitt, Irving. *Literature and the American College: Essays in Defense of the Humanities*. Boston and New York: Houghton Mifflin Co., 1908.

Bair, Deidre. *Anaïs Nin: A Biography*. New York: G. P. Putnam's Sons, 1995.

Barzun, Jacques. "Reminiscences of the Columbia History Department, 1923–75." In *Living Legacies at Columbia*, edited by Theodore de Bary, 370. New York: Columbia University Publications, 2006.

———. "The Tenth Muse." *Harper's Magazine* 303, no. 816 (September 2001): 73–80.

———. *From Dawn to Decadence: 500 Years of Western Cultural Life*. New York: Harper Collins, 2000.

———. "The Great Books." *The Atlantic Monthly* 190 (December 1952): 79–84.

Beam, Alex. *A Great Idea at the Time: The Rise, Fall, and Curious Afterlife of the Great Books*. New York: Public Affairs, 2008.

Beck, Clyde. "Erskine Cites Immoral Book." *Detroit News*, January 6, 1937.

Boardman, Von W. "After Class." In *A History of Columbia College on Morningside*, edited by Irwin Edman. New York: Columbia University Press, 1954.

Boas, Norman F. *Nod Hill, Wilton, Connecticut: Reminiscences*. Mystic, CT: Privately Published, 1997.

Bourne, Randolph. "The Professor." *The New Republic*, July 10, 1915, 257–258.

———. "The Two Generations." *The Atlantic Monthly* 107 (May 1911): 591–598.

———. "From Olympus." *Columbia Monthly* 8 (December 1910): 71.

Boyd, Ernest. "Readers and Writers." *The Independent*, November 8, 1925, X15.

Bradley, William A. "Two Young Poets of Idealism." *The New York Times Review of Books*, March 2, 1907, 132.

Brooks, Van Wyck. *America's Coming of Age*. New York: E. P. Dutton, 1915.

Brown, Alan Willard. "The Columbia College Colloquium on Important Books." *Journal of General Education*, July 1, 1948, 278–286.

———, ed. *Classics of the Western World*. Chicago: American Library Association, 1943.

Buchler, Justus. *A History of Columbia College on Morningside*. New York: Columbia University Press, 1954.

Bullert, Gary. *The Politics of John Dewey*. Buffalo: Prometheus Books, 1983.

Bush, Wendell T. "Reviews and Abstracts of Literature." *The Journal of Philosophy, Psychology and Scientific Methods*13, no. 25 (December 7, 1916): 696.

Butler, Nicholas Murray. *Across the Busy Years: Recollections and Reflections*. New York: Scribner's, 1939.

———. *Scholarship and Service*. New York: Scribner's and Sons, 1921.

Campbell, Oscar James. "The Department of English and Comparative Literature." In *The Faculty of Philosophy*, edited by Jacques Barzun, 79, 84–85. New York: Columbia University Press, 1957.

Cane, Melville. *All and Sundry: An Oblique Autobiography*. New York: Harcourt, Brace & World, 1968.

Carter, John. "The Wit and Wisdom of Helen of Troy." *New York Times*, November 8, 1925, X15.

Chaddock, Katherine R. "A Canon of Democratic Intent: Reinterpreting the Roots of the Great Books Movement." In *The History of Higher Education Annual*, Vol. 22, edited by Roger Geiger, 203. Pascataway, NJ: Transaction Publishers, 2002.

"Class Day at Columbia." *New York Times*, June 12, 1900.

Clayton, Bruce. *Forgotten Prophet: The Life of Randolph Bourne*. Baton Rouge: Louisiana State University Press, 1984.

Cohen, Helen Louise, ed. *More One-Act Plays by Modern Authors*. New York: Harcourt, Brace & Co., 1927.

"Colleges Reap 'Softies,' John Erskine Is Afraid." *Philadelphia Inquirer*, April 7, 1935.

Commager, Henry Steele. *The American Mind: An Interpretation of American Thought and Character Since the 1880's*. New Haven & London: Yale University Press, 1950.

Committee on Plans. *A College Program in Action: A Review of Working Principles at Columbia College*. New York: Columbia University Press, 1946.

Conn, Peter. *The Divided Mind: Ideology and Imagination in America, 1898–1917*. New York: Cambridge University Press, 1983.

Coon, Horace. *Columbia: Colossus on the Hudson*. New York: E. P. Dutton & Co., 1947.

Cornebise, Emile. *Soldier-Scholars: Higher Education in the AEF, 1917–1919.* Philadelphia: American Philosophical Society, 1997.

"Courses at Columbia 'Razzed' by Students." *New York World* 28 (April 1927): 4.

"Criticises Butler and Quits Columbia." *New York Times,* February 4, 1904, 16.

"Critics in Recital: Musicians as Critics." *New York Times,* January 22, 1927, 10.

Cross, Timothy P. *An Oasis of Order: The Core Curriculum at Columbia College.* New York: Office of Columbia University Publications, 1995.

Cuess, Claude M. *Amherst: The Story of a New England College.* Boston: Little, Brown, 1935.

"Culling the Sweet and Bitter Fruits of Six Months' Fiction." *New York Times,* December 5, 1926, Book Review 5.

Davis, Elmer. "Guinevere Runs Off with Mr. Erskine's 'Galahad'." *New York Times,* November 14, 1926, Book Review 2.

Dawidoff, Robert. *The Genteel Tradition and the Sacred Rage: High Culture vs. Democracy in Adams, James, & Santayana.* Chapel Hill: The University of North Carolina Press, 1992.

De Bary, William Theodore. *The Philosophy of the Curriculum.* Buffalo, New York: Prometheus Books, 1975.

De Bary, William Theodore, Jerry Kisslinger, and Tom Mathewson, eds. *Living Legacies at Columbia.* New York: Columbia University Press, 2006.

Denby, David. *Great Books: My Adventures with Homer, Rousseau, Woolf, and Other Indestructible Writers of the Western World.* New York: Simon & Schuster, 1996.

Downes, Olin. "Helen Retires Has Premiere at the Julliard School." *New York Times,* March 1, 1934, 22.

———. "Erskine's Libretto: Author and Musician Returns to Helen of Troy for Delectable Comic Opera." *New York Times,* June 15, 1930.

"Dr. Erskine Heads Juilliard School." *New York Times,* February 23, 1928, 17.

"Dr. Erskine on Democracy." *New York Evening Post,* September 4, 1920, 6.

"Dr. Harris on Football." *Boston Evening Transcript,* February 6, 1906, 2.

"Dr. Lowell Puts His Approval on Students' Tests." *Christian Monitor,* January 23, 1931.

"Dr. Wise Denounces Erskine's Novels." *Literary Digest* (December 13, 1926): 24, 31.

Eberle. "Erskine Writes Biography of François Villon." *Dayton Journal,* August 1, 1937, Editorial Section, 3.

Edman, Irwin. "The College: A Memoir of Forty Years." In *A History of Columbia College on Morningside Heights,* edited by Dwight C. Miner. New York: Columbia University Press, 1954.

————. *Philosopher's Holiday*. New York: Penguin, 1938.

Elgin, Elinore. "I Blame Wives' Physical Decline for Husbands' Seeking New Loves." *New York Evening Graphic*, August 28, 1926, Magazine Section, 1–2.

Eliot, Charles W., ed. *The Harvard Classics*, 50 vols. New York: P. F. Collier, 1909–1910.

"Elizabethan Songs: John Erskine's Study of Their Poetry and Music." *New York Times*, October 24, 1903, BR5.

"Erskine Completes Books for 2 Operas." *New York Times*, June 10, 1930, 35.

"Erskine O.K.'s Lewis Award." *Supreme American*, January 18, 1931.

"Erskine Sees Drys and Bible at Odds." *New York Evening Sun*, December 9, 1927, 3.

"Erskine to Marry Newspaper Woman." *New York Times*, June 30, 1945.

F. F. K. "Ladies: Mr. Erskine." *New York Times*, February 9, 1936, BR23.

Fadiman, Clifton. "Some Recollections of Great Teachers." In *University on the Heights*, edited by Wesley First. New York: Doubleday & Co., 1969.

————. *Reading I've Liked*. New York: Simon and Schuster, 1941.

Fitch, Noel Riley. *Anaïs: The Erotic Life of Anaïs Nin*. Boston: Little Brown & Co., 1993.

Flexner, Abraham. *The American College: A Criticism*. New York: The Century Co., 1908.

"For a Salzburg Here." *New Orleans Times-Picayune*, November 15, 1936.

Ford, Corey. "The Jester and the Times." In *University on the Heights*, edited by Wesley First. New York: Doubleday & Co., 1969.

"40,000 in Air Piano Course." *New York Times*, April 1, 1931, 4.

Freeman, Joseph. *An American Testament: A Narrative of Rebels and Romantics*. London: Victor Gollancz Ltd., 1938.

"George Harris Speaking at the Boston Alumni Dinner." *Boston Evening Transcript*, February 6, 1906, 1–10.

Gershwin, George. "Critic Artist, Artist Critic in This Review of Concert." *New York World*, January 22, 1927, 10.

Gildersleeve, Virginia. *Many a Good Crusade*. New York: Macmillan Co., 1954.

Graff, Gerald. *Professing Literature: An Institutional History*. Chicago: The University of Chicago Press, 1987.

Green, Ashbel, ed. *My Columbia: Reminiscences of University Life*. New York: Columbia University Press, 2005.

Greenslet, Ferris. *Under the Bridge: An Autobiography*. Boston: Houghton Mifflin, 1943.

"Greenwich House Music School to Give Reception." *New York Times*, October 27, 1929.

Hadas, Moses. "The Department of Greek and Latin." In *A History of the Faculty of Philosophy, Columbia University*, edited by Dwight Miner, 177. New York: Columbia University Press, 1957.

Harrison, Frederic. *Choice of Books*. New York: MacMillan, 1893.

Harrison, Henry S. *Queed*. Boston: Houghton Mifflin, 1911.

"Helen and Galahad Under Fire." *The Literary Digest* 92 (January 8, 1927): 26–27.

Hellman, George S. "The A.E.F. Schools of Art." *New York Times*, July 17, 1919, 70.

Hoeveler, J. David. *The New Humanism: A Critique of Modern America, 1900–1940*. Charlottesville: University Press of Virginia, 1977.

Hofstadter, Richard. *Anti-Intellectualism in American Life*. New York: Alfred Knopf, 1963.

Horowitz, Helen Lefkowitz. *Campus Life: Undergraduate Cultures from the End of the Eighteenth Century to the Present*. New York: Alfred A. Knopf, 1987.

Hutchins, Robert M., ed. *Great Books of the Western World*. Chicago: Encyclopedia Britannica, 1955.

James, William. "The Moral Equivalent of War." *McClure's Magazine* 35 (August 1910): 463–468, P29.

"John Erskine Favors Music Festival Here." *New Orleans Tribune*, November 11, 1936.

"John Erskine President of Juilliard School." *The Music Leader*, March 1, 1928.

"John Erskine Returns to Find Himself a Wit." *New York World*, January 24, 1926, 2.

"John Erskine to Speak Here." *Milwaukee Leader*, January 24, 1931.

"John Erskine to Tour as Symphony Soloist." *New York Herald-Tribune*, January 15, 1928.

Juilliard's Bargain." *Time Magazine* (March 18, 1935).

"Juilliard School to Give New Opera." *New York Times*, October 7, 1937, 30.

Kass, Amy Apfel. Radical Conservatives for a Liberal Education. PhD diss., Baltimore: The Johns Hopkins University, 1973.

Kennedy, David M. *Over Here: The First World War and American Society*. New York and Oxford: Oxford University Press, 1980.

Keppel, Frederick P. *The Undergraduate and His College*. Boston and New York: Houghton Mifflin Co., 1917.

———. *Columbia*. New York: Oxford University Press, 1914.

Kilmer, Joyce. "The College Student Has Changed Greatly." *New York Times*, February 21, 1915, SM21.

Knickerbocker, William S. "John Erskine: Enough of His Mind to Explain His Art." *Sewanee Review* 35 (April 1927): 154–174.

Krupnick, Mark. *Lionel Trilling and the Fate of Cultural Criticism*. Evanston, IL: Northwestern University Press, 1986.

Krutch, Joseph Wood. "Pseudo-Classic." *The Nation*, August 15, 1923, 168.

Krystal, Arthur. "Annals of Letters: Age of Reason." *The New Yorker*, October 22, 2007, 94–103.

Kurtz, Benjamin P. *Charles Mills Gayley*. Berkeley: University of California Press, 1943.

Le Duc, Thomas. *Piety and Intellect at Amherst College*. New York: Columbia University Press, 1946.

Lee, Virginia. "Treating Women as Gentlemen." *Davenport (Iowa) Democrat & Leader*, January 8, 1937.

Leese, David J. The Pragmatic Vision: Columbia College and the Progressive Reorganization of the Liberal Core—the Formative Years, 1880–1941. PhD diss., Columbia University, 1987.

Liebling, Jerome, Christopher Benfey, Polly Longworth, and Barton Levi St. Armand. *The Dickinsons of Amherst*. Hanover, NH: University Press of New England, 2001.

Levine, David O. *The American Culture and the Culture of Aspiration, 1915–1940*. Ithaca, NY: Cornell University Press, 1986.

Levine, Lawrence W. *Highbrow/Lowbrow: The Emergence of Cultural Hierarchy in America*. Cambridge: Harvard University Press, 1988.

Lewisohn, Ludwig. *Upstream: An American Chronicle*. New York: Horace Liveright, 1922.

Lubbock, John. *The Hundred Best Books*. London: Keegan Paul, 1897.

Macdonald, Dwight. "Masscult and Midcult: I." *Partisan Review* 27 (Spring 1960): 203–233.

———. "Masscult and Midcult: II." *Partisan Review* 27 (Fall 1960): 589–631.

Mackendrick, Alex. "Intelligence as a Moral Obligation." *The Dial*, February 3, 1916, 118.

Mangione, Jerre. *The Dream and the Deal: The Federal Writers' Project, 1935–1943*. Syracuse, NY: Syracuse University Press, 1996.

Marble, Annie Russell. *A Study of the Modern Novel, British and American, Since 1900*. New York and London: D. Appleton and Co., 1928.

Martin, George. *The Damrosch Dynasty*. Boston: Houghton Mifflin Company, 1963.

Martin, Jay. *The Education of John Dewey: A Biography*. New York: Columbia University Press, 2002.

Matthews, Brander. *These Many Years: Recollections of a New Yorker*. New York: Charles Scribner's Sons, 1917.

———. "Literary Men and Public Affairs." *The North American Review* (April 1909): 533.

Matthews, Brander. *The Historical Novel and Other Essays*. New York: Charles Scribner's Sons, 1901.

———. "The Study of Fiction." In *Counsel Upon the Reading of Books*, edited by Henry Van Dyke, 175–212. Boston: Houghton, Mifflin and Company, 1901.

McCaughey, Robert A. *Stand, Columbia: A History of Columbia University in the City of New York, 1754–2004*. New York: Columbia University Press, 2003.

Meiklejohn, Alexander. "College Education and the Moral Ideal." *Education* 28 (May 1908): 552–557.

Melnick, Ralph. *The Life and Work of Ludwig Lewisohn*. Detroit: Wayne State University Press, 1998.

Menand, Louis. "Browbeaten: Dwight Macdonald's War on Midcult." *The New Yorker*, September 5, 2011, 72–78.

———. *The Marketplace of Ideas*. New York: W.W. Norton, 2010.

———. *The Metaphysical Club*. New York: Farrar, Straus & Giroux, 2001.

Moorhead, Hugh S. The Great Books Movement. PhD diss., Chicago: University of Chicago, 1964.

"More Music Study Is Urged by Erskine." *New York Times*, June 5, 1928, 28.

Morris, Lloyd. *Not So Long Ago*. New York: Random House, 1949.

———. *A Threshold in the Sun*. New York: Harper & Brothers, 1943.

———. "Professor Erskine Drops the Literary Sounding-Line." *New York Times Book Review* (May 6, 1923): 9.

———. "Review." *International Book Review* (December 1922): 32.

"Music: Juilliard's Bargain." *Time*, March 18, 1935, 58–60.

"Negroes Held Neglected." *New York Times*, April 26, 1933, 4.

"The New Columbia Professor." *Harper's Weekly* (April 1882): 268–269.

"New Type Relief Agency Is Organized by John Erskine." *Wheeling West Virginia News*, December 2, 1933, 56.

Nin, Anaïs. *The Early Diary of Anaïs Nin: Volume Four, 1927–1931*. New York: Harcourt Brace Jovanovich, 1985.

———. *The Early Diary of Anaïs Nin: Volume Two, 1920–1923*. New York: Harcourt Brace Jovanovich, 1983.

———. *The Early Diary of Anaïs Nin: Volume Three, 1923–1927*. New York: Harcourt Brace Jovanovich, 1983.

Norton, Charles Eliot, ed. *The Heart of Oaks Books*. Boston: D. C. Heath and Co., 1902.

Oliver, Lawrence J. *Brander Matthews, Theodore Roosevelt, and the Politics of American Literature, 1880–1920*. Knoxville: University of Tennessee Press, 1992.

Olmstead, Andrea. *Juilliard, A History*. Urbana, IL: University of Illinois Press, 1999.

Outline of Readings in Important Books. New York: Columbia University Press, 1924.

Paterson, Isabel. "Reviews." *New York Herald Tribune*, November 14, 1926, 5.

Patterson. *Fifth Avenue: The Best Address*. New York: Rizzoli International, 1998.

Porter, Noah. *Books and Reading: Or What Books Shall I Read and How Shall I Read Them*. New York: Charles Scribner, 1881.

"Professor Erskine in Hospital." *The New York World*, March 18, 1927, 3.

R. G. E. "Sincerity." *The New Republic* 61 (January 8, 1930): 204.

Radway, Janice. "The Scandal of the Middlebrow: The Book-of-the-Month Club, Class Fracture, and Cultural Authority." *South Atlantic Quarterly* 89 (Fall 1990): 714.

"Recent Essays." *Springfield Republican*, December 26, 1915, 27.

"Reviews." *Boston Transcript*, December 24, 1915, 6.

"Revived Interest in Pianos and Potential Sales Seen in Daily Enrollment of 4,000 Students in NBC Weekly Radio Broadcasts of Instruction Series." *Talking Machine and Radio Weekly*, April 1, 1931.

Reynolds, Katherine Chaddock. "A Canon of Democratic Intent: Reinterpreting the Roots of the Great Books Movement." *History of Higher Education Annual* 22 (2002): 5–32.

Richardson, Charles F. *The Choice of Books*. New York: American Book Exchange, 1881.

Riesman, David, N. Glazer, and R. Denney. *The Lonely Crowd: A Study of the Changing American Character*. New Haven: Yale University Press, 1950.

"Rites at Columbia for John Erskine." *New York Times*, June 5, 1951, 31.

Robbins, F. L. "Book Review: Sincerity." *The Outlook* 153 (November 13, 1929): 428.

Roberts, R. Ellis. "The Personal Preferences of John Erskine." *The Saturday Review* 26 (April 1943): 8.

Robinson, Henry Morton. "John Erskine as i Knew Him." *Columbia Alumni News* (March 1954): 8–10.

———. "John Erskine—A Modern Actaeon." *Bookman* 65 (August 1927): 613–618.

Rohfeld, Rae W. "Preparing World War I Soldiers for Peacetime: The Army's University in France." *Adult Education Quarterly* 39 (1989): 187–198.

Rosenthal, Michael. *Nicholas Miraculous: The Amazing Career of the Redoubtable Dr. Nicholas Murray Butler*. New York: Farrar, Straus and Giroux, 2006.

Rubin, Joan Shelley. *The Making of Middlebrow Culture*. Chapel Hill: The University of North Carolina Press, 1992.

Rudel, Anthony. *Hello, Everybody: The Dawn of American Radio*. Orlando, Florida: Harcourt, 2008.

Sandeen, Eric J., ed. *The Letters of Randolph Bourne: A Comprehensive Edition*. Troy, NY: The Whitston Publishing Company, 1981.

Santayana, George. "The Genteel Tradition in American Philosophy (1911)." In *Nine Essays by George Santayana*, edited by Douglas L. Wilson. Cambridge: Harvard University Press, 1967.

———. "The Genteel Tradition in American Philosophy." *University of California Chronicle* 12, no. 4 (October 1911): 358.

Seinfel, Ruth. "Erskine Sees Broadway Shows Guiding Our Future Opera." *New York Evening Post*, September 25, 1930, 3.

"Several Careers in the Arts Are Combined in Work of John Erskine." *Kansas City Star*, March 25, 1946.

Shoben, Jr. Edward Joseph. *Lionel Trilling*. New York: Frederick Ungar Publishing Co., 1981.

Sinclair, Upton. *The Goose-Step*. Pasadena, CA: Published by the Author, 1922.

Smith, Helen Huntington. "Professor's Progress." *The New Yorker*, December 27, 1927, 27–29.

"Social Notes." *New York Times*, June 9, 1910.

Spingarn, Joel. "George Edward Woodberry." In *Dictionary of American Biography, Volume X*, edited by M. Dumas. New York: Charles Scribner's Sons, 1937.

———. "Harry Thurston Peck." *The International* 8, no. 4 (April 1914): 107.

Steegmuller, Francis. "Oldest Hotels." *The New Yorker*, September 22, 1934, 18.

Stephens, H. Morse, Arthur T. Hadley, Hamilton W. Mabie, Brander Matthews, and Agnes Repplier. *Counsel Upon the Reading of Books*. Boston and New York: Houghton, Mifflin & Co., 1900.

Stokes, Anson Phelps. "Educational Memorandum No. II: Report Giving Approved Plan for Work during Demobilization." In *Educational Plans for the American Army Abroad*, edited by A. P. Stokes. New York: Association Press, 1918: 31–40.

Strehlau, F. W. "Baltimore Symphony Orchestra Pleases Record Audience in First Appearance of Season." *Baltimore Evening Sun*, November 19, 1928, 3.

Sugrue, Thomas. "A Civilized Man's Guide to Culture." *The New York Times*, April 25, 1943, Book Review, 9.

Susman, Warren I. *Culture as History*. New York: Pantheon, 1984.

"To Lecture Here." *Boston Transcript*, April 2, 1931.

Trent, William Peterfield, John Erskine, Stuart Pratt Sherman, and Carl Van Doren. The Cambridge History of American Literature. New York: George Putnam's Sons, 1917.

Trilling, Diana, ed. *The Last Decade: Essays and Reviews, 1965–1975/Lionel Trilling*. New York: Harcourt, Brace, Jovanovich, 1979.

Trilling, Lionel. *The Moral Obligation to Be Intelligent: Selected Essays*, edited by Leon Wieseltier. New York: Farrar, Straus, & Giroux, 2000.

———. "Notes for an Autobiographical Lecture." In *The Last Decade: 1965–75*, edited by Diana Trilling. New York: Harcourt, Brace, Jovanovich, 1978.

———. *The Last Decade: Essays and Reviews, 1965–1975.* New York: Harcourt Brace, 1977.

———. "The Van Amringe and Keppel Eras." In *A History of Columbia College on Morningside*, edited by Irwin Edman. New York: Columbia University Press, 1954.

"Trouble at Columbia." *New York Times*, April 28, 1902, 2.

Van Doren, Mark. *The Autobiography of Mark Van Doren.* New York: Harcourt, Brace & Co., 1939.

Vanderbilt, Kermit. *American Literature and the Academy.* Philadelphia: University of Pennsylvania Press, 1986.

Veysey, Laurence R. *The Emergence of the American University.* Chicago: The University of Chicago Press, 1965.

"Wants Fewer Virtuosos." *New York Times*, July 20, 1928, 23.

Whicher, George F. *Mornings at 8:50: Brief Evocations of the Past for a College Audience.* Northampton, MA: The Hampshire Bookshop, 1950.

Wiebe, Robert H. *The Search for Order: 1877–1920.* New York: Hill and Wang, 1967.

Wiggins, Debois K. "Made Helen a Real Person." *Sunday Brooklyn Eagle Magazine* (October 31, 1926): 5.

Wofford, Harris, Jr., ed. *Embers of the World.* Santa Barbara, CA: Center for the Studies of Democratic Institutions, 1969.

Woodberry, George Edward. *Selected Letters of George Edward Woodberry.* Boston and New York: Houghton Mifflin Co., 1933.

———. *Heart of Man, and Other Papers.* New York: Harcourt, Brace and How, 1920.

———. *The Appreciation of Literature.* New York: Baker & Taylor Co., 1907.

———. "Introduction." In *One Hundred Books Famous in English Literature*, n.a, xiii. New York: The Grolier Club of the City of New York, 1902.

Worden, Helen. *Round Manhattan's Rim.* Indianapolis: Bobbs-Merrill, 1933.

———. *The Real New York.* Indianapolis: Bobbs-Merrill, 1932.

Wright, Cobina. "John Erskine Turns from Novels to Discuss Musical Education." *West Palm Beach Post*, July 7, 1928, 3.

"Young Artists Hold Show in Erskine's Barn." *New York Herald Tribune*, September 8, 1929.

Zinsser, Hans. *As I Remember Him: The Biography of R.S.* Boston: Little, Brown & Co., 1940.

INDEX